"In this volume, significant voices within the Southern Baptist Convention candidly engage the denomination's turbulent past surrounding race and gender roles. The essays are at once historical, biblical, personal, and practical. These are not easy or comfortable discussions, but the authors write with an irenic spirit that should encourage ongoing dialogue and constructive change."

—**M. Daniel Carroll R.**, Blanchard Professor
of Old Testament, Wheaton College

"Oh, how our generation needs the mind and voice of Walter Strickland and Dayton Hartman! They have come to the rescue again. I have long wrestled with what I sense is a kind of theological imperialism imposed upon people of color in these yet to be United States. It's a fragile matter handled with care and depth in these pages. We say that we believe that all mankind is made in the image and likeness of God. This text gives us a way to align our explicit theology with our implicit action. Read it and weep."

—**Charlie Dates**, senior pastor, Progressive Baptist Church

"The American church has not always loved people well, and as followers of Jesus, we have an opportunity to change this not only within our churches but within ourselves as well. To become people who seek true kingdom diversity by living our lives in a way that values all people. As someone who not only wants to love everyone well, and as someone who wants to teach others to love him well, I found this book to be a wealth of information and encouragement. There were parts of which I found myself reading over and over again, sometimes in disgust and sometimes in awe. Pick this book up only if you are willing to acknowledge where we have gone wrong and willing to forge a new path full of love, grace, and truth for all people made in the image of God."

—**Jamie Ivey**, podcast host of *The Happy Hour with Jamie Ivey*

"I commend the contributors to this timely and challenging volume for tackling some of the most confounding issues facing the church today. Regardless of your perspective on those issues, you will profit from reading this book."

—**Thomas S. Kidd**, distinguished professor of history and James
Vardaman Endowed Professor of History, Baylor University

"Human cultures and ethnicities reflect the abundance and creativity of God's nature. Yet, at the same time, they create barriers that we sometimes struggle to overcome. *For God So Loved the World* addresses the challenges and gifts of human difference and diversity, along with the unity that comes—or should come—for all who are in Christ. I don't think I've ever read a book that so holistically, comprehensively, and convincingly addresses the beauty and richness of God's kingdom, both now and to come."

—**Karen Swallow Prior**, research professor of English and Christianity & Culture, Southeastern Baptist Theological Seminary

"*For God So Loved the World* is a much-needed entry in literature on diversity within the church. It needs to be read by anyone who wants to be part of making our Christian communities more diverse. The all-star lineup of writers provides important information and challenges us to do what we can to enhance diversity within the body of Christ. The book is theologically sound and will resonate with those who take seriously the Word of God. Read this book and then give it to a friend. Think about these issues. That is how we are going to find solutions that move us away from Sunday morning being the most segregated time of the week."

—**George Yancey**, professor of the social sciences, Baylor University

"*For God So Loved the World: A Blueprint for Kingdom Diversity* is so thoughtful and so affective I could not put this *tour de force* down until every word was consumed. Rooted in Scripture, these inerrantists also listen carefully to the cultures they engage for the Great Commission. Today's most important theological locus—anthropology—is treated in its biblical, historical, and practical dimensions. The voices of African, Anglo, Asians, and Hispanic Americans, both women and men, advance human dignity better than anyone has yet done. Strickland and Hartman, Akin and Ashford, and Bowen and Whitfield, along with many others, paint a vision that I pray all Baptists and Evangelicals will now embrace and never relinquish."

—**Malcolm B. Yarnell III**, research professor of systematic theology, Southwestern Baptist Theological Seminary, and teaching pastor, Lakeside Baptist Church

FOR GOD
SO LOVED
THE WORLD

A BLUEPRINT FOR KINGDOM DIVERSITY

FOR GOD SO LOVED THE WORLD

Editors:

WALTER R. STRICKLAND II AND DAYTON HARTMAN

ACADEMIC
NASHVILLE, TENNESSEE

CONTENTS

Part 3: A Practical Theology

FOREWORD

J. D. Greear

"*Kairos*" is one of those Greek words that my pastor used all the time in the church I grew up in. He explained that it was a special word for time, implying a specially appointed moment in history. A time when God was up to something. A moment when God rewrites the narrative. I wasn't sure exactly what it all entailed, but I knew I really wanted to be part of one.

I believe the American church is in a *kairos* moment regarding race and gender, a moment God has appointed for the church to rise up and demonstrate a unity in Christ for which the world yearns.

Our society is not short on its declarations of intent for unity and harmony. We hear words like *postracial, color-blind, color-brave, empowering*, and *woke*. We memorialize the words of Dr. King, who longed for a day when our children would "not be judged by the color of their skin but by the content of their character."[1] We remind ourselves that our very nation was founded on the idea that all men—and, we should add, all *women*—are created equal.

---

[1] Dr. Martin Luther King Jr., "I Have A Dream", August 28, 1963.

But then we discover a cache of emails from a university president that reveal clear racial discrimination in hiring practices. We see evidence of bias in the entertainment industry. Or the media. Or something like *Charlottesville* happens.

Or we hear story after story of leaders abusing their power to assault women—and then further traumatizing victims by covering it up. We listen, with heartache and incredulity, as the #MeToo and #ChurchToo movements highlight the persistent ways that some males still use their power to prey on the vulnerable and protect their positions of power. And not only "out there," in Hollywood or on Wall Street. But in our very pews. And, God help us, in our very pulpits.

At moments like these, we realize that our declarations of racial reconciliation and gender equality are but thin veneers papered on a society still very much divided and broken.

It is in this broken moment that we realize we have entered a *kairos* moment.

What our society is unable to produce through declarations of intent, the gospel produces through the new humanity.

The gospel teaches us that all people are created equal because they are each alike made in the image of God. All people suffer from a common problem, sin, and look toward a common hope, Jesus.

That gospel creates a new humanity, a redeemed people made in Christ's image.

In the gospel alone, we find the resources to achieve multiethnic harmony.

In the gospel alone, we find the power to experience gender complementarianism the way God meant it to be—as an act of service, focused on loving, serving and protecting the other and not ourselves.

The book of Romans, Paul's longest treatment of the gospel, was written to a church experiencing ethnic division between Jew and Gentile, showing that through the cross God created a brand-new humanity. The book of Galatians (in many ways a miniature version of Romans) reminds us that men and women are, alike, equal and indispensable partners in the gospel. Their complementary roles exist to bless and serve, not domineer or abuse.

Unity in Christ outweighs any divisions we experience—racial, gender, economic, class, and everything else.

Whenever we experience ethnic strife and sexism in our churches, it's not that our inherent differences are too big for God to overcome. It's that our sense of the gospel is too small.

God, you see, created a diversity of ethnicities to display his glory like a multisplendored diamond. He made men and women as complementary and necessary partners in his mission. The two are not exactly the same—if so, one would be unnecessary. The image of God is more fully revealed in both genders than it is in one gender alone.

We should see that glory and experience that partnership, first and foremost, in the church.

Around the great throne of Christ in Revelation, we will worship the risen Son with people from every tribe, tongue, and nation. With men and women, rich and poor. The church, God's "Plan A" for rescuing the world, must stand as a place of refuge for people of every color, of every background, of every segment of society.

At our church, we say we want to reflect the diversity of our community and proclaim the diversity of the kingdom.

We want to see men and women become everything God has created, and redeemed, them to be.

The makeup of our attendance on the weekend should unequivocally declare:

We are one race—the human race.

United under one Savior—Jesus Christ.

With one problem—sin.

United with one hope.

Resurrection.

We look forward to one glorious consummation: when we reign eternally with Christ on high as brothers and sisters.

ACKNOWLEDGMENTS

We want to express our deep gratitude to Jim Baird, Chris Thompson, and Sarah Landers for their vital contributions to the project. Their encouragement and partnership in taking this project from idea to publication will serve the church for years to come. Additionally, we are thankful for all the work, research, and efforts put forth by each of the contributors. Our work in this project was merely to pull together leading thinkers and experts to speak to complex issues with clarity and authority.

General Introduction

Walter R. Strickland II

There are two ways to ruin pleasant conversation in America: introduce the topic of race or religion. This volume does both. The legacy
of race in America causes some to recoil viscerally for fear of being
accused of complicity; it causes others to engage with intense passion
because the conversation is long overdue. These innate responses dis-
close the vexing nature of this topic. Christians must skillfully navigate these emotions and the realities that cause them to God's glory.
In the spirit of ministering to and catalyzing God's people for his mission, this volume also raises the question, "what can women do?" This
question stands in contrast to the common complementarian disposition that is prone to focus on what women cannot do in the church
and beyond.[1]

Churches, Christian schools, and parachurch ministries ought
to be driven by Scripture, in contrast to the broader culture in which
actions are too often motivated by social or political pressure. The reac-
tive nature of the contemporary race and gender discussions foster an
inherently negative and punitive tone. The goal of this book is to be

---

[1] See the appendix for a statement on gender roles.

descriptive and constructive. To that end, this introduction is devoted to establishing biblical and theological foundations for pursuing Christ-centered unity and diversity.

The theological premise of this volume is most effectively communicated in the form of motivating factors to pursue reconciliation. Proper motivation will empower your journey through these pages and the application of its content in your ministry. These motivators include biblical warrant, personal sanctification, and the church's corporate witness.

Biblical Warrant

According to the apostle Paul in Ephesians 2, the gospel unifies a diverse people in Christ. Paul's words examine new life in Christ by exploring two implications of the gospel.[2] First, Paul addresses the redemption of individual people to God (vv. 1–10); then he examines the gospel's unifying implications in the redeemed community (vv. 11–22). Paul's argument culminates with a unified, yet diverse, community despite humanity's initial plight of being "dead in your trespasses and sins" (v. 1). Fortunately, God, who is gracious and merciful, made a way for salvation through faith in the resurrected Christ that united humanity to God and one another (vv. 8, 16).

After describing the means of humanity's restoration to God, Paul transitions to the gospel's ability to mend broken relationships between brothers and sisters. Christ-centered unity addresses every stumbling block that divides the people of God. In Ephesus, a significant source of discord was the Jew and Gentile divide. Paul describes how Christ's resurrection overcame that division (vv. 14–17). Paul's logic in Ephesians 2 is instructive today as God's people strive to value male and female image bearers from all cultures within the family of God.

---

[2] The gospel is simply defined as God redeeming all things to himself through the death and resurrection of Jesus Christ.

Personal Sanctification

Christians are not all-knowing, and the quest to be like God, "knowing good and evil" (Gen 3:5) began in the creation account. This ill-advised quest fractured humanity's ability to know ourselves, others, and God rightly. In 1 Cor 13:12, Paul describes the human condition by declaring that people "see only a reflection as in a mirror." These limitations emerge from human particularity as each person is influenced by certain geographic regions, economic realities, upbringing, and cultural background. Each of these characteristics dims our lenses to some earthy realities and makes us keenly aware of others.

Limitation is essential to what it means to be human. In the incarnation, Christ set aside some of his divine prerogatives (like omnipresence) to take on flesh. The incarnation demonstrates that limitation is not sinful but integral to the meaning of humanity. But in practice, many people deny their limitations and subconsciously insist that they have the ability to transcend their humanity. Because humanity is imperfect, any effort to insist that a particular person or cultural perspective is purely objective denies Scripture's teaching about fallen humanity and asserts humanity into the role of God. The human condition generates *blind spots* that cannot be denied. As a result, the question is not, do I have blind spots?, but rather, what are my blind spots?

In an effort to overcome our blind spots, Prov 27:17 says that "iron sharpens iron, as one person sharpens another." Scripture also notes that iron sharpens iron most effectively across the lines of difference. This dynamic is evident in 2 Tim 2:2 (older and younger men) and in Titus 2 (older and younger women) as they benefit from the age gap. In the contemporary American church, learning from older generations is held in relatively high regard compared to gleaning from those of a different culture or across gender lines (mainly brothers learning from their sisters). Unfortunately, believers rarely reap the benefits of this mutual sharpening because of the unconscious yet prideful assumption that those from different cultures and women have nothing insightful to offer.

Iron sharpening iron across difference is best illustrated in the marriage relationship. Two sinners come together and are refined and sanctified because of that relationship. Despite the difficult and awkward moments, on the whole, Christians cherish the opportunity to be sanctified and uphold their marriage covenant before God. Many times, the benefits of relationships between brothers and sisters of different backgrounds are forfeited the moment conversation becomes uncomfortable or a misunderstanding occurs. All efforts of coming together are suspended. After well-intended attempts to unify, believers reconvene in their segregated spaces because their allegiance to American segregated cultural norms is seemingly greater than their commitment to the people of God.

The slow pace of the American church to pursue racial reconciliation reveals a gaping hole in the pursuit of sanctification. In America, the struggle for racial reconciliation is perhaps the premier litmus test for spiritual maturity. A body of believers that worships across racial lines, resembling their community, and expresses the "one anothers" of the New Testament paints a wonderful picture of the gospel's ability to tear down the walls that divide. Moreover, it is a people who have heeded Paul's admonition in Phil 2:3–5a: "Do nothing out of selfish ambition or conceit, but in humility consider others as more important than yourselves. Everyone should look out not only for his own interests, but also for the interests of others. Adopt the same attitude as that of Christ Jesus."

People who worship in multiethnic spaces are more likely to have put on Christ in a way that overcomes historical baggage, heals grudges, and forces them to think on behalf of the other. This requires the forgiveness and patience that have been exemplified in Christ. Although human effort will not realize John's multiethnic vision of Rev 5:9 on this side of the kingdom, the Lord *will* do that when he returns. Efforts to pursue biblical diversity are not about achieving kingdom promises now, but about the work done in and among his people in the process. This refining makes Christians more like Jesus, and this is why racial reconciliation and gleaning from men and women alike are essential.

The Church's Corporate Witness

Christ's followers live between his first coming and second coming and have experienced the fruit of the resurrection in salvation, but God's people look forward to experiencing the fullness of God's kingdom when all of creation is under God's rule and reign. Until the kingdom is here in full, God's people are to live as those actively seeking to manifest the riches of Christ's future kingdom reign in the present.

The church's collective witness either clarifies or obscures the gospel of Jesus Christ and the hope of John's Rev 7:9 vision. In the area of unity, the American church has positively, but all too often negatively, embodied the gospel. Christians are called to serve as a beacon of hope to one another and to the world by consistently living the redeemed life that encompasses both word and deed on an issue where there is a desperate need for hope.

Helpful Definitions

Ethne, translated "ethnicity" (sometimes "nations"), is a biblical term used to describe the "peoples" of the earth. Two of the best-known occurrences of *ethne* are Matt 28:19 and Rev 7:9. Ethnicity refers to the biological origins of a person's birth and is part of God's good creation (Gen 1:31). Together, humanity's countless ethnicities reflect the fullness of God's intention for his image bearers.

Despite its association with ethnicity, *culture* is a nonbiological phenomenon that shapes common behaviors and thought patterns shared by a people group. Cultural norms help elucidate humor, guide food preferences, and determine things like what constitutes being "on time." Ethnicity and culture alike will appear in the kingdom; however, an important distinction is that although every ethnicity will be present only God-honoring aspects of culture will appear in eternity, because culture is generated by fallen humanity.

Race is a socially constructed reality that attributes negative or positive meaning to biological characteristics and cultural manifestations that are used to categorize people. This categorization creates "in"

and "out" groups. Inhabiting the "in" group is prerequisite for gaining
social influence and requires diminishing distinctions within it (i.e.,
fabricating homogeneity) and simultaneously highlighting the distinctions among the "out" groups to ensure their perpetual marginalization.
This type of categorization is unbiblical and will not appear in God's
kingdom.[3]

It follows that *racism* is a sinful attitude that perpetuates this categorization. Unfortunately, church practice and the Christian faith itself
have been employed to uphold these categories in sacred and secular
environments. Racism appears individually, communally, and structur-
ally. Individual racism (or bias) is something that is done by one individual to another.[4] As a result, racism is increasingly covert and hides
within mental categorization and communication.[5] Scripture warns of
the negative and positive influence of individuals in community (Prov
13:20), and racial bias is negatively compounded in homogeneous communities. It's easy for homogeneous communities to abdicate their
responsibility to apply the gospel to racism and contrive theological
justification to dismiss sinful activity.

Systemic (or structural) racism is the means by which systems,
organizations, and enterprises grant advantages and influence to some
and disadvantage others.[6] Beneficiaries of systems rarely appreciate
the value received and can unknowingly perpetuate such structures.
By contrast, those disadvantaged by depressing systems consistently
feel the negative effects of inequitable structures. I'm convinced that

---

[3] National identities are neither inherently good nor evil. Racialization is
when national designations are given meaning that promotes or marginalizes
over against other people groups.

[4] George Yancey, *Beyond Racial Gridlock: Embracing Mutual Responsibility*
(Downers Grove, IL: InterVarsity Press, 2006), 20.

[5] Michael O. Emerson and Christian Smith, *Divided by Faith: Evangelical
Religion and the Problem of Race in America* (New York: Oxford, 2000), 9.

[6] Michael O. Emerson and Christian Smith, *Divided by Faith: Evangelical
Religion and the Problem of Race in America* (New York: Oxford University
Press, 2001), 89. In a ministry environment, this often looks like programming,
preaching, and developing practices with a single demographic in mind.

the vast majority of systemic bias is perpetuated unintentionally, but must be taken captive by well-meaning believers. Each aspect (individual, communal, and structural) of racial bias must be redressed by the restorative power of the gospel to engender progress in ethnic relations.

The most common use of *race* in this book is not in affirmation of the social categories it produces; it is, rather, an admission of the negative influence derived from these secular categories. *Race* is also used to reference a common humanity shared by every image bearer. Thus, *racial reconciliation* is participating in the redemptive power of the gospel by dismantling individual, communal, and structural racism in a world that bears the marks of sin. Essential to this work is the task of deploying the Christian faith as a balm in a nationwide, enduring wound.

The Book's Scope and Sequence

In a well-intended flurry of activity, the challenges that impede reconciliation are often oversimplified. We must understand the complexity and depth of the issues before sprinting toward solutions. When short-sighted decisions are made, symptoms of more sophisticated problems are addressed and long-term progress is frustrated, breeding frustration and a sense of defeat. This book offers three sections to help understand the dynamics at play and move forward with informed zeal.

Part 1 offers insight on current racial tensions in light of the past. Following Stephen Eccher's introduction, which calls attention to underheard and obscured voices in the Christian tradition, the essays explore how these omissions occurred. Dayton Hartman demonstrates how theological voices were overlooked, showing how theological formulation became the property of the Anglo West. Steven Harris's chapter discusses the development of segregation in America; his purpose is to facilitate ministry to people in the midst of attitudes and structures that have kept people apart. As Christian leaders move toward healing the systemic brokenness that plagues the American landscape, Keith Harper explores a denominational partnership forged to heal race relations that served to fortify segregation.

Josh Wester introduces part 2 on public theology by calling readers to examine how Christians from different racial backgrounds have navigated our common life together. Bruce Ashford explores a comprehensive pro-life ethic that transcends the "single issue" of any demographic. Alan Cross continues engaging the church's public affirmation of image bearers by prescribing ways to minister both to and with immigrants. Part 2 concludes with D. A. Horton's treatment of the nature and content of urban apologetics.

The final part of the book answers the practical question about how to pursue kingdom diversity in ministry. After an introduction by Jarvis Williams, Chris Williamson offers principles for shepherding toward racial reconciliation in the local church. Central in the church's ministry is preaching from Scripture. Walter Strickland demonstrates how to read and teach the Bible with a broad audience in mind while affirming scriptural authority. God's kingdom vision includes men and women alike. Then Amber Bowen laments the contested nature of the gender conversation in church life. She exhorts believers to offer one another courage to pursue God's mission by his design. Tony Merida builds upon Bowen's chapter by describing specific ways that men and women can be missional partners in the local church. The final chapter offers several "tales from the trenches" that are intended to be both instructional and encouraging testimonies from saints who have facilitated healing in areas where America has been historically divided. In the appendix, Matthew Emerson describes a spectrum within complementarianism over against the assumption that it is monolithic.

Part 1

Historical Context

Introduction

Stephen Brett Eccher

And they sang a new song: You are worthy to take the scroll
and to open its seals; because you were slaughtered and you
purchased people for God by your blood from every tribe and
language and people and nation. You made them a kingdom
and priests to our God, and they will reign on the earth.
—Revelation 5:9–10

John's portrait of God's culminating work in redemptive history is both beautiful and stirring. It brings to fruition a salvation history that began in a garden with Adam and Eve but ends in a heavenly city with throngs of people from every tribe, tongue, and nation worshipping the Lamb. This redemptive activity was and will be the realized blessing of the Son, Jesus Christ, entering into human history by means of the incarnation.

Alongside God's work in salvation history, the Bible sets forth a complementary narrative for God's people. The bride of Christ, the church, was set apart by God to be a people living in community as a temporal reflection, albeit an imperfect reflection, of that future eschatological reality prophesied by John. As the church awaits the return of Messiah, believers worship their King Jesus corporately and labor together to make him known among the nations.

Despite its biblical foundation and purpose, the history of the church is replete with examples whereby this important and God-ordained call has been forgotten, even grossly undermined by professing Christians. In fact, rather than offering a visible expression of that heavenly kingdom, in the two thousand years since Jesus's ascension, the church has mostly presented a distorted reflection of this biblical pattern. Rather than exemplifying unity, diversity, and community, the church has too frequently been characterized by discord and division. As Martin Luther King Jr. once famously opined, "It is one of the tragedies of our nation, one of the shameful tragedies, that eleven o'clock on Sunday morning is one of the most segregated hours, if not the most segregated hours in Christian America."[1] Dr. King's statement was a telling observation about his contemporary American church, yet it is also relevant to Christian history as a whole. Division has cast a long shadow over the church's history and been manifest in myriad ways extending as far back as the Jewish-Gentile divide seen in the New Testament. Sadly, King's experience from the mid-twentieth century was a microcosm of the much larger problem of bias, which has plagued the church's history in its global footprint. All too often ethnic, gender, and cultural diversity have been eschewed, even vilified, by Christians.

Despite the historic and repeated failings of the church to realize its diverse scriptural calling, there remains hope for a greater affinity between the church's fallen, present state and its glorified, promised future. Recognizing that the church's makeup and mission have been distorted throughout history and understanding what led to these distortions is crucial for creating a contemporary corrective. Until both the depths and cause of the church's brokenness in the area of unity amid diversity are identified, a remedy will remain undefined and elusive.

---

[1] This statement was made by Dr. Martin Luther King Jr. during a *Meet the Press* NBC interview, April 17, 1960.

"Until the lions have their historians, tales of the hunt will always glorify the hunter."[2] This anonymous African proverb suggests that without a critical examination of those with the power to write history it is impossible to understand the stories of those who are without power. Unfortunately, those with a platform to write history have traditionally for their own selfish gain repeatedly and purposefully omitted, erased, and silenced those at the margins of society. Those in power rarely like to cede their authority and what it affords them. Sadly that tactic has been applied within a church context as well. In fact, this proverb captures in a pithy and clever way the situation that the modern Christian church faces, given its history. More important, it serves as a reminder that other stories, just as complex and compelling as the dominant one preserved in history, do exist. Those untold accounts have value and need to be told.

Before considering how to access divergent cultural traditions and experiences to realize a more biblical church, it is helpful to know why these nonmajority voices have been historically absent from the dominant culture. A number of contextual factors have served to systemically silence many Christians throughout history. Some of those silencing influences are subtle, even assumed by many, given certain cultural norms that are frequently taken for granted. The harsh realities of illiteracy or economic cycles of poverty, for example, create environments where certain sectors of society are not afforded the means, time, or platform to tell their stories. Unless the proverbial lion is valued enough to have its story told and given the medium to record that narrative, how will the history of the hunt be told from its perspective?

Other forms of oppression are more visible, blatant, and purposeful in their intention. Consider the people who have been forgotten in church history because of slavery and human trafficking. Or ponder the number of women throughout history who had their stories squelched

---

[2] The twentieth-century Nigerian author Chinua Achebe helped popularize this quotation while providing commentary on the political situation in his native country in 1994. Chinua Achebe, "The Art of Fiction," interview by Jerome Brooks, *Paris Review* 133 (Winter 1994): 143–66.

by forms of patriarchalism and sexism.[3] In the case of women, that is roughly 50 percent of the population that has for centuries been muzzled by its oppressors. Their unique accounts and memoirs were unwritten, lost, or ignored, while those of their male counterparts have had a more dominant voice that has shaped the historical narrative.

Beyond these modes of oppression and a host of others, Christianity's historical record has also been purposefully skewed and altered for centuries by those in power. Until recent years, it was not merely permissible but expected that history was retold in order to shape the way Christianity was understood and perceived. As James Bradley and Richard Muller have argued, "Before the mid-eighteenth century, the study of church history was uncritical; it was invariably written from a confessional viewpoint and it was anything but detached or neutral."[4] For centuries, historical method has favored the hunter over the lion. In the case of Christianity, this has most often benefited the Western tradition, as well as certain ethnicities, especially those of European-Anglo descent, and men. For example, consider the myriad medieval icons, images, and artistic renderings that depict Athanasius and Augustine with light skin tones, when both church fathers were of North African descent. The fictitious story these artistic pieces told perpetuated the notion of a certain type of Christianity, one in which lighter skin was normal.

In the end, bias was and will always be a part of the human experience. That truth is inescapable regardless of one's era. Nevertheless, there is a path forward to a more robust and biblical picture of the church. Perhaps that path begins by imagining that hunted lion with a quill in its paw. The beauty of that imagery, and of the entire proverb,

---

[3] *Patriarchalism* here denotes a social and/or political program whereby men were historically understood as superior in personhood to women, which directly led to the elevation of men in society as unique purveyors of governance, beneficiaries of social privilege, and caretakers of moral supremacy. *Sexism* is used to highlight the purposeful discrimination of female voices specifically on the basis of sex alone.

[4] James E. Bradley and Richard A. Muller, *Church History: An Introduction to Research Methods and Resources*, 2nd ed. (Grand Rapids: Eerdmans, 2016), 9.

is that the corrective to historical bias has been cleverly woven into its comedic critique. The lion telling its side of the story? Is it that preposterous? Along similar lines, what if the church valued the voices of those who had for centuries been demeaned, disenfranchised, and dehumanized? Their stories, though different from the more familiar ones, are no less real or respectable. What if those on the margins of society were not merely told but also shown that they were of value? What if these were granted a seat at the table of change or given access to positions of influence and authority? What if they were celebrated for their great value as image bearers and then empowered to use their voices to help create a more biblical church? The following essays will consider these ideas and more. And although these subsequent chapters do not purport to solve the problem of historic bias for the church, they do offer helpful thoughts along these lines as a means of considering a productive path forward, a path that God desires and one that eventually will lead to that stunning sight once glimpsed by the apostle John.

Chapter 1

The Shaping of the Western Christian Mind

Dayton Hartman

Vignette 1

"Does he have good theology?" I felt the blood drain from my face as I stood awkwardly, unsure how to respond. A question like this from a fellow pastor was not out of the ordinary, except for the context of the question. What elicited this inquiry was my mentioning that I had invited an area pastor to begin meeting with our growing cohort of ministers. It was not uncommon for us to invite new pastors into our meetings. What was different is that this was the first time I was asked about a man's theology. This was also the first time I invited an African-American pastor to our monthly roundtable.

I responded, sounding slightly befuddled, "Good. He believes the Bible. I'm curious, why do you ask?" The response was telling: "Well, I just know that a lot of black churches don't have very good theology." This statement reflected a level of subtle (or not-so-subtle) white

supremacy. We had never discussed the theological bona fides of the
Anglo pastors invited. Why now?[1]

This exchange occurred many years ago. However, this same
assumption has recently reared its head in a public fashion. A well-
known blogger advocating for our African-American brothers and sisters was lambasted for denying the "fact" that Anglos are responsible for
establishing and preserving theological orthodoxy for the ages.[2] This
is not subtle white supremacy; this is historical ignorance mixed with
"sanctified" and seemingly pious racism.

It is true that much of Christianity's theological enterprise has
become the product of white men. However, we must ask two questions: (1) Has this always been the case? (2) If not, why is it now true?

My aim in this chapter is to demonstrate that orthodoxy was
birthed and preserved by a diverse people, and it is only because of
our historical ignorance, and sometimes blatant sin, that the present
theological landscape in the West is dominated by the voices of one
particular ethnicity.[3]

---

[1] The truth is that bad or sub-biblical theology is found in many church
traditions, regardless of the ethnicities that are attached to those traditions.

[2] In 2019, the United Methodist Church (UMC) became embroiled in
controversy when its member churches were invited to vote on a plan to formally allow congregations to embrace, advocate, and celebrate LGBTQ life-
styles. This effort, largely pushed by UMC churches in the West, was struck
down by a strong consensus among UMC churches in Africa that sought to
affirm and uphold biblical orthodoxy on issues of sexual practice and ethics.
It would seem that Africa has once again acted as the safeguard of historic
orthodoxy. See Kathy L. Gilbert, Heather Hahn, and Joey Butler, "2019 General
Conferences Passes Traditional Plan," *UM News*, February 26, 2019, www
.umnews.org/en/news/gc2019-daily-feb-26.

[3] I am encouraged by the progress made in recent years toward a global
and diverse influence in the Western church's theological enterprise. What I
am arguing for is a reclaiming of the theological contributions of the global
church, outside the Anglo West. These themes have been explored in works
such as Craig Ott and Harold Netland, eds., *Globalizing Theology* (Grand
Rapids, MI: Baker Academic, 2006); Timothy Tennent, *Theology in the
Context of World Christianity* (Grand Rapids, MI: Zondervan, 2007); Lamin
Sanneh, *Whose Religion is Christianity?: The Gospel Beyond the West* (Grand

The Early Years

Most Christians are guilty of anachronistic thinking, meaning that we assume the past was largely like the present.[4] One obvious instance of this is in medieval art. Paintings of Jesus present him as a European male, often wearing medieval European garb, rather than a first-century Jewish attire. We do this today as well, perhaps in a more insidious fashion. When you pick up a children's Bible, complete with artwork that illustrates every major character of the Scripture, what do you notice? Most of the artwork depicts the men and women of the Bible as white. Some Westerners assume that the central figures of our faith were Anglo-Westerners. However, the central characters of the Bible were all Middle Eastern and African. Additionally, the history of our faith, until recent centuries, was marked by ethnically diverse voices.

The church at Antioch is often identified as *the* missionary church of the New Testament. What is encouraging about this church? It's not just their emphasis on sending missionaries to the nations (as wonderful as that is); it's that their local assemblies comprised the nations. As the first of the sending churches in the New Testament, their heart *for* the nations was reflected in their congregation that was composed of men and women *from* the nations. Even their leadership reflected multiple ethnicities and cultures (Acts 13:1). Ethnically diverse leadership can be a catalyst toward encouraging a church to be a missionary people. The church that most modeled obedience to the Great Commission was also the most diverse church in the New Testament.

In the post-New Testament era, the contours of Christian orthodoxy were forged by a diverse people. The wording and shape of the

---

Rapids, MI: Eerdmans, 2003); Gene Green, Stephen Pardue, and K. Yeo, eds., *Jesus without Borders: Christology in the Majority World* (Grand Rapids, MI: Eerdmans, 2014); Jeffrey Greenman and Gene Green, eds., *Global Theology in Evangelical Perspective: Exploring the Contextual Nature of Theology and Mission* (Downers Grove, IL: InterVarsity Press, 2012).

[4] One of the clearest examples of this is in medieval Christian art. Every biblical character is presented as a European with a contemporary, to the period, hairstyle.

most influential Christian creed was not steered by the thoughts or words of a theologian from the Anglo West but from Africa. For instance, one of the most important shapers of Christian orthodoxy is Athanasius (296–373). His nickname, "the black dwarf," reflected both his height and his skin tone. Much of what has shaped the outline of Christian orthodoxy was because of Athanasius's influence at Nicaea and beyond, which earned him the designation "the father of orthodoxy."[5] The irony of this moniker is that for much of American history a man of Athanasius's ethnicity would have been forbidden from studying in seminaries that championed historic orthodoxy. Every Trinitarian statement of faith has been influenced by and echoes the theology of Athanasius.[6]

The creeds, particularly the Apostles' and Nicene,[7] define the contours of orthodoxy, not because they have authority, but because they accurately summarize the content of Scripture. The relationship between Scripture and creeds is best described as a highway with guardrails for theological exploration and explanation.[8] In short, the

---

[5] Samuel Macauley Jackson, ed., *The New Schaff-Herzog Encyclopedia of Religious Knowledge: Embracing Biblical, Historical, Doctrinal, and Practical Theology and Biblical, Theological, and Ecclesiastical Biography from the Earliest Times to the Present Day* (New York: Funk & Wagnalls, 1908–14), 52–53.

[6] The value of looking to the early church to shake us out of our inaccurate assumptions is stated succinctly by Michael Haykin: "Every age has its own distinct outlook and presuppositions that remain unquestioned even by opponents. The examination of another period of thought forces us to confront our innate prejudices, which would go unnoticed otherwise." *Rediscovering the Church Fathers* (Wheaton, IL: Crossway, 2011), 17.

[7] Certainly the ecumenical creeds are all important. However, these earliest creeds demonstrate the core of orthodox doctrine and faith.

[8] "Scripture is our starting point. It defines the direction and content of biblical orthodoxy. Our journey in biblical orthodoxy must take place within the lanes provided by Scripture. Within those lanes, Christians can disagree and remain on the safe road of biblical orthodoxy. Think of the lanes as different Christian traditions—Reformed, Wesleyan, or Charismatic, for example. Guardrails—the creeds—protect those traveling along the highway of biblical orthodoxy. While allowing for diversity on non-essential issues, the

creedal guardrails of orthodoxy were built by men and women outside the Anglo West.[9]

Many argue that Martin Luther, the father of the Protestant Reformation, ought to be regarded as history's most important theologian. However, *the* most influential theologian was Augustine of Hippo (354–430), a native of North Africa. Luther was an Augustinian monk who represented a reclaiming of Augustine's legacy. Augustine is not merely the most important post-New Testament theologian; his thought is largely what gave birth to the worldview that enabled the rise of Western culture. As Jonathan Hill observes, Augustine's "influence over Western thought—religious and otherwise—is total; he remains inescapable even over fifteen centuries after his death."[10]

As the Roman Empire met its demise, accusations circulated that Christianity led to the empire's downfall. In response, Augustine wrote his defining work, *The City of God*, which engages paganism both politically and theologically. Augustine's argumentation served as the basis for what became the defining features of Western thought. How, then, is it that the North African father of Western thought spawned a tradition in which African voices are absent?

Three Worldview Planks

I will briefly argue that the absence of non-Western voices in the dominant-culture Christianity is linked to the development of three worldview "planks" that are fundamental to Western Christian thought: philosophical, theological, and cultural.

---

creeds prevent us from veering off the highway of biblical orthodoxy." Dayton Hartman, *Church History for Modern Ministry: Why Our Past Matters for Everything We Do* (Bellingham, WA: Lexham, 2016), 16.

[9] See Thomas Oden, *How Africa Shaped the Christian Mind: Rediscovering the African Seedbed of Western Christianity* (Downers Grove, IL: InterVarsity Press, 2010).

[10] Jonathan Hill, *The History of Christian Thought* (Downers Grove, IL: InterVarsity Press, 2003), 79.

The Philosophical Split between the Eastern and Western Churches

A growing rift between the Western (increasingly Roman Catholic) and Eastern (Orthodox) churches brewed for centuries. The impetus for the schism was multifaceted and ranged from issues emerging from the *filioque* controversy[11] to the diminished influence of Eastern patriarchs, and ever-expanding linguistic differentiation. Perhaps the most easily identified historical cause was the rise of Charlemagne (ca. 742–814). This soon-to-be emperor dominated much of Europe and worked relentlessly to unite the disparate peoples throughout the Western portions of the continent. In 800, Pope Leo III (750–816) inaugurated Charlemagne as the emperor of the Holy Roman Empire. This moment established the Western church's intermingling with the governmental powers of Europe, a marriage that was not mirrored, in the strictest sense, among the churches of the East. The Western (European) church's love affair with governmental power gave it a platform and prominence that the Eastern church did not match. In 1054, the split or schism was formally pronounced, and the global church became a divided church.

Centuries in the making, the East-West schism served to accelerate a growing sense of "otherness" among Eastern believers. The philosophically oriented theology of the East was "othered." The power structure and the ethnic groups that dominated the East were eventually

---

[11] The *filioque* controversy was a philosophical-theological dispute over whether the Western versions of the creeds were correct in their clarification that the Holy Spirit proceeded from the Father and the Son rather than the Eastern rendition of the creeds that stated that the Holy Spirit proceeded from the Father. The issue at hand was not so much a divide over doctrine or philosophy as it was a division over language due to linguistic barriers. See Steve Strauss, "Creeds, Confessions, and Global Theologizing," in *Globalizing Theology: Belief and Practice in an Era of World Christianity*, ed. Craig Ott and Harold Netland (Grand Rapids: Baker Academic, 2006), 140–56.

obscured. It could be argued that this schism heavily contributed to the otherness of Eastern philosophical presuppositions.[12]

In his excellent work *The Lost History of Christianity*, Philip Jenkins makes an interesting statement regarding this "otherness": "In modern terminology, the Eastern churches were thoroughly enculturated, presenting their faith in the languages of the culture they encountered, sharing their artistic and literary forms."[13] The Eastern churches were in constant contact with Muslims, Buddhists, and Hindus as well as local and regional tribal religions. The consistent interaction with other religions necessitated that Eastern churches become experts in contextualization.[14] This resulted in a Christianity that employed biblically appropriate cultural expressions of worship, art forms, and theological priorities.

The insular nature of the Western churches diminished the need for contextualization and therefore led to a greater sense of uniformity among churches in practice and theological priorities. The uniformity of the West further propelled the sense of otherness inherent to the people of the Eastern churches.

The centuries following the East-West schism witnessed the near-extinction of the Eastern church. Through the advance of Islam, the brutality of regional rulers, diseases, and disasters, the churches of the East were utterly decimated across the three hundred years between AD 1200 and 1500. By the dawn of the Reformation, Christianity had a stronghold on Europe. As the Western church became a politically significant power, its theological pronouncements also increased in their

---

[12] For full disclosure. I side with the formulation of the Western church regarding the nature of the Spirit's procession.

[13] Philip Jenkins, *The Lost History of Christianity* (New York: HarperOne, 2008), 14.

[14] Contextualization is the process by which theological categories are expressed in forms and language that make use of the existing culture's definitions and linguistic norms. The content of the theology is not changed to adapt to the culture around it, but the mode of expression is adapted to the communication forms of the prevailing culture.

power and effect. As Philip Jenkins notes, by 1500 Christianity had become distinctly European. What began as a divide over philosophy resulted in distinction in theology.[15]

The Theology of the Protestant Reformation Reformed the Western Church, Not the Eastern

The amount of theological material produced early in the Reformation reflected the concerns and philosophical categories of the West. There was no concern for the Christians of the East, because the Reformation was relegated to the Western church. The Protestant Reformation and the ensuing backlash within Roman Catholicism served to reinforce the dominance of the Anglo West in the production of theological works. Much of the Eastern church was insulated from the Reformation (although not entirely). As the Reformation's influence grew and its leaders rose in prominence, they developed traditions that further pushed the center of Christian theology westward.

This observation is not to cast the Reformation in a negative light. Protestants are grateful for the *solas* of the Reformation. Nevertheless, the Reformation reinforced the centrality of Western thought for the Christian world. This was certainly not Martin Luther's intention. Around the time the Protestant Reformation formalized (1517), Luther developed a fascination with the history and theology of Ethiopian Christianity. Ethiopia, in Luther's estimation, provided a glimpse into what was in Christianity's past and what ought to be in her future: a church divorced from the papacy and all that comes with Romanism. In 1534, Luther met a representative of the Ethiopian church, Michael the Deacon; the details of this encounter reinforced Luther's positive appraisal of the Ethiopian church.[16] But the Reformation did not result in unifying the divided church; rather, it served to unintentionally reinforce the schism. Although the church of the East was viewed

---

[15] Jenkins, *Lost History of Christianity*, 25.

[16] Martin Brecht, *Martin Luther, vol. 3: The Preservation of the Church, 1532–1546* (Minneapolis: Fortress, 1993), 59.

with overall positivity, the Reformation was a phenomenon of the Western (Roman) church. This was not out of spite or animosity to the Christians of the East, but simply one of the ongoing ramifications of the East-West schism.

If the East-West schism resulted in the philosophical presupposition of the East's otherness, the Reformation established the theological otherness of the East. To be Christian was to be among those seeking the reform of the Western church. Of course, this was not Luther's intention (as his engagement with Michael the Deacon demonstrates). However, this assumption became an unintended consequence. The Western church has and continues to be dominated by Anglo thought, priorities, and theological emphases.

Cultural: The Rise of Colonialism Served to Establish the Cultural Divide between the East and West

Colonialism is the process of Europeans exercising dominance and control over non-European lands and people groups. Not only did colonialism result in the dominance of non-European peoples, but it eventually meant the forced importation of Western or predominately Anglo culture on the peoples impacted by colonialism. There was an undeniable presupposition that if it was Anglo, it was better.[17] As a system, colonialism resulted in genocides, overt racism, slave trading, and other horrifically evil practices.

The otherness of those outside the reach of the Protestant Reformation did nothing to dull the subtle, and at times overt, sense of Anglo supremacy.[18] Instead of carrying a contextualizable gospel to the

---

[17] This assumption often carried with it theological overtones that included the belief that those with dark skin were cursed by God and were inherently inferior to whites. Theologians and public thinkers charged those with dark skin as bearing the curse of Ham.

[18] One of the clearest examples of this was a Bible produced for slaves in the West Indies. This heavily edited version of the Scriptures removed any

nations, colonization assumed the Anglo way of life was inherent in the gospel. The cultural assumptions of colonization made it common for Western missionaries to force new believers to give up their previous ways of life in order to accept the gospel, rather than suggesting that the gospel redeem preexisting culture.[19]

The intermingling of Christianity and colonization resulted in baffling absurdities, such as imploring Africans to renounce the use of drums and to use the organ (keyboard) in their worship services. Missionaries encouraged converts to leave behind their previous modes of dress and adopt distinctly Anglo clothing styles. Sadly, the pressure to assimilate sometimes continues to this day. I recall sitting in a missions conference during the early 2000s for a fundamentalist-leaning organization; the language of convincing tribal groups in Africa to adopt a "godly lifestyle" included forcing them to stop clapping in worship and requiring them to dress like Anglo businessmen from suburban America.

On American soil, up until the end of the Civil War, Protestantism was largely an Anglo phenomenon. Following the war, the theological climate necessitated that African-American Christians produce written materials meant to provide counter-exegesis to the overtly racist and contradictory expositions employed by former slave holders.[20] Protestantism was linked with the evils of slavery. A reformation was needed, and its reformers were former slaves.[21]

---

text that could lead to slaves desiring freedom, even passages pertaining to the gospel. The Slave Bible has been on display at the Museum of the Bible (Washington, DC) in conjunction with Fisk University, accessed August 22, 2019. See www.museumofthebible.org/exhibits/slave-bible.

[19] If the Eastern church pursued enculturation, the church of the West pursued culture importation.

[20] Mark Noll, *The Civil War as a Theological Crisis* (Chapel Hill: University of North Carolina Press, 2006), 64–65.

[21] An excellent representation of the theological rigor among former slaves can be found in Charles Octavius Boothe, *Plain Theology for Plain People* (Bellingham, WA: Lexham, 2017).

Vignette 2

In 2014, my church established a partnership with an indigenous church-planting movement in India. I was overwhelmed to hear of the numbers of people coming to faith in Christ. I traveled to India, my first experience outside of an Anglo-dominated nation state, and I was horrified by what it revealed in my soul. I found myself silently questioning the orthodoxy and philosophy of men and women who professed faith in Jesus. Why? Because their philosophical categories differed from mine. Additionally, their cultural expressions of worship and biblical community were not my own. By the end of my trip, I was painfully aware of my own distinctly Anglo-centric presuppositions about what it means to be a Christian. On the flight back, I spent time in prayer and repentance.

Following that trip, I embraced something I already knew but had not applied to my heart and soul: Theology is not formed in a vacuum. Its priorities and contours are constantly shaped by the issues of our age and the questions raised by our culture. In short, there is no way to escape the distinct influence of culture in shaping and establishing theology.

This is a good thing! The content of the gospel does not change when it is expressed in a different cultural context. The guardrails of orthodoxy remain consistent, but the gospel's implications changes based upon the specific cultural sins, idols, and needs that the gospel answers, corrects, or redeems.

This means we need each other. A robust theological guardrail cannot be purely Anglo-centric in culture and heritage, nor can it be strictly African or Asian. It must be global in scope, diverse in application, and yet unified in its central convictions.

The Result: Philosophy + Theology + Culture

The philosophical differences that developed between the churches of the East and West culminated in a schism. The decimation of the Eastern churches, coupled with the Western church embracing

European powers by intermingling the church with the state, preserved the church in the West but rendered it distinctly European. The
Protestant Reformation accomplished the necessary work of reform-
ing the Roman Catholic Church. However, an unfortunate corollary is
that it solidified orthodoxy's distinctly Anglo-centric expression in the
West. The philosophical and theological divides culminated in a cultural divide that tied together Western philosophy, theology, and culture as the standard for what is Christian.

It is nearly impossible for Western Christians to be divorced from
the results of this divide. In the present, these three factors were exacer-
bated by proliferation of common sense realism. This system proposes
that human beings are capable of examining the world around them
and making judgments that are free from bias. In short, the world truly
is how it is perceived. So if the churches of the East appear to be other
in their philosophy, theology, and culture, it is because they are as truly
"other" as they appear. This epistemological assumption dismisses,
often unintentionally, the need for special revelation to understand the
world as God says it actually is.[22]

The aim of common sense realism was good, as it

> sought to refute both the skepticism of David Hume (1711–
> 1776) and the idealism of George Berkeley (1685–1753) by
> arguing that ordinary people may gain accurate knowledge of
> the real world through responsible use of their senses. While
> man's physical senses could discover truth about the outside
> world through empirical study and induction, an innate "moral
> sense" common to all humans allowed for intuitive knowledge
> of certain foundational principles of morality.[23]

But denying the possibility of bias in an individual's thinking fundamentally rejects the reality that for those living in the Anglo West

---

[22] Noll, *Civil War*, 56–64.
[23] "Scottish Realism" in *Dictionary of Christianity in America*, ed. Daniel
G. Reid et al. (Downers Grove, IL: InterVarsity, 1990), Logos ed.

(particularly the United States) our assumptions are shaped by Anglo-centric historical realities.

As will be explored in the next chapter, our nation's history will be scarred forever by the evil of slavery. Mark Noll describes it this way:

> The interpretive practices that had grown up with the great antebellum denominations favored democratic, republican, antitraditional, and commonsensical exegesis. Against this historical background, the biblical proslavery argument seemed very strong, the biblical antislavery argument seemed religiously dangerous, and the nuanced biblical argument against slavery in its American form did not comport well with democratic practice or republican theory.[24]

With the fall of slavery in the United States, there should have been hope for the church and theological enterprise of America to reclaim the diversity of Antioch. Alas, it did not happen. Instead, the effects of the three planks of the West's ethnocentric worldview continued. In short, the fall of slavery did not result in the fall of racism or white supremacy.

An example of the three planks is at work in the world's largest Protestant denomination, the Southern Baptist Convention (SBC). The SBC was born out of a dispute over slavery. Convention organizers supported the commodification of human beings based upon their skin color. As result, Southern Baptist seminaries were born to train white men.[25]

At the dawn of the twentieth century, those institutions that convictionally clung to the authority and inspiration of the Bible (including SBC seminaries) were paradoxically the schools that reflected Darwin's

---

[24] Noll, *Civil War*, 49.

[25] Having repented of the racism present at the birth of the Southern Baptist Convention, the transforming work of the gospel has produced increasingly diverse student populations in our seminaries. Even so, seminaries have taken steps to publicly acknowledge the sins of the past. The Southern Baptist Theological Seminary's December 2018 release of *Report on Slavery and Racism in the History of The Southern Baptist Theological Seminary* demonstrates this historical reality with painful but necessary detail. See www.sbts.edu/southern-project/.

racist worldview by barring nonwhites.[26] As Germanic higher criticism flooded American seminaries and the so-called battle for the Bible began, the seminaries that undermined biblical authority became the most ethnically inclusive.[27]

As the twentieth century marched toward the watershed period of civil rights legislation, the eventual leaders of the Civil Rights Movement were trained in schools and seminaries that had jettisoned biblical orthodoxy. Many who remained committed to theological orthodoxy were largely silent in the face of Jim Crow segregation.

The cessation of racist laws did not overturn the Anglo-centric worldview that was shaped by the three worldview planks (philosophy, theology, culture) for centuries.

The goal of this brief chapter is to help the reader understand that each of us carries assumptions that have historical roots (some good and some bad) and these roots shape the way we think theologically. The remaining chapters in this section serve to help readers extricate themselves from these assumptions.

---

[26] One of the most unsettling discoveries of my adult life was when I was exposed to the personal correspondence of the famed champion of orthodoxy, J. Gresham Machen. The famed theologian wrote to his mother, lamenting the efforts of B. B. Warfield toward desegregating student housing. For the contents of this 1913 letter, along with the historical narrative that provides the context for the occasion of the letter, see Fred G. Zaspel, "Reversing the Gospel: Warfield on Race and Racism," *Themelios* 43, no. 1 (April 2018), http://themelios.thegospelcoalition.org/article/reversing-the-gospel-warfield-on-race-and-racism; Timothy I. Cho, "A Tale of Two Machens," *Faithfully*, September 8, 2018, https://faithfullymagazine.com/tale-of-two-machens/.

[27] Interestingly, the schools advancing Darwinian evolution (an inherently racist ideology that has ungirded much of the West's genocidal and eugenic evils) were the most welcoming to those who were not white.

Chapter 2

The Segregated States of America

Steven M. Harris

Typically when one thinks of racial segregation in the United States, historical references orient around its de jure and de facto representations in what are commonly called the Jim Crow and civil rights eras. In addition to Black Codes and Jim Crow laws, landmark Supreme Court cases such as *Plessy v. Ferguson* (1896) and *Brown v. Board of Education of Topeka* (1954) help us periodize the trials and triumphs of our collective, national memory. However, it is important to understand that *legal* doctrines such as "separate but equal" emerged from a distinctive religio-racial history, replete with its own set of *theological* doctrines that both informed and animated public life. This relationship between the theological, political, and racial can be seen from the nation's earliest days. With a particular focus on Protestants, this chapter traces the seeds of Sunday morning segregation from the Revolutionary period through the post-Reconstruction era, exposing the befouling effects of white supremacist ideology and racial hierarchy on the church in America.

The Revolutionary Era:
A Fragmented Foundation

By the time George III had informed the British Parliament of the expanding colonial rebellion in October 1775, revolutionary sentiment had pervaded New England and the rejection of British tyrannical power was increasingly viewed with providential and prophetic significance.[1] Given that a large portion of early- to mid-eighteenth-century white society could be found in ecclesial settings on Sunday mornings, one would expect that the emerging revolutionary ideas would be assessed and articulated through a biblical lens. Although the Great Awakening of the 1730s had both unsettled radical revivalists' faith in the legitimacy of established churches and bequeathed a Calvinistic evangelical theology rooted in egalitarian principles—principles that dovetailed with the notions of equality and liberty espoused by Thomas Paine, John Locke, and Thomas Jefferson—many were unwilling to readily apply revolutionary ideas to the issue of slavery.[2]

Slavery was widespread in the late eighteenth century, with both the northern and southern economies invested and dependent on its survival. As a result, most religious leaders expressed little disapproval of the institution. Religious leaders of this period defended the presumption that Christianity and slavery were compatible. The groundwork for

---

[1] See Mark Noll, *In The Beginning Was the Word: The Bible in American Public Life, 1492–1783* (New York: Oxford University Press, 2016); James P. Byrd, *Sacred Scripture, Sacred War: The Bible and the American Revolution* (New York: Oxford University Press, 2013).

[2] Thomas S. Kidd, *God of Liberty: A Religious History of the American Revolution* (New York: Basic Books, 2010), 131–46. See Mark Noll, *Christians in the American Revolution* (Vancouver, BC: Regent College Publishing, 2006). It was the Baptists of the Revolutionary period who especially focused on the issue of religious liberty as they found themselves on the underside of religious establishment and subject to ongoing persecution. The turn of the nineteenth century saw most white Baptists enthusiastic at the election of Thomas Jefferson due to his commitment to the issue as evidenced by his 1786 religious freedom bill in Virginia. See Thomas S. Kidd and Barry Hankins, *Baptists in America: A History* (New York: Oxford University Press, 2015).

such reasoning had been laid in the previous century, with slaveholding Christians moving from initial conceptions of freedom being reserved for Protestants who were not cursed with "hereditary heathenism" (e.g., Africans) to notions of "Christian slavery" in which conversion did not disrupt the racial hierarchy of slavery but rather accommodated it.[3] Earlier in the eighteenth century, Puritan minister Cotton Mather had published *The Negro Christianized* (1706) in which he simultaneously argued against segregation, that Africans did indeed possess souls, and that Christianity allowed slavery. "They are *Men*, and not *Beasts* that you have bought, and they must be used accordingly," he argued.[4] In 1741, Jonathan Edwards—himself a slave owner—took precious time amidst Awakening fervor to issue a defense on behalf of fellow New England pastor Benjamin Doolittle who was apparently receiving criticism from his congregation for his owning of slaves. This defense was never published but noteworthy, nonetheless, given the fact that Doolittle was both Arminian in his soteriology and unsupportive of the revivals—two qualities that Edwards did not view favorably.[5]

To be sure, some Christians expressed critical commentary against a military campaign waged for the liberty to enslave—or, to put it another way, the freedom to hold others in bondage. Phillis Wheatley, the former New England slave turned famous published author, arguably had slaves in view when she wrote to George Washington expressing her support of him being elected the commander-in-chief of the newly formed Continental Army. Wheatley was, perhaps, "hoping that even the most eminent slave owner in the colonies would ultimately apply the revolutionary ideology of equality and liberty to people of

---

[3] See Rebecca Anne Goetz, *The Baptism of Early Virginia: How Christianity Created Race* (Baltimore: Johns Hopkins University Press, 2012); Katharine Gerbner, *Christian Slavery: Conversion and Race in the Protestant Atlantic World* (Philadelphia: University of Pennsylvania Press, 2018).

[4] Cotton Mather, *The Negro Christianized: An essay to excite and assist the good work, the instruction of Negro-servants in Christianity* (Boston: B. Green, 1706), 23.

[5] George P. Marsden, *Jonathan Edwards: A Life* (New Haven, CT: Yale University Press, 2003), 256.

African as well as European descent."[6] In addition to northern black writers such as Wheatley and the former slave turned Revolutionary soldier and Congregationalist minister, Lemuel Haynes, white Congregationalist ministers such as Jonathan Edwards Jr. and Samuel Hopkins indicted slaveholders for their hypocrisy, warning that the British threat constituted divine judgment due to the sin of slavery.[7] Nevertheless, the overwhelming majority of religious leaders took no issue with the institution of slavery as they supported and engaged in the forming of a new republic.

It is commonly held that the document that came out of the Constitutional Convention neither authorized nor prohibited slavery, largely because it goes to great lengths to avoid mentioning the word altogether. Though it did not mention slavery explicitly, three provisions solidified racial disunity in this period and paved the way for the massive expansion of slavery in the next: The Three-Fifths Clause (Art. 1 § 2) stipulated a taxation level and representation in Congress based on adding 60 percent, or three-fifths, of the number of slaves of a given state to the total number of free persons. The Migration and Importation Clause (Art. 1 § 9) prohibited Congress from ending the transatlantic slave trade for twenty years. The Fugitive Slave Clause (Art. 4 § 2) mandated the return of fugitive slaves. In an effort to prioritize the replacement of the Articles of Confederation and appeal to southern slaveholding sensibilities, the newly formed nation chose to commence its experiment in free government not in consideration of its enslaved

---

[6] Vincent Carretta, *Phillis Wheatley: Biography of a Genius in Bondage* (Athens: University of Georgia Press, 2011), 154.

[7] Kidd, *God of Liberty*, 148–54. For more on Samuel Hopkins and antislavery thought in eighteenth-century New England, see Joseph A. Conforti, *Samuel Hopkins and the New Divinity Movement: Calvinism, the Congregational Ministry, and Reform in New England between the Great Awakenings* (Grand Rapids: Christian University Press, 1981); Samuel Hopkins, *A dialogue concerning the slavery of the Africans; shewing it to be the duty and interest of the American colonies to emancipate all their African slaves: with an address to the owners of such slaves. Dedicated to the Honorable The Continental Congress* (Norwich, CT: Judah P. Spooner, 1776).

population but in service to political expediency. Commenting on this moment of American history, essayist John Jay Chapman referred to slavery as the "sleeping serpent" that lay "coiled up under the table during the deliberation of the Constitutional Convention in 1787."[8] Like any cunning snake, the sleeping serpent of slavery would lie in wait until the inopportune time at which it would issue a deadly strike and further divide the nation.

The Long Antebellum Era: The "Peculiar" and the "Invisible" Institutions

Most black slaves remained untouched by the influence of Christianity at the close of the eighteenth century. But the ongoing revivalist mood coupled with the rise in visibility and effectiveness of Baptist and Methodist evangelism efforts eventuated in significant waves of slave converts during the first decades of the nineteenth century.

Conversion to Christianity during this period, however, was not a simple matter. Attendant to the revivalist fervor of what is often called the Second Great Awakening was the expansion of the internal slave trade— what historian Ira Berlin called the Second Middle Passage. Between the elections of Thomas Jefferson in 1800 and Abraham Lincoln in 1860, approximately a million black slaves were relocated to the southern interior via auction blocks and chains. Berlin described the impact of this massive deportation on black life as devastatingly extensive:

> Like those who had been forcibly transported across the Atlantic, the lives of men and women ensnared in the second great migration were changed forever. Husbands and wives were separated, and children orphaned. As some families were torn apart, others forged new domestic relations, marrying or remarrying, becoming parents and adoptive parents, and creating yet new lineages and networks of kin. Migrants came to

---

[8] John Jay Chapman, *William Lloyd Garrison* (New York: Moffat, Yard, 1921), 9.

speak new languages, practice new skills, worship new gods, and sing new songs, as thousands of men and women abandoned beliefs of their parents and grandparents and embraced new ideas.[9]

The forced evacuation of the seaboard southward was driven by the sugar and cotton revolutions and eventuated in the transition of southern states into massive slave societies.[10]

Space will not allow for a comprehensive treatment of plantation life. However, it is important to understand the fundamental nature of the "peculiar" institution that circumscribed black existence, and the chattel principle that allowed for the violent exploitation of labor from black bodies. In his seminal study of slavery in the antebellum South, historian Kenneth Stampp outlined a series of steps that characterized slaveholders' methodology for fashioning ideal slaves. "Here, then, was the way to produce the perfect slave," Stampp explained, "accustom him to rigid discipline, demand from him unconditional submission, impress upon him his innate inferiority, develop in him a paralyzing fear of white men, train him to adopt the master's code of good behavior, and instill in him a sense of complete dependence."[11] Preeminent among these qualities was the eradication of personhood and the reduction of the slave status to that of property—a marketable commodity to be bought and sold.[12] The ends to which slaves were trafficked were fun-

---

[9] Ira Berlin, *The Making of African America: The Four Great Migrations* (New York: Penguin Books, 2010), 100–101.

[10] Ira Berlin draws a distinction between "societies with slaves" (particularly in the North) and "slave societies" to highlight the difference between a society not centered on slaveholding as an economic and social order and one that is. See Ira Berlin, *Generations of Captivity: A History of African-American Slaves* (Cambridge, MA: Belknap, 2003), 8–9.

[11] Kenneth M. Stampp, *The Peculiar Institution: Slavery in the Ante-Bellum South* (New York: Vintage Books, 1989), 148.

[12] See Walter Johnson, ed., *The Chattel Principle: Internal Slave Trades in the Americas* (New Haven, CT: Yale University Press, 2005), 1–31. For an in-depth treatment of the various ways slaves were assigned monetary value, including in some cases the procurement of life insurance policies by

damentally economic. In fact, it can be argued—and has been argued—that it was due to the violent innovations of plantation torture and the overseer's whip that, via the ever-increasing efficiency of slave labor, the new nation became a powerful participant in the global cotton market as a modernizing, capitalistic economy.[13] Faced with the difficult task of remaking their social lives amidst the threat of social death, plantation slaves reevaluated their *sacred* world. In short time, "men and women whose ancestors had ignored Jesus for nearly two centuries embraced Christianity."[14]

The Christianity that the slaves embraced, however, was not the Christianity that was regularly put before them on plantations across the South. Consistent with the development of proslavery theology bequeathed from previous eras, slave owners and plantation missionaries sought to at once combine religious instruction with social and institutional control. There was an increasing concern that any kind of "Christian fellowship between master, unless very carefully regulated, would corrode the proper social hierarchy—the essential inferiority of blacks and superiority of whites—upon which the system rested."[15] Fears generated by the foiled revolt of Denmark Vesey in 1822 and the unforgettably bloody rebellion led by Nat Turner in 1831 sparked the development of a "vigorous theological defense of the enslavement of black men and women."[16] The Turner revolt was not the only event of 1831 that gave slave owners pause. That same year, William

---

slaveholders on account of the enslaved, see Daina Ramey Berry, *The Price for Their Pound of Flesh* (Boston: Beacon Press, 2017).

[13] See Edward E. Baptist, *The Half Has Never Been Told: Slavery and the Making of American Capitalism* (New York: Basic Books, 2014), xvi–xxiii; 116–44; Sven Beckert, *Empire of Cotton: A Global History* (New York: Vintage Books, 2014).

[14] Berlin, *Generations of Captivity,* 162.

[15] Albert Raboteau, *Slave Religion: The "Invisible Institution" in the Antebellum South,* updated ed. (New York: Oxford University Press, 2004), 168–69.

[16] Paul Harvey, *Christianity and Race in the Antebellum South: A History* (Chicago: University of Chicago Press, 2016), 73.

Lloyd Garrison published the first edition of his influential newspaper, *The Liberator*. (Two years prior, antislavery activist David Walker had published his highly inflammatory *Appeal . . . to the Coloured Citizens of the World*.) In response to the direct assault on slavery issued by immediatist abolitionists in the increasingly free North, southern theologians marshaled a variety of arguments to solidify social order and justify slavery's existence—from invocations of the "Hamitic curse" of Gen 9:18–27 (more accurately, the curse on Canaan, son of Ham) to rehearsals of the apostle Paul's directive that slaves were to obey their earthly masters (with an accompanying argument that "the condition of the servant of the Roman empire was much less free than that of the southern negro").[17]

On the question of independent black congregations in this period, the master class vacillated between temperaments of consent and constraint. To be sure, there had been separate worship communities established in Kentucky, Virginia, North Carolina, Alabama, Mississippi, and, as early as the late eighteenth century, Silver Bluff, South Carolina. However, the actual degree of independence of these black churches, along with their ministers, was always limited by imposed restrictions.[18] With the rise in black converts among Methodist and Baptist churches in the nineteenth century, it was not uncommon to see an increase in mixed, albeit segregated, congregations. Regardless of whether one was enslaved or free, blacks usually sat in back pews or separate galleries. It would be this abiding of white supremacist logics in the name of Christianity that moved Richard Allen to vacate the white Methodist community of which he was a part and help found the African Methodist Episcopal Church in 1816, becoming its first bishop.[19]

---

[17] Harvey, *Christianity and Race*, 77. For more on Hamitic rhetoric and its relationship to racial identity, see Sylvester A. Johnson, *The Myth of Ham in Nineteenth-Century American Christianity* (New York: Palgrave Macmillan, 2004).

[18] Raboteau, *Slave Religion*, 133–50.

[19] See Richard Allen, The Life, Experience, and Gospel Labours of the Rt. Rev. Richard Allen. To Which is Annexed the Rise and Progress of the African Methodist Episcopal Church in the United States of America. Containing a

In addition to the visible forms of black Protestantism manifested in the nineteenth century, just beyond the view of the slave master an "invisible institution" came into being. Historian Albert Raboteau describes the organizing principles of this institution:

> The religious experience of the slaves was by no means fully contained in the visible structures of the institutional church. From the abundant testimony of fugitive and freed slaves it is clear that the slave community had an extensive religious life of its own, hidden from the eyes of the master. In the secrecy of the quarters or the seclusion of the brush arbors ("hush harbors") the slaves made Christianity truly their own. The religion of the slaves was both institutional and noninstitutional, visible and invisible, formally organized and spontaneously adapted. Regular Sunday worship in the local church was paralleled by illicit, or at least informal, prayer meetings on weeknights in the slave cabins. Preachers licensed by the church and hired by the master were supplemented by slave preachers licensed only by the spirit.[20]

Interpreting together the writings of Phillis Wheatley and Lemuel Haynes, the persistence and entrepreneurial spirit of independent black church and denominational founders, and the boldness and imagination of plantation slaves stealing away to nighttime religious meetings, it becomes clear that the "black church" was birthed in protest—protest against the transatlantic slave trade and chattel slavery, and protest against white supremacy and the theo-logics of racial hierarchy. Though often unrecognized, the issue of religious freedom is an additional motivating factor alongside these more commonly acknowledged reasons for protest. C. Eric Lincoln and Lawrence Mamiya make the compelling case that "from the very beginning of the black experience in America, one critical denotation of freedom has remained constant:

Narrative of the Yellow Fever in the Year of Our Lord 1793: With an Address to the People of Colour in the United States (New York: Abingdon, 1960).

[20] Raboteau, *Slave Religion*, 212.

freedom has always meant the absence of any restraint which might compromise one's responsibility to God."[21] Once slaves caught wind of the story of Israel's exodus from Egypt, the narrative became a central theme of slave religion, making it possible to foster a new imaginative of black life beyond the boundaries of bondage.

The Civil War and Reconstruction Eras: A Costly Campaign, a Promising Project

In 1845, John O'Sullivan, then editor of the *Democratic Review*, coined a phrase, *manifest destiny*, that represented the fusion of a puritanical conception of divine providence to the expansionist aims of an emerging empire. O'Sullivan argued that it was "America's manifest destiny to overspread the continent allotted by Providence for the free development of our yearly multiplying millions."[22] The presumed national distinctiveness inherent in O'Sullivan's words—today popularly referred to as "American exceptionalism"—constituted the ideological context in which the sectional tensions of the Civil War era played out. The mission of westward expansion, therefore, was constantly frustrated by a moral question intentionally left unanswered.

John Jay Chapman's sleeping serpent had been on the move years before the Confederate cannons fired on Fort Sumter. The great

---

[21] C. Eric Lincoln and Lawrence H. Mamiya, *The Black Church in the African American Experience* (Durham, NC: Duke University Press, 1990), 4.

[22] John D. Wilsey, *American Exceptionalism and Civil Religion: Reassessing the History of an Idea* (Downers Grove, IL: InterVarsity Press, 2015), 17, 76. The notion of inevitability that lies at the heart of Manifest Destiny is rooted in the seventeenth-century belief that God had covenantally elected the Puritans and had agreed to exchange providential blessing for obedience as they set out to establish a purely Christian community in view of ushering in the kingdom of God. Beginning in the Revolutionary era and persisting until today, the theological vision that characterized the New England way lost its ecclesiastical overtones in the religious and social transitions of the early period and was subsequently applied to the developing nation—not as the Puritans realizing a model Christian community, but as the United States realizing a model democratic and free society.

Compromise of 1850, although perhaps responsible for delaying the approaching conflict, was yet another patchwork of legislative "solutions" aimed at temporarily relieving sectional tensions. The most controversial aspect of this compromise was, by far, the passage of a revised Fugitive Slave Act, which mandated that citizens of northern states assist in the capture of alleged runaway slaves, while denying slaves the right to a jury trial.[23] The Fugitive Slave Act effectively meant that any black person, at any given moment, could be captured and enslaved in a southern state. Northern antislavery activists and abolitionists were outraged at the degree to which the federal government catered to the demands of slaveholding states. In the September 27, 1850, issue of *The Liberator*, Garrison introduced the new law with the following statement: "It is a Bill to be resisted, disobeyed, and trampled under foot, at all hazards."[24] Less than a month after Garrison's published, radical commentary, Frederick Douglass engaged in his own fiery rhetoric. He admonished an audience of northern blacks that if they were ever faced with possible capture to be "resolved rather to die than to go back." If the slave catcher persisted, Douglass suggested that he should be "murdered in your streets."[25] One other antislavery voice that emerged in the wake of the Fugitive Slave Act took the form of a sentimental novel to sensitize apathetic white northerners to the abolitionist cause. Though a romantic racialist text to the core—with condescending stereotypes of blacks laced throughout—Harriet Beecher Stowe's *Uncle Tom's Cabin*

---

[23] The Fugitive Slave Clause of the original Constitution (Art. 4 § 2) lacked the operational details requisite for enforcement. Moreover, the Fugitive Slave Act of 1793 remained largely unenforced and was further weakened by the Supreme Court ruling in *Prigg v. Pennsylvania* (1842).

[24] William Lloyd Garrison, "Refuge of Oppression," *The Liberator*, September 27, 1850, in *Slavery and Anti-slavery: A Transnational Archive*, accessed April 7, 2019, https://www.nypl.org/collections/articles-databases/slavery-and-anti-slavery-transnational-archive.

[25] David W. Blight, *Frederick Douglass: Prophet of Freedom* (New York: Simon & Schuster, 2018), 241. With Douglass's rhetoric being increasingly suggestive of violent abolitionism during this time, it is no wonder that authorities sought to arrest him as a conspirator with John Brown in the raid on Harpers Ferry. See Blight, *Frederick Douglass*, 305–9.

(1852) was probably, outside of the Bible, the best-selling book of the nineteenth century.[26] In 1862, Stowe was invited to a White House gathering; upon meeting the president, she was allegedly greeted with the comment, "So you are the little woman who wrote the book that started this great war."[27] Republican Abraham Lincoln had been elected in 1860, and his antislavery stance, coupled with the fallout from the Kansas-Nebraska Act (1854) and the Dred Scott decision (1857), incited the secession of southern states.[28]

Although the historiography on the cause of the Civil War is long and debated, it is undeniable that the architects of the Confederacy "sought nothing less than to build the first independent slaveholders' republic in the Western Hemisphere and to launch it into a leading role in the game of nations."[29] Racial hierarchy was at the heart of the Confederate endeavor. The initial Union "rested upon the assumption of the equality of races," Confederacy Vice President Alexander Stephens explained. He went on to describe his contrasting vision:

> Our new government is founded upon exactly the opposite ideas: its foundations are laid, its cornerstone rests, upon the great truth that the negro is not equal to the white man; that

[26] For a discussion of romantic racialism and *Uncle Tom's Cabin* within the discourse of black religion, see the introduction to Curtis J. Evans, *The Burden of Black Religion* (New York: Oxford University Press, 2008), 3–16. For more on *Uncle Tom's Cabin* as a sentimental novel, see Dale M. Bauer and Phillip Gould, eds., *The Cambridge Companion to Nineteenth-Century American Women's Writing* (Cambridge: Cambridge University Press, 2001), 221–43.

[27] For a discussion of the apocryphal, albeit possible, nature of this exchange, see, David B. Sachsman, S. Kittrell Rushing, and Roy Morris, eds., *Memory and Myth: The Civil War in Fiction and Film from Uncle Tom's Cabin to Cold Mountain* (West Lafayette, IN: Purdue University Press, 2007), 8.

[28] The Kansas-Nebraska Act essentially nullified the Missouri Compromise of 1820 by stipulating that the two states decide for themselves whether slavery would be allowed within their borders. *Dred Scott v. Sanford* was a landmark Supreme Court decision that ruled that blacks were not US citizens and therefore could not bring suit in court.

[29] Stephanie McCurry, *Confederate Reckoning: Power and Politics in the Civil War South* (Cambridge, MA: Harvard University Press, 2010), 11.

slavery is his natural and moral condition. This, our new government, is the first, in the history of the world, based upon this
great . . . truth.[30]

Curiously enough, Stephens's argument assumed that the foundational
character of the first union was racial equality and that the Confederacy's
project was the formation of an entirely new social arrangement. It
seems more accurate, however, to consider the secessionist aspiration
of proslavery nationalism to be quite American at its core. According
to Drew, "The political system white Southerners proposed to export
was simply, as many claimed, the original republic of the United
States redeemed and perfected."[31] Such an analysis accords well with
Jefferson Davis's views as he sought on several occasions to reassure
Mississippians of the original, intended meaning of the Declaration of
Independence—a document that had nothing to do with slaves, according to him. With regard to the official documents that emerged from
secession conventions, "no attempt was made to hide concern over the
fate of the South's slave system in a United States ruled by a Republican
majority."[32] In others words, as states officially departed from the Union,
they made sure to indicate formally their fundamental concern for the
fate of the slaveholding society that defined their way of life—a way of
life for which they were ultimately willing to die.

In the Civil War of the United States, a "harvest of death" was
reaped. During its height, almost every household in the South was
mourning at least one loved one. To draw out a sobering perspective,
historian Drew Gilpin Faust made the following observation:

> In the middle of the nineteenth century, the United States
> embarked on a new relationship with death, entering into a civil
> war that proved bloodier than any other conflict in American

---

[30] McCurry, *Confederate Reckoning,* 12.
[31] McCurry, *Confederate Reckoning,* 13.
[32] Charles B. Dew, *Apostles of Disunion: Southern Secession Commissioners
and the Causes of the Civil War* (Charlottesville: University of Virginia Press,
2017), 17.

history, a war that would presage the slaughter of World War I's Western Front and the global carnage of the twentieth century. The number of soldiers who died between 1861 and 1865, an estimated 620,000, is approximately equal to the total American fatalities in the Revolution, the War of 1812, the Mexican War, the Spanish-American War, World War I, World War II, and the Korean War combined.[33]

Soldiers in both the North and the South reminded themselves that they were fighting for "God and for country"—with black soldiers often asserting, for "God, race, and country." From the battle of Bull Run in 1861 where "Stonewall" Jackson first emerged as a force to be reckoned with, to the battle of Antietam, which became the bloodiest day in American military history with more than twenty thousand dead, wounded, or missing, the war was filled with not a few significant events that reflected the sobering weight of war.

However, it was the Emancipation Proclamation of 1863 and the subsequent battle and address at Gettysburg, Pennsylvania, that literally defined the military campaign and served as the major turning point in its history. Due to a mixture of motivating factors, both military and moral—the weight assigned to each being debated until today, though the military expediency being particularly obvious—Lincoln increasingly became convinced to definitionally transition the Union's cause from merely a war against a slaveholding rebellion to a war against the peculiar institution itself. On January 1, he freed all of the slaves being held in territory controlled by rebel states—approximately three million of the nation's four million slaves.[34] Following a successful, albeit massively bloody, Union victory over the course of three days in July

---

[33] Drew Gilpin Faust, *This Republic of Suffering: Death and the American Civil War* (New York: Vintage Books, 2009), xi. New estimates suggest that the toll may have been about 20 percent higher. See https://www.nytimes.com/2012/04/03/science/civil-war-toll-up-by-20-percent-in-new-estimate.html.

[34] Eric Foner, *Reconstruction: America's Unfinished Revolution, 1863–1877* (New York: HarperPerennial, 2014), 1.

at Gettysburg, Lincoln returned to that consecrated field to dedicate a Union cemetery. What Lincoln ended up providing, however, was a particular historical frame that established the war as a fight for the founding principles of liberty and equality, and, with slavery presumably on its way out, the pathway to a "new birth of freedom."[35] Historian David Blight, in chronicling Frederick Douglass's reaction to emancipation, commented that "at that moment, and for its duration, the cruel and apocalyptic war had become holy."[36]

Religion was indeed the site at which personal and communal meaning was to be found. "Union and Confederate soldiers alike were heirs of the Second Great Awakening," and all of the theo-political history that defined the young nation.[37] Moreover, both sides "invoked God's favor and each at first was confident that God was on its side."[38] Historian Mark Noll was correct to regard the Civil War not merely as a political crisis but as a *theological* crisis. Denominational splits had occurred more than a decade prior to the start of the war, with the Southern Baptist Convention being formed in 1845 by Baptists in the South fed up over moral criticism and desirous of affirming a slaveholding Christianity. During the war, southern slaveholders and religious leaders employed providentialist reasoning to argue for the legitimacy of slavery and the justice of the Confederate cause. According to one southern divine, it was God who had "caused the African Race to be planted here under our political protection and under our Christian nurture, for his own ultimate design."[39] As the war progressed, battle victories and losses were interpreted as a fulfillment of God's plan. Abolitionism, moreover, was declared to be "an interference with the

---

[35] "The Gettysburg Address," accessed April 9, 2019, http://rmc.library .cornell.edu/gettysburg/good_cause/transcript.htm.

[36] *Frederick Douglass*, 384.

[37] James M. McPherson, "Afterword," in *Religion and the American Civil War*, ed. Randall M. Miller, Harry S. Stout, and Charles Reagan Wilson (New York: Oxford University Press, 1998), 409.

[38] McPherson, "Afterword," 411.

[39] Harvey, *Christianity and Race*, 94.

plans of Divine Providence."[40] To be sure, slaves and northern Christians employed the language of providence as well. They were just as convinced of the common phrase "God is in history."[41]

The outcome of the war itself would raise both sociopolitical and theological questions for everyone involved. The Union officially secured victory in 1865. By year end, the Thirteenth Amendment to the Constitution was ratified. Having in many ways commenced two years prior with the Emancipation Proclamation, the period known as Reconstruction was in full swing, and the institution of slavery, abolished. The overarching questions of the era could be summarized in the following way: Was abolition alone sufficient for the newly freed to take their place in American democracy? Or "did their unique historical experience oblige the federal government to take special action on their behalf?"[42] The Reconstruction project was a promising effort energized by the latter ideological conviction. In addition to the Bureau of Refugees, Freedmen, and Abandoned Lands—commonly referred to as the Freedmen's Bureau—the federal government passed two additional amendments guaranteeing the rights of citizenship and the right to vote (to black men), respectively. This period also saw unprecedented black participation in politics and public life. Moreover, white Christians and abolitionists in the North enthusiastically assisted with the organization of agencies, founding of schools, and building of churches.[43] It was, in fact, the formation of truly independent black congregations that served as one of the defining features of religious

[40] https://books.google.com/books?id=IENpLaRkoCUC&pg=PA339&dq=an+interference+with+the+plans+of+divine+providence&hl=en&newbks=1&newbks_redir=0&sa=X&ved=2ahUKEwji2cjl18nlAhVvQt8KHXWiC-IQ6AEwBXoECAMQAg#v=onepage&q=an%20interference%20with%20the%20plans%20of%20divine%20providence&f=false

[41] Mark Noll, *The Civil War as a Theological Crisis* (Chapel Hill: University of North Carolina Press, 2006), 82.

[42] Foner, *Reconstruction*, 67.

[43] Michael O. Emerson and Christian Smith, *Divided by Faith: Evangelical Religion and the Problem of Race in America* (New York: Oxford University Press, 2000), 38.

life in the Reconstruction era. After the war, white Christians in the South continued to insist on the legitimacy of racial hierarchy within their churches. This prejudice was expressed in ongoing segregated seating and overall unjust ecclesiological practice. Robert Lewis Dabney, an influential Presbyterian minister and former Confederate chaplain, vigorously objected to black participation in Presbyterian churches in the South—particularly in church leadership. In an 1867 Virginia synod speech arguing against the equality of black preachers and their right to rule over white Christians, Dabney lamented that the formerly enslaved were "almost universally banded to make themselves the eager tools of the remorseless enemies of my country, to assail my vital rights, and to threaten the very existence of civil society and the church, at once."[44] The response from black Christians across the South to such sentiments was a massive exodus from white Baptist, Methodist, and Presbyterian churches. This formal wave of black rejection of the institutional instantiation of second-class spiritual citizenship in favor of ecclesial autonomy marked a major turning point in American evangelicalism.

Consistent with, and in many ways heralding, the emerging segregationist ideologies of the post-Reconstruction era, southern Christians eventually saw the separation of churches as consistent with their own racialized theology. Though blacks were voluntarily establishing separate churches, white Christians began to agree that such was best given their belief that God had in fact differentiated the two races along hierarchical lines. Moreover, segregated churches provided a sense of assurance that one of the greatest fears of the era would be prevented: interracial marriage.[45] As the racial and economic realities of the new South set in, white Christians buttressed the revisionist "lost cause" mythology by invoking the biblical theme

---

[44] Robert Lewis Dabney, *Ecclesiastical Relation of Negroes* (Richmond, VA: Office of the Boys and Girls' Monthly, 1868), 4.

[45] Paul Harvey, *Freedom's Coming: Religious Culture and the Shaping of the South from the Civil War through the Civil Rights Era* (Chapel Hill: University of North Carolina Press, 2005), 27.

of redemption as an apologetic for their resentment of, and opposition to, Reconstruction. Historian Luke Harlow well exposes the racial center of redemption ideology:

> Instead of atoning for the sin of slavery, it referred to atoning for the North's sins of the Civil War and Reconstruction. The war destroyed slavery and was a war against the Christian God's biblical design for the ordering of human societies. . . . "Redemption" therefore meant what started in the 1870s: the restoration of southern "home rule," shorthand for white Democratic governments that would restore white supremacy in the South. It happened through nothing less than a terrorist counter-revolution against interracial democracy.[46]

This terroristic response from whites in the South rendered Grant's Enforcement Acts of the early 1870s—designed to protect black rights against Klan obstruction—all but null and void. Moreover, the Civil Rights Act of 1875 proved no match for the emerging reconciliation between southern and northern whites that eventuated in the election of Rutherford B. Hayes and the removal of federal troops from the South in 1877.[47] With this compromise, the period known as Reconstruction had officially ended.

---

[46] Luke E. Harlow, "The Civil War and the Making of Conservative American Evangelicalism," in *Turning Points in the History of American Evangelicalism*, ed. Heath W. Carter and Laura Rominger Porter (Grand Rapids: Eerdmans, 2017), 127.

[47] Racism was never a problem exclusive to the South. Before Reconstruction ended, many (if not most) whites in the North mirrored southern whites in their sentiments concerning the place of blacks in the developing democracy. Harriet Wilson's sentimental novel *Our Nig* (1859)—considered to be the first novel published by an African-American—is a creative excavation of the racial realities of life in the North for free blacks. See Harriett E. Wilson, *Our Nig: Or, Sketches from the Life of a Free Black*, ed. Henry Louis Gates Jr. and Richard J. Ellis (New York: Vintage Books, 2011); Paul D. Escott, *"What Shall We Do with the Negro?": Lincoln, White Racism, and Civil War America* (Charlottesville: University of Virginia Press, 2009).

New Eras, Old Territories

A caricature of a black slave popularized through minstrel song and dance would serve as the symbol for a period of racial terror unknown since the days of chattel slavery. Although the heading *Jim Crow era* does not quite capture the devastating depths of the ordeal, it does speak to the fundamental driver of the violence meted out on blacks in the period between 1877 and the rise of the Civil Rights Movements in the 1950s—white supremacy. The conviction of white superiority led to the establishment—and in *Plessy v. Ferguson* (1896), the legal codification—of Jim Crow laws. In the words of C. Vann Woodward, these segregation statutes "constituted the most elaborate and formal expression of sovereign white opinion upon the subject" of black inferiority.[48]

One cannot discuss the era of Jim Crow laws without an extended consideration of the lynching of black bodies, blackface, and the film *The Birth of a Nation*—the latter two serving as an apologetic for the first. That is to say, perceptions rooted in racist imaginations fueled violent acts against blacks, the worst of which were lynching (of mostly black men) and sexual assault (of mostly black women).[49] *The Birth of a Nation* premiered in 1915 and was afforded a private White House screening by President Woodrow Wilson. The film is considered to be one of the most racist films ever made. Historian David Blight explained the implication of the film in the following way:

> The lasting significance of this epic film is that by using powerful imagery, buttressed by enormous advertising and political endorsement; it etched a story of Reconstruction that has lasted long in America's historical consciousness. The war was noble on both sides, the film says, but Reconstruction in

---

[48] C. Vann Woodward, *The Strange Career of Jim Crow* (New York: Oxford University Press, 2002), 7.

[49] For an extended discussion of the sexualized perception of blacks, the phenomenon of blackface, and the film *The Birth of a Nation*, see Henry Louis Gates Jr., *Stony the Road: Reconstruction, White Supremacy, and the Rise of Jim Crow* (New York: Penguin Press, 2019), 125–57.

the South was directed by deranged radicals and sex-crazed blacks. . . . The very lifeblood of civilization, of familial survival, was at stake for the exploited South; hence, white Southern men had to take law and history into their own hands. The South not only wins in the end in *Birth of a Nation*; it also transforms emancipation, the potential second founding of the American nation, into a reign of racial terror and the necessity of a third creation by the heroic, hooded riders of the Ku Klux Klan.[50]

White theologians in the South endorsed the status quo of the Jim Crow era. White churches not only capitulated to, but helped propagate, the logics of the Jim Crow era as an extension of the cosmic battle between righteousness and unrighteousness, a rightly ordered civilization or one given over to barbarism. For this reason, many had no problem attending racial terror lynchings. They not only served as a public spectacle that performed the cultural work of reinforcing white supremacy, but they also functioned as communal purification rite, signifying the commitment to divine justice and a virtuous society.[51] For many blacks, enduring this society became their lot for the next several decades, witnessing the gains of Reconstruction run backward, rights lost, and freedom diminished. Black Christians in Alabama and Tennessee had founded the National Baptist Convention in 1880 and the Church of God in Christ in 1897, representing the commitment to foster theologically reflective religious communities and not simply acquiesce to white ones. For many others, the status quo in the South motivated them to seek a better life in the North. By 1930, 1.3 million blacks had vacated the South, abandoning its racist reasoning and hypocritical religion.[52]

---

[50] David W. Blight, *Race and Reunion* (Cambridge, MA: Harvard University Press, 2009), 395.

[51] Harvey, *Christianity and Race*, 115–16; Amy Louise Wood, *Lynching and Spectacle: Witnessing Racial Violence in America, 1890–1940* (Chapel Hill: University of North Carolina Press, 2009).

[52] See Berlin, *Making of African America*, 152–200.

The black community—and its central institution, the black church—turned inward in pursuit of racial uplift.[53]

The first few decades of the twentieth century saw many national changes. Two world wars that profoundly altered geopolitics were surrounded by theological controversies and social shifts. At the time when women were finally enfranchised and African-Americans were creatively laying claim to previously unacknowledged cultural dignity in Harlem, notions of biblical and theological "fundamentals" were met by a severe liberal backlash, all while the country was headed toward a decade of economic depression. The church in America was yet fractured along racial lines. Predominately black denominations and predominately white denominations, though many times sharing a distinctive theological conservatism, viewed social and political realities differently and parsed divergent priorities and projects in response to those realities.[54]

In the run-up to the Civil Rights Movement, these priorities would feature in familiarly regional and racialized ways. The meaning of the Civil War and emancipation would be contested anew in a *second* reconstruction, with significant gains and severe setbacks following. The church in America would once again betray an inability to reckon with its sordid past—a past in which religion and race each gave definition to the other, informing respective meanings and motivations, and sanctioning various courses of action. The co-constituted nature of the religious and the racial in American history continues to impact us today, often times in ways we fail to perceive.

---

[53] See Barbara Dianne Savage, *Your Spirits Walk beside Us: The Politics of Black Religion* (Cambridge, MA: Belknap, 2008); Evelyn Brooks Higginbotham, *Righteous Discontent: The Women's Movement in the Black Baptist Church, 1880–1920* (Cambridge, MA: Harvard University Press, 1993).

[54] See Mary Beth Swetnam Mathews, *Doctrine and Race: African American Evangelicals and Fundamentalism between the Wars* (Tuscaloosa: University of Alabama Press, 2017).

Chapter 3

The 1995 Resolution on Race; the Defunding of the American Baptist College; Nashville, Tennessee; and the End of Southern Baptist Paternalism[1]

Keith Harper

In 1995, the Southern Baptist Convention (SBC) celebrated its 150th anniversary. As they observed this milestone, Southern Baptists also stunned the nation by issuing a formal apology for their past racism and participation in slavery. They acknowledged that racism was both divisive and destructive, and they asked African-Americans to forgive them. Further, they pledged to "eradicate racism in all its forms from Southern Baptist life and ministry" and to "be doers of the Word

---

[1] The contents of this essay were delivered in a slightly different form in a meeting of the Conference on Faith and History, Grand Rapids, MI, October 6, 2018.

(Jas 1:22) by pursuing racial reconciliation . . . especially with our brothers and sisters in Christ."[2]

Messengers to that same convention also voted to end their connection with the American Baptist College (ABC) in Nashville. It was an extraordinary measure that was overshadowed by the resolution on race. Southern Baptists had shared both governance *and* financial support of the ABC, an African-American institution, with the National Baptist Convention, USA, Inc. (NBC), since 1924. Now, seventy-one years later, they were quietly parting ways. It is ironic that in owning up to their complicity in slavery and persistent racism, Southern Baptists were also moving away from their most tangible tie to African-American Baptists.

When viewed together, these events reflect broader currents in SBC life. In 1995, Southern Baptists had just emerged from a protracted battle over denominational control. Conservatives/fundamentalists had supplanted moderates/liberals in denominational leadership, and plans for denominational restructuring were already underway. Such restructuring aside, the now-famous resolution on race and the defunding of the ABC demonstrate a keen awareness that racism continued to plague Baptist life. Equally significant, they represent a departure from past practices that relied on a select group or groups of individuals working within specific organizational structures, such as special committees and commissions, to address social issues. In other words, the 1924 agreement between the NBC and the SBC to share governance and support of the ABC signaled an end to the ad hoc, paternalistic approach to race relations that had characterized Southern Baptists since 1845. But by severing ties with the ABC in 1995, Southern Baptists were moving away from the denominationally oriented kinds of mechanisms they had designed to address matters bearing on race.[3]

---

[2] *Annual* of the Southern Baptist Convention (1995), 80–81. See Mark Newman, *Getting Right with God: Southern Baptists and Desegregation, 1945–1995* (Tuscaloosa: University of Alabama Press, 2001), 9, 23, 134, 168.

[3] Newman, *Getting Right with God*, 292–95.

Background

How does one reckon with race and American history? In 1944, Gunner Myrdal deemed race an "American Dilemma." The United States claimed abundant resources and offered seemingly boundless opportunity, but not for African-Americans. The nation's black population consistently struggled to gain a place at the nation's social, cultural, political, and economic table. Race becomes even more complicated when considered from a religious perspective. At times, Baptists have boasted that they were people who believed in "the Book, the blood, and the blessed hope." When queried about the greatest commandment of all, Jesus responded, "Love the Lord your God with all your heart, with all your soul, and with all your mind." To that he quickly added a second that was like the first: "Love your neighbor as yourself" (Matt 22:37, 39). Who better than religiously minded folk to model brotherly love for the world?[4] But a cursory reading of Baptist history indicates that loving one's neighbor is often easier from a distance. The same Southern Baptists who embraced international mission work around the globe frequently struggled with loving their African-American neighbors across the street.

Defining social and cultural space for people of color has been an issue throughout American history. In the wake of the Civil War, historian C. Vann Woodward argued that southerners lived in a hard-soft period of race relations. It was an awkward dance of social give and take as blacks and whites struggled to find their respective places in a new, postwar reality. Unfortunately, the line between the races became increasingly "hard" over time, as whites reasserted white supremacy. Other scholars, such as historian Joel Williamson, maintain that among southern whites there existed three broadly defined attitudes toward race, each emphasizing one's "place" in society. Impressed by the

---

[4] Gunner Myrdal, *An American Dilemma: The Negro Problem and Modern Democracy* (1944; reprt., New York: Harper & Row, 1962). See Matt 22:37–39. Jesus went on to say that the Law *and* Prophets hang on these two commandments.

progress blacks had made since emancipation, Williamson identified "liberals" as those who believed that blacks enjoyed a bright future with almost unlimited potential. At the opposite end of the spectrum, "radicals" maintained that blacks had no future in the South.

A third group, the "conservatives," claimed a broad middle ground between the two extremes. Conservatives tended to be paternalists who were cautiously optimistic about the future, provided that African-Americans were led properly. Among Southern Baptists, leaders of this third, conservative mind-set worked with African-Americans to foster closer ties between their respective communities.[5] In the broadest sense, white southern conservatives claimed that whites had a duty to assist African-Americans in finding their proper place in society. As historian Joseph H. Cartwright put it, "To most whites, the enslavement of blacks and their lack of education, property, and political experience rationalized the need for a policy of white paternalistic guidance. Such a policy offered progress for blacks but at a pace and in a direction dictated by whites."[6]

Linking respective mind-sets with actual points in time requires effort, but for relations between white and black Baptists in the southern states, 1894 serves as a pivotal year. After the Civil War ended, many of the nation's Baptists continued their own internecine "warfare" through two of their missionary agencies, the Home Mission Society (HMS, North) and the Home Mission Board (HMB, South).[7] Northern

---

[5] See C. Vann Woodward, *The Strange Career of Jim Crow* (New York: Oxford University Press, 1974); Joel Williamson, *The Crucible of Race: Black/White Relations in the American South since Emancipation* (New York: Oxford University Press, 1984).

[6] Joseph H. Cartwright, *The Triumph of Jim Crow: Tennessee Race Relations in the 1880s* (Knoxville: University of Tennessee Press, 1976), 163. Charting the contours of paternalism can be a challenge. See Christian Coons and Michael Weber, eds., *Paternalism: Theory and Practice* (Cambridge: Cambridge University Press, 2013); Joe Soss, Richard C. Fording, and Sanford F. Schram, *Disciplining the Poor: Neoliberal Paternalism and the Persistent Power of Race* (Chicago: University of Chicago Press, 2011).

[7] Keith Harper, "The Fortress Monroe Conference and the Shaping of Baptist Life in America at the End of the Nineteenth Century," in *Mirrors and*

denominations and missionary societies were eager to rescue benighted southerners. In some cases, they dispatched missionaries southward even before hostilities officially ended. Many missionaries started schools to educate freed people of color. Northern Baptists were no exception, but by 1890 they found themselves in a bind. Certain HMS board members were ready to cut ties to their southern schools. How long, they wondered, should the HMS fund such ventures? Financing multiple schools proved to be expensive; they fretted—there would be no end to expenditures.[8]

Society board members were not the only ones complaining. Many African-Americans chafed under condescending white paternalism, the attitude of white superiority coupled with the assumption that African-Americans needed guidance to find their way in life. They also resented what they considered tight-fisted control of *their* schools, especially when the HMS doled out advice more freely than money. Additionally, white Southern Baptists, especially those affiliated with the HMB, resented northerners invading "their field"; it was no secret that they wanted northerners to leave. Finally, the costs of evangelizing immigrants on both coasts and ministering to Native Americans, not to mention establishing new churches, were soaring. With finances stretched increasingly thin, economics alone dictated that something had to be done.[9]

In 1894, representatives from the HMS and the HMB met near Norfolk at Fortress Monroe, Virginia. The HMS agreed to leave the South, provided that Southern Baptists confined their work to areas where they were already working, and they would assist with African-American education. The HMB readily accepted the terms, but it is significant to note that there were no African-American Baptists at

---

Microscopes: Historical Perceptions of Baptists, ed. C. Douglas Weaver (Milton Keyes, UK: Paternoster, 2015), 110–28.

[8] Harper, "Fortress Monroe Conference."

[9] Harper, "Fortress Monroe Conference." For northern missionary work in the South, see Joe M. Richardson, *Christian Reconstruction: The American Missionary Association and Southern Blacks, 1861–1890* (Athens: University of Georgia Press, 1986).

Fortress Monroe, and one year later, African-American Baptists formed the National Baptist Convention (NBC).[10]

After Fortress Monroe, Southern Baptists occasionally contributed financially to existing African American schools, but they preferred to focus on training ministers to serve in churches rather than supporting more classically-oriented education. They also experimented with "New Era Schools," an innovative approach to education that brought black ministers to a central location for a brief time, usually a week or two, whereupon they returned to their home churches and communities. Advocates for the New Era Schools believed that black ministers would be more influential in their communities than white missionaries. They also discussed long-term options. These discussions led to a partnership between the SBC and the recently formed NBC to create the American Baptist Theological Seminary (ABTS).[11]

The American Baptist Theological Seminary

Discussions for a brick-and-mortar school for African-American ministerial education began as early as 1904. In 1913, however, E. Y. Mullins, president of the Southern Baptist Theological Seminary in Louisville, Kentucky, offered a resolution calling for Southern Baptists to help build such a school. Mullins noted that the NBC had appointed a committee to consider building a school, and they had reached out to the SBC for advice and support. The Convention appointed its own committee to investigate the possibilities of working together, and the ABTS opened its doors in 1924. The records pertaining to ABTS are housed at the Southern Baptist Historical Library and Archives, Nashville, Tennessee.[12]

---

[10] Harper, "Fortress Monroe Conference."

[11] For a brief overview of New Era Schools, see Keith Harper, *The Quality of Mercy: Southern Baptists and Social Christianity, 1890–1920* (Tuscaloosa: University of Alabama Press, 1996), 97, 124–31. The New Era Schools were part of the SBC's approach to racial uplift.

[12] Steve Hoskins, *Tennessee Encyclopedia*, s.v. "American Baptist College," March 1, 2018, https://tennesseeencyclopedia.net/entries/american-baptist

It is significant to note that early-twentieth-century Southern Baptists relied increasingly on organizational means to achieve denominational ends. In 1913, the HMB noted, "Southern Baptists are engaged in no Home Mission effort more fully sanctioned by precedent and their own official pronouncement than the work which they are doing for religious uplift of the Negroes. The conscience of the denomination has always responded to the appeal of the religious needs of this dependent people."[13] Unfortunately, the report offered no substantial suggestions for uplifting African-Americans beyond vague declarations that something needed to be done. "The situation is delicate," the report intoned, "because while it is primarily religious, it is also the most vexing and portentious [sic] civil and social question in Southern political ideals and Southern character."[14] One year later, the newly formed Social Service Commission (SSC) made its first report to the SBC. Institutionally, the SSC was established to promote Southern Baptist social engagement, especially temperance and related issues. In that initial report, the SSC observed, "Social righteousness is to be attained through the leaven of individual righteousness. Social life is to be cleansed by cleansing life of the social unit."[15] At the same Convention, the Committee on a Negro Theological Institution requested at least $50,000 to operate the school. That committee supported the formation of a separate committee "to consider in general the status of the negro industrially, economically and religiously in the South, and that such information be secured and reported to the Convention on this subject as may tend to promote a

-theological-seminary/. The Southern Baptist Historical Library and Archives has thirteen *full* records center boxes of material on the ABTS. The materials are housed under AR 630, The Southern Baptist Convention Commission on the American Baptist Theological Seminary. All references to primary material bearing on this institution are in this collection. The ABTS does not have an archive, per se, and the NBC has no real centralized way to collect, store, and retrieve records from affiliated agencies.

[13] *Annual*, SBC (1913), 325–26.

[14] *Annual*, SBC (1913), 326–27.

[15] *Annual*, SBC (1914), 38. See *Encyclopedia of Southern Baptists* (*ESB*), s.v. "Christian Life Commission."

better understanding between the white and colored races and which may tend to the welfare of the negro race."[16]

Thus, the tone for the ABTS was set at least ten years before it became a reality. As progressive era reformers sought the state's assistance in curbing what they deemed as destructive behavior, the NBC and SBC sought at least one avenue whereby they could work together for the betterment of both races. Upon closer examination, one sees that the ABTS represented two different approaches to America's racial issues—namely, white paternalism and black uplift. On the one hand, white Southern Baptists could lend their assistance to African-Americans as benevolent "parents." At its best, paternalism could be nurturing, if condescending; at its worst, it could be domineering. On the other hand, the ABTS afforded National Baptists with the opportunity to engage in racial uplift. The ABTS was an institution for African-Americans who would serve in segregated congregations. Both denominations hoped the ABTS would play a leading role in creating a better society by creating a better, that is, Christian, people.

The ABTS might have opened before 1924 had it not been for two issues that nearly scuttled the project before it could be launched. First, as the NBC and SBC entered negotiations to build the school, the NBC split over who controlled denominational agencies. Were the agencies held privately or owned and maintained by the denomination? It was a complicated disagreement that cannot be recounted in detail here, but essentially, the Boyd faction called for private control while the Morris faction called for denominational control. Ultimately the SBC sided with the faction that favored denominational control.[17]

---

[16] *Annual*, SBC (1914), 25–26. The Committee on a Negro Theological Institution would become the Commission on the American Baptist Theological Seminary.

[17] For a fuller explanation of the Boyd-Morris Controversy and the NBC schism, see Edward R. Crowther and Keith Harper, "A Heart to Heart Talk with You over This Matter: Richard Henry Boyd, Elias Camp Morris, James Marion Frost, and the Black Baptist Schism of 1915," *History Research* 7, no. 1 (January–February 2017, serial no. 24): 20–29.

Post-war economic hardship posed the second, equally serious hurdle for the ABTS. The American economy suffered immediately following World War I, and southerners soon felt the squeeze. Between 1919 and 1924, Southern Baptists entered into a five-year fund-raising effort known as the 75 Million Campaign. It was an optimistic effort rooted in an artificially stimulated pre-war economy. Nonetheless, if everyone met their pledge, Southern Baptists would have made their goal and the ABTS would have received $200,000. Unfortunately, the final tally indicated total receipts of just over $58 million. There is no record of what the ABTS received from the $58 million, but it was nowhere near the anticipated $200,000.[18]

Economic issues notwithstanding, both the NBC and SBC were committed to building a school for training African-American ministers. From the outset, SBC representatives made it clear that the NBC maintained majority control over this school. As interested parties from both sides looked for the most opportune time to admit the first class, they worked out a five-point agreement on how the school should be maintained. The ABTS would have two governing bodies, one over buildings and grounds and one to oversee seminary affairs. The former would have twelve members, eight from the SBC, four from the NBC. The composition of the seminary governing body would be determined by the NBC and maintain a membership ratio of 2:1, NBC to SBC. The ABTS president would be affiliated with the NBC.[19]

Choosing a location for the ABTS also posed challenges. The SBC and NBC considered Memphis, Louisville, Atlanta, and Birmingham, before settling on Nashville as the best site for the ABTS. Nashville offered easy travel options for potential students and served as a hub for both denominations. In another ironic twist, however, the ABTS

---

[18] Andrew Christopher Smith, *Fundamentalism, Fundraising, and the Transformation of the Southern Baptist Convention, 1919–1925* (Knoxville: University of Tennessee Press, 2016). According to a brief paper titled "Significant Events in the History of Negro Education . . ." a successful 75 Million Campaign would have meant $200,000 for ABTS; see Records for the SBC and ABTS, box 7, folder 21.

[19] See "American Baptist Theological Seminary," *ESB*, vol. 1.

was located on land adjacent to Roger Williams University, an African-American institution originally sponsored by the HMS. Unfortunately, Roger Williams closed its doors in 1929, citing low enrollment and poor finances, issues that the ABTS would battle for the next seven decades (covering the scope of this chapter).

The ABTS faced challenges from the outset, but not because of its unique governance. Stated simply, this school faced the same issues as any other school. For example, the administration felt a constant pressure to recruit and retain both faculty and students. An examination of the school's history indicates that the ABTS struggled to maintain a consistent enrollment. As one example, between 1955 and 1965, ABTS enrollment averaged slightly more than seventy students with an average of about thirteen graduates per year.[20] Maintaining institutional viability with such low enrollment and graduation rates was extremely difficult.

Over that same period, at least two issues arose involving faculty. First, in 1965, Troy Woodbury, chairman of the Southern Baptist Commission on the ABTS, noted that the school's dean was serving a Presbyterian church as pastor. He did not think this was appropriate, seeing that ABTS was a Baptist school. Even worse, another instructor was a member of a local Church of Christ. The existing records do not indicate what specific action, if any, was taken in either instance, but the minutes for that meeting include the institution's Statement of Faith from 1924. It seems fair to say that the Southern Baptists on the Commission expected something to be done.[21]

One year later, the ABTS administration acknowledged obvious stress and strain. They did not mention it specifically, but they had always suffered from administrative issues beginning in the president's

---

[20] See *Minutes* of Executive Committee of the Commission on the ABTS (SBC), 1955–1965. The exact figures are 71.56 and 13.2. One might examine records for any period and see similar numbers. I am using the mid-50s to mid- and later-60s because that material has been pulled together for reports and is easily accessible. The ABTS made annual reports to the SBC Commission on the American Baptist Theological Seminary.

[21] *Minutes,* ABTS (SBC) meeting, April 15, 1965, box 2, folder 49.

office. Sutton Griggs, the first president of ABTS served from 1925 to
1926. He was followed by William Amiger (1927–29). J. H. Garnett, who
had served as acting president in 1924, served ABTS as dean and president from 1930 to 1932; he was followed by Roy A. Mayfield (1932–34).
Such instability continued throughout most of the twentieth century.
In fact, Odell McGlothlan Sr., inaugurated in 1980, was the eleventh
president in the institution's first fifty-six years.[22]

The report also acknowledged that the ABTS struggled to recruit
and retain students. Young African-Americans who wanted to enter
the ministry could receive training from a number of different schools.
Unfortunately, the ABTS was seldom high on their priority list.
Moreover, institutions like Morehouse and Spelman offered remedial
programs for students who needed academic assistance. The ABTS
did not offer such programs and could not compete with other, better-
funded institutions in remedial education. As for faculty, the administration had discussed seeking out advanced students from Vanderbilt
Divinity School as potential faculty members. There was no mention
of the Statement of Faith and no recorded challenge from the SBC's
representatives.[23]

As time passed, the ABTS experienced several high points. It was
accredited by the American Association of Bible Colleges in 1971. Upon
accreditation, the ABTS also changed its name to the American Baptist
College. In 2013, the ABC was officially recognized as a Historically Black
College/University. Meanwhile, enrollment continued to fluctuate, and

---

[22] *Minutes*, ABTS (SBC), 1966. See L. S. Sedberry, *ESB*, s.v. "American
Baptist Theological Seminary," 1:42–44; George E. Capps Jr., *ESB*, Supplement
2, 1984, s.v. "American Baptist Theological Seminary," 2027–28. In fairness to
everyone concerned, the Depression hit the ABTS hard. For a time, the school's
property was up for sale.

[23] *Minutes*, ABTS (SBC), 1966. It is hard to explain why the SBC did not
push back more aggressively against the proposal to look to Vanderbilt Divinity
School (officially Methodist). Of course, meeting minutes seldom convey the
extent of a given discussion, but it could be that SBC committee members
relented when presented with the stark reality of how difficult it was to hire
competent faculty.

the institution never really enjoyed good financial health. By the end of the 1980s, the ABC could claim to be stable, trending slightly upward. Nonetheless, its existence remained tenuous.

Conclusion

Between 1924 and 1995, the ABC proved to be a unique institution that defies easy categorization. Historian William A. Link claims that toward the end of the nineteenth century, progressive era reformers began looking to governmental power to curb behavior they believed was harmful to society; in the process, they began advocating for societal reform over individual reform.[24] In the early twentieth century, many of those same reformers debated whether blacks would be better served by classical or mechanical education. The ABC was neither a classical nor mechanical institution, seeing that it was dedicated to training ministers for service in churches. Moreover, whatever influence the ABC exercised over society would come primarily through African-American churches. The ABC charted a course that allowed it to remain true to its commitment to change society from within, especially in its earliest years.

Perhaps more significantly, the ABC's biracial leadership drawn from two different denominations distinguished it from other schools. Here again, the ABC defies easy categorization. For African-Americans, the school was neither separatist, wanting no white involvement, nor accommodationist, bowing to the directives of white influence. The ABC operated as a black school under predominantly black leadership, which raised no red flags with respect to Jim Crow legislation.

Here is where the lingering effects of Southern Baptist paternalism became most apparent—and troubling. Even though the NBC and SBC shared governance of the ABC, the Southern Baptists

---

[24] William A. Link, *The Paradox of Southern Progressivism, 1880–1930* (Chapel Hill: University of North Carolina Press, 1992), 50–51. See Dewey W. Grantham, *Southern Progressivism: The Reconciliation of Tradition and Progress* (Knoxville: University of Tennessee Press, 1983).

contributed a disproportionate amount of the school's funding. Thus, the ABC afforded Southern Baptists the opportunity to furnish financial assistance and advice in unlimited measure, thereby serving African-Americans as white benefactors.[25] But apart from hearing the Commission's annual report to the SBC, most Southern Baptists scarcely knew they supported such a school, and they seldom, if ever, interacted with the ABC's faculty, staff, or student body. In assessing racial uplift in the early twentieth century, historian Kevin K. Gaines observes, "Although there were exceptions, discussions of race and class by blacks and whites, albeit contested, remained separate and unequal, reinforcing racial essentialism."[26] In this case, the Southern Baptist's Commission on the ABC, an institutional arm of the SBC tasked with fostering racial harmony and cooperation, inadvertently kept African-American and white Baptists apart by perpetuating a racially segregated status quo. Ironically, by relying on a commission to act on the denomination's behalf, the organizational instrument Southern Baptists created to help bridge a racial gap had insulated rank-and-file Southern Baptists who sought racial harmony and essentially hindered racial reconciliation and healing since 1924.

By 1995, circumstances within the ABC permitted the SBC to divorce itself from this progressive era arrangement.[27] The Southern Baptist Commission on the ABC convened a special session in January, just months ahead of the passage of the Resolution on Slavery and

---

[25] Emmanuel L. McCall describes the relationship between the NBC and SBC as transitioning from paternalistic to fraternal. It was obviously a long, slow transition. See Emmanuel L. McCall, "Home Mission Board Ministry to the Black Community," *Journal of African American Southern Baptist History* 1, no. 1 (June 2003): 44–59.

[26] Kevin K. Gaines, *Uplifting the Race: Black Leadership, Politics, and Culture in the Twentieth Century* (Chapel Hill: The University of North Carolina Press, 1996) xvi.

[27] For opposing views on the SBC controversy/fundamentalist takeover, see David Morgan, *New Crusades, New Holy Land: Conflict in the Southern Baptist Convention, 1969–1991* (Tuscaloosa: University of Alabama Press, 1996); Jerry Sutton, *The Baptist Reformation: The Conservative Resurgence in the Southern Baptist Convention* (Nashville: Broadman & Holman, 2000).

Racism. The Commission was troubled by what they saw in the school or, more precisely, what they did not see. Commission member Tom McCoy set the tone for the meeting. According to McCoy:

> Spring enrollment is down at the college from 200 to approximately 125. This is mostly due to loss of prison program, loss of Pell Grants and students whose accounts were not paid in full were not allowed to enroll. Heating system is functioning but with leaks that are causing large utility bills. Estimates for a new heating system are in the $400,000.00 range. Wiring in building will not support any quick fixes such as units that fit below window or space heaters. Food services will be discontinued June 1 if $54,000.00 is not paid.[28]

Once again, the institution was in trouble and needed help.

It was an all-too-familiar refrain. So as Southern Baptists prepared to sever ties with the ABC the Commission offered an eleven-point recommendation that would transfer complete control of the school to the National Baptist Convention, USA, Inc. On a positive note, the Commission observed that since 1924 "America had moved from a racially segregated society and an era of white patronage of black institutions to a time when the colleges and seminaries of Southern Baptist general bodies are open to all who would study there without regard to race." Even more encouraging, the NBC's leadership had "expressed an interest in assuming full responsibility for selecting trustees to govern the Seminary." When the motion to surrender SBC interests in the ABC was presented to the SBC, messengers overwhelmingly approved it and Southern Baptists officially turned control of the college over to the NBC.[29]

Some participants characterized the divestiture as racial progress, but there was more to the story. Beyond finances and low enrollment, Commission members unleashed a litany of criticisms against the school in their early-1995 meeting. Paul Hill complained about the

---

[28] *Minutes,* ABTS (SBC), January 1995.

[29] *Annual* of the SBC (1995), 294.

school's direct oversight. He wondered if the institution's trustees even received accurate information on the institution, and he doubted that Southern Baptists "can effectively function as half of the Board [seeing that] office positions are continually given to the same National Baptists who do not have a rotation procedure." William Rorer added that, in his opinion, National Baptists were not kept informed of the school, and Lloyd Brown "expressed concern with the small scale of fund raising activities by the College."[30]

The Commission prepared a resolution for the upcoming SBC. It was similar but not identical to the one approved by the Convention. Originally the Commission stipulated, "The National Baptist Convention, U.S.A., Inc. is fully capable of supporting and selecting those who govern this Seminary *without any assistance from the Southern Baptist Convention*."[31] This "observation" was not included in the resolution affirmed by the SBC.

Looking back, the ABC represents a significant moment for Southern Baptists and race relations. At a time when the NBC could have gone its own way and started a school by itself, it chose to partner with the SBC. At a time when the nation seemed to be coming apart socially and culturally, the SBC apparently never considered cutting ties with the ABC even though the school served as a civil rights staging and training ground. In reflecting on the ABC (ABTS), in 1980, Joseph H. Jackson, pastor of Olivet Baptist Church in Chicago and longtime president of the National Baptist Convention, USA, Inc., said, "Dr. (L. K.) Williams and Dr. (O. L.) Hailey worked together on making this school at Nashville, Tennessee a possibility. It still stands as a concrete illustration of the Convention's belief in cooperation, and in Dr. Williams' emphasis on fellowship."[32]

But in the end, sluggish enrollment, finances, and the NBC's willingness to assume full control of the school coupled with SBC reorganization

---

[30] *Minutes*, ABTS (SBC), January 1995.

[31] *Minutes*, ABTS (SBC), January 1995, emphasis mine.

[32] J. H. Jackson, *A Story of Christian Activism: The History of the National Baptist Convention, U.S.A., Inc.* (Nashville: Townsend Press, 1980), 172.

did what the Great Depression, World War II, and the social turmoil of the 1960s could not do. The Southern Baptist Convention of 1995 marked an end to fostering cordial race relations through cooperative organizational structures. Of course, this parting of the ways had a far deeper meaning. Throughout the twentieth century, the SBC *Annuals* reported interdenominational work between the NBC and SBC under headings such as "Negro Work." After 1960, the nomenclature for inter-racial cooperation changed several times until 1998, when there was no separate report of cooperative work with the NBC. By choosing to end their relationship with the ABC, Southern Baptists appear determined to pursue racial reconciliation on their own terms.

If the American South is changing, one might argue that Southern Baptists are changing, too. Unfortunately, the SBC failed to follow up on any positive momentum they may have gained from their apology for slavery in 1995. The long-term implications of the SBC's institutional paternalism and committee-led, structural attempts to foster positive race relations remains undetermined, but there are no indications that racial reconciliation is happening on its own.[33]

---

[33] For change in the American South, see Charles P. Roland, *The Improbable Era: The South since World War 2* (Lexington: University Press of Kentucky, 1976); Numan V. Bartley, *The New South, 1945–1980* (Baton Rouge: Louisiana State University Press, 1995).

Part 2

A Public Theology

Introduction
A Public Theology

Josh Wester

Public Theology

Public theology is the work of bringing the riches of the gospel to bear upon our common life in the world. It is built upon a simple proposition: the Christian faith is a public faith because Jesus has set out to redeem the whole world from the curse of sin (Gal 3:13).

Central to Jesus's work of redemption is the establishment of his kingdom on the earth. This is why Jesus taught us to pray in Matt 6:10, "Your kingdom come. Your will be done on earth as it is in heaven." This work, establishing his kingdom on earth, was the task at which Jesus labored in his ministry. But as the Scriptures tell us, his work would not find its completion until the day of his return (Matt 16:28).

The future of the world is thus bound up with the coming of God's kingdom. This is because in announcing the coming of his kingdom, Jesus lays claim to the whole earth. All of creation belongs to him. At his return, all of the peoples and rulers of the earth will bow down before him and recognize his rule; he will be king and will reign over all (Phil 2:10). But until that day, Jesus has not left his people to stare idly into the sky. We do not wait passively for his arrival and the consummation of his kingdom. Instead, in establishing the church, Jesus has established on earth an embassy of his kingdom to represent his rule and reign.[1]

As an embassy of the kingdom, the church therefore is a political body. A redeemed, blood-bought people whose very lives and worship testify to the reality of Jesus's reign, the church is the visible manifestation of the kingdom of God on the earth. In the witness of the church, the world can glimpse its future, a future where the will and actions of every creature, indeed of the whole creation, are conformed unto the will of Christ (Rev 21:27). And it is here that public theology comes into play. Beyond its duty to confront the world with a vision of its future under Jesus's reign, the church is entrusted with wisdom the world needs in the present.

The Marks of the Church's Public Witness

The church has wisdom the world needs (Eph 3:10). Over the course of two millennia, the church has imparted to the world the benefits of its wisdom concerning both the world's destiny and design. Jesus is, after all, not only the agent of redemption but of creation as well.

Consider the concept of human dignity. We take it for granted in our culture today that human beings possess inherent dignity and worth, and that all people are therefore equal in value. This understanding of the human person is cemented into our consciences and codified (albeit imperfectly) in our laws. The roots of this concept, however, are fundamentally Christian.

The Christian doctrine of *imago Dei* teaches that every person bears the image of God (Gen 1:26–27). Because human beings bear

---

[1] By granting the church the keys to his kingdom, Jesus gives his church the right to speak with his authority and represent his rule on the earth (Matt 16:19; cf. 18:18).

God's divine image, we possess intrinsic value and fundamental, unassailable dignity. And this concept has had a profound impact upon the course of Western society. From the foundations of liberal democracy to the oratory of the great emancipator of the nineteenth century to the message of America's twentieth-century prophet Martin Luther King Jr., the ongoing struggle to achieve the ideals of human dignity and equality is everywhere influenced by this explicitly Christian doctrine.

Similar positive attributions can be credited to the church's witness in any number of cases, including the abolition of the slave trade in Great Britain, the broader Civil Rights Movement in America, and the decades-long international struggle to defend the lives of the unborn against the barbarism of abortion. But as we take stock of the church's influence in history, and what it thereby has to offer in the modern age, we must be quick to acknowledge its many failures in the public arena.

The church has, too often, not only failed to mitigate or prevent tragic developments in human history but has sadly been complicit or even instrumental in those very events. I have in mind the recent genocide in Rwanda, the acquiescence of the German church to the rise of Nazism, the Dutch Reformed Church's embrace of apartheid in South Africa, and, most relevant to us, the active support much of the American church exhibited toward the slave trade, America's peculiar institution, and subsequently Jim Crow. Though we celebrate the Civil Rights Movement as an ecclesial movement—and it was—we do so with a wince, realizing that even as so many Christians and churches were struggling to advance the movement's call for justice and equality, all the while a significant portion of white churches and white Christians actively opposed their progress.

Fittingly then, the church's public theology should be marked by a posture of humility even as we seek to impart the treasures of the gospel unto the world. Though we rightly strive to manifest the reign of Christ by working to promote human flourishing as we await his return, we are chastened by the lessons from our past and reminded to pursue such efforts from a humble posture.

Race, the Church, and the World

If one were looking for an area in which our culture needs the church's public witness, few examples more clearly exhibit this need than the issues of racial harmony and racial justice in the United States today. Racial division shows up in many places in American life. These divisions are manifest in our politics, in our neighborhoods, and in our own hearts. Even worse is the fact that it is not uncommon for animus and discord to arise from those same divisions within the church.

One of the central aspects of the gospel is the concept of unity. In the gospel, we experience the counterintuitive idea of taking that which is other or different from us and being intimately united with it. This is the mystery of the gospel Paul talks about in Colossians, that God long ago planned to unite within one body two disparate and sharply divided groups of people—in this case, Jews and Gentiles (1:27). Further, Paul tells us that Jesus, through his redemptive work, breaks down the walls of hostility and division between these groups (Eph 2:14).

This is what a Christian public theology has to offer the world on matters of racism and ethnic division. Within its walls, the church is to be for the world a model of unity. The world should see a picture of a united and diverse people as the church gathers regularly for worship to practice the rhythms and liturgies of a (political) family—rendering their lives and worship unto their king. And in the public square, Christians should work to promote racial unity by endeavoring to manifest in the world the unity that already—though imperfectly—defines the church.

In many cases, our work in the public square should be less about specific policies or initiatives than it is about a posture. When it comes to public theology, the posture of the Christian should be marked by humility and love: humility that is quick to listen, giving ear to the voices of the oppressed and the marginalized, and love that is willing to stand up and speak out in order to secure liberty and justice for all people. With this posture, the church can manifest the rule of Christ and bring forth the riches of its wisdom to the world.

Chapter 4

Bearing Witness to a Whole-Life, Pro-Life Ethic

Bruce Riley Ashford

Everything Christians hope for, everything Christians pray for, everything Christians work toward in this world is a precursor to, and anticipation of, our blessed hope. It is premised upon Christ's promise that he will return one day to set the world to rights. On that day, he will gather the redeemed from among all tribes, tongues, people, and nations, wiping away every tear from every eye. Everything that darkens the world and degrades our life will pass away. All things will be made new.

This is the blessed hope that, from the early church until today, sustains the greatest cause of our time—that of human dignity. Confessing that God created humanity in his image and redeemed us by the blood of his Son, any Christian ethic worthy of the name must contend for the dignity of every person created in God's image—man or woman, born or unborn, black or white, rich or poor, useful or inconvenient. As Richard John Neuhaus wrote,

> We [must] contend, and . . . contend relentlessly, for the dignity of the human person, of every human person, created

in the image and likeness of God, destined from eternity for eternity—every human person, no matter how weak or how strong, no matter how young or how old, no matter how productive or how burdensome, no matter how welcome or how convenient. Nobody is a nobody; nobody is unwanted. All are wanted by God, and therefore to be respected, protected, and cherished by us.[1]

Indeed, we must fight the good fight, opposing relentlessly the perverse tendency of our age to deny, minimize, or otherwise undermine the dignity bestowed upon all humanity by none other than God himself.

In *Evangelium Vitae*, Pope John Paul II spoke of an encroaching "culture of death" in the West in which immoral acts such as elective abortion and euthanasia are viewed as individual rights. "Choices once unanimously considered criminal and rejected by the common moral sense are gradually becoming socially acceptable," the pope declared.[2] Moreover, we would add that the West's culture is one of degradation in which we see a growing and widespread tendency to devalue entire classes of humanity based upon their birth status, usefulness, nationality, ethnicity, class, religion, ideology, or political affiliation.

The Emergence of a Secular Age

Several factors have hastened the maturation of the West's culture of death. Chief among them has been the West's increasing rejection of its Judeo-Christian heritage. It is in fact a *secular* age, an era in which

---

[1] Richard John Neuhaus, "Appendix C: We Shall Not Weary, We Shall Not Rest," *Human Life Review* 34, no. 3 (2008): 104. This address, which Princeton law professor Robert P. George called "the greatest pro-life speech ever given," was delivered as the closing remarks for the 2008 convention of the National Right to Life Committee. In honor of Neuhaus's memory and in recognition of the brilliance of his speech, the current essay follows closely the Neuhaus pattern of argument.

[2] John Paul II, "*Evangelium Vitae*," March 25, 1995, http://w2.vatican.va /content/john-paul-ii/en/encyclicals/documents/hf_jp-ii_enc_25031995 _evangelium-vitae.html.

Christianity has not only been displaced from the default position, but now is positively contested by countless religions, ideologies, and "takes" on life. This secularization process was spearheaded by elite cultural power brokers, but has now cascaded down to the street level, desacralizing the worldviews and "social imaginaries" of everyday people.[3] Indeed, as political philosopher Ryszard Legutko has recently argued, this secularizing process has been so successful that the Communists of old would be envious to witness such a total embrace of anti-Christian dogma in their own day.[4]

Secularization's poisonous fruits are abundant in our society, extending death to education, politics, family, economics, and every other sphere of public life. But nowhere has the impact been more profound than in the West's view of the human being. Secular anthropologies encroach upon the Judeo-Christian anthropology, unable to fund human dignity and human rights with anything other than self-authorization. Accompanying these anthropologies are secular moral philosophies, which likewise reject transcendence and reduce morality to convention.[5] So although our secular age is increasingly concerned

---

[3] The phrase *social imaginaries* in the thought of prophetic philosopher Charles Taylor refers to a set of conditions in society that determine not simply what individuals believe about God and the universe, but, more important, what they consider to be even imaginable. We inhabit a time in which not only is belief in God contested, but is in fact unimaginable. One cannot even imagine that life frame around belief transcendent truth is possible, given the way modernity has so construed truth in materialist, immanent terms. This is contrasted with a time when, before the Enlightenment, society could not imagine life without God. For more on Taylor's reading of the times, see Bruce Riley Ashford, "Tayloring Christian Politics in Our Secular Age," *Themelios* 42, no. 3 (2017): 446–51.

[4] Ryszard Legutko, *The Demon in Democracy: Totalitarian Temptations in Free Societies* (New York: Encounter Books, 2016), 31. For more on secularism and its devastating effects on the metaphysical foundations of modern society, see Charles Taylor, *A Secular Age* (Cambridge, MA: Belknap, 2009); Philip Rieff, *My Life among the Deathworks: Illustrations of the Aesthetics of Authority*, ed. Kenneth S. Piver, Sacred Order/Social Order, vol. 1 (Charlottesville: University of Virginia Press, 2006).

[5] Taylor, *Secular Age*, 580–89.

with codes of permissions and prohibitions, it is decreasingly able to justify them.[6] As a result, the secularized, fragilized individual cannot articulate *why* "the other" should submit to his or herself-authorized moral code. Taylor, referring to this as the "extraordinary inarticulacy" of modern culture, provides an explanation for the West's vitriolic and effluvial public discourse in which citizens and commentators do little other than shout each other down.[7]

The Legalization of Lethal Violence

In tracing the evolution of America's culture of death and degradation, one of the most natural recent starting points is 1973. In perhaps the most perverse ruling in the Supreme Court's history, the majority in *Roe v. Wade* implicitly categorized the unborn being in the womb as the "personalty"—a legal term referring to one's private property—of the mother, explicitly legalizing abortion on the basis of a woman's right to privacy in relation to her personalty. We should not miss the tragic irony of the timing of this ruling. Only a few years after the Civil Rights Movement, seven begowned lawyers bypassed the legislature to declare that an entire class of citizens—unborn human beings—had no guarantee of justice and equality.

Roe v. Wade was the equivalent of an environmental disaster on the moral ecology of our country. It degraded our nation by multiplying death to a level unmatched by both world wars. In fact, the number of unborn Americans killed via legal abortion—approximately sixty million—is more than *forty times higher* than the combined number of Americans killed in every war in our nation's history.

Roe v. Wade and ensuing legal decisions ensured that an unborn baby in a hospital today enjoys less legal protection than an endangered animal species in the wildlife reserve next door. To camouflage

---

[6] Taylor, *Secular Age*, 605–6.
[7] Charles Taylor, *The Malaise of Modernity* (Toronto: House of Anansi, 1991), 18.

this violent reality, Planned Parenthood and other death-care providers engage in linguistic deception, referring to the baby as "the products of conception" and to the use of lethal violence as "the termination of pregnancy."

As horrific as this death count is, the devastation wrought by the abortion industry extends even further. It harms *women* by justifying the use of lethal violence against the child, leaving them with long-term emotional and psychological damage, and by encouraging male irresponsibility and sexually predatory behavior. It harms *men* by leaving them with no legal say, whatsoever, in the decision of whether or not to kill their children. It harms romantic relationships and *marriages and families* by snuffing out the life of a family member, marginalizing motherhood and fatherhood, and depriving the children of the right to know and love their sibling. It undermines *law-governed democracy* by denying justice and equality to an entire class of people—unborn human beings—by teaching that it is legally and morally acceptable to use lethal violence against the weakest and most vulnerable among us, and by bypassing the legislative process and fabricating a constitutional right to abortion.

Indeed, the abortion industry harms society in innumerable ways. It erodes the moral foundations of our civic community, numbs our collective consciences, and sets the stage for a more expansive use of lethal violence against lives we consider inconvenient or burdensome. Instead of reinforcing our intuitive desire to protect society's most vulnerable persons, it goes against the grain of our consciences with relentless reassurances of the moral acceptability of the abortive deed.

The Twentieth Century's Racial and Ideological Cleansings

And yet, the origin of the West's culture of death and degradation goes further back than abortion laws of the late twentieth century. We think of the racial and ideological cleansings of the early- and mid-twentieth centuries that, as any number of commentators have noted, were built

on faulty anthropologies that rejected the *imago Dei* and the corre-
sponding doctrine of human dignity. Nobody who has read Alexandr
Solzhenitsyn's *The Gulag Archipelago* can forget "The Ascent," a har-
rowing chapter in which he describes how the Communist Party
viewed human beings as animals who existed merely to serve the state,
even calling the least useful ones "swarming lice" instead of "the crown
of creation," beings in whom there exists "a little spark of God," as
Solzhenitsyn and historic Christianity would have it.[8]

Soviet anthropology made these callous views possible. Built on
Marxist ideology, this anthropology conceived of human beings as
determined entirely by historical or material circumstances rather than
by divine action or inner conscience. With no transcendent order, there
was no transcendent creator. And with no transcendent creator, there
is no transcendent dignity for humanity. Humans become tools in an
immanent fight toward some material salvation.

In such a view, it became easy to justify any destruction or degradation of human beings so long as it served the purposes of the
Communist state. Dissenters are not merely people who disagree; they
are sinners who need to be punished or eliminated.[9] Religious people
are not merely individuals who worship a supernatural deity; they are
the enemy of progress and thus must be neutralized or exterminated.

In its own way, National Socialism (Nazism) also rejected the biblical doctrine of universal human dignity. Having just emerged from the
First World War and the Great Depression, the German people were
especially susceptible to utopian solutions, which in Germany's case
involved a nationalist-socialist ideology that ascribed to the Aryan race
alone a spark of the divine, denying to the Jewish people the same dignity. Reflecting on the Nazis' brutal degradation of the Jews and the
widespread destruction unleashed by Hitler and his party, Jewish survivor Hannah Arendt's classic *Origins of Totalitarianism* argued that the

---

[8] Alexandr Solzhenitsyn, *The Gulag Archipelago*, trans. Thomas P.
Whitney and Harry Willets, abridged by Edward E Ericson Jr. (New York:
HarperCollins, 2007), 299–313.

[9] Legutko, *Demon in Democracy*, 44.

West needed to find a "new guarantee [of human dignity] whose valid-
ity this time must comprehend the whole of humanity."[10]

The Institution of Slavery

But the culture of death and degradation goes back much further than
the genocides of the twentieth century. The founding of our own nation
was marred irreparably by the institution of chattel slavery, in which
black human beings were declared to be subhuman property. They
were sold, bought, punished, sexually abused, and even lynched at the
whim of their masters. Like abortion, slavery was an environmental
disaster on the moral ecology of our country, a disaster for which the
complicated "cleanup operation" is far from over.

The collective sins of white slave owners and many other Americans
combined at the societal level to harm America's black community in
innumerable ways.[11] It harmed black *children* in that, from their first
moments of self-consciousness, they understood that they and their
families were perceived as less than human. It harmed black *women*,
who were valued not as human beings created in God's image, but as
wombs, workers, and sex toys. It harmed black *men*, who were viewed

---

[10] Hannah Arendt, *The Origins of Totalitarianism* (New York: Harcourt,
1976), ix.

[11] James Q. Wilson makes a compelling argument that compared to
other minority groups subject to racial and cultural discrimination, America's
black community is disproportionately disadvantaged in a number of categories, such as out-of-wedlock births, low marriage rates, absentee fathers, etc.
Further, Wilson argues that these cannot be accounted for simply by African
cultural values that the community inherited from pre-slavery days. Rather, the
institution of slavery uniquely caused these disadvantages through the specific
familial and social harm it enacted. James Q. Wilson, "Slavery and the Black
Family," *Public Interest*, 147 (2002): 3–23.

Wilkins et al.'s research demonstrates similar conclusions, arguing for
observable "residual effects of slavery," which mental healthcare providers
should take into consideration of their treatments of African-Americans suffering from PTSD. Erica J. Wilkins et al., "Residual Effects of Slavery: What
Clinicians Need to Know," *Contemporary Family Therapy* 35 (2013): 14–28.

as animals or machines, valued primarily for their labor and reproductive potential. It harmed black *families*, many of whom were ripped apart as mothers or fathers or children were sold down the river at the whim of their masters; often, a man was allowed no real responsibility for his wife or children.

Furthermore, the institution of slavery *undermined* law-governed democracy, making a mockery of America's claim to guarantee "justice and equality for all," given that there existed an entire group of human beings who were classified as property. It warped and weakened our cultural institutions; not only were the executive, legislative, and judicial branches of our government complicit in this evil, but so were families, churches, businesses, educational institutions and nearly every other cultural institution.

Sadly, Christian *pastors* often strengthened the institution of slavery. Even when they did not own slaves or defend slavery, pastors sometimes encouraged social passivity in the face of slavery, watching quietly as their black neighbors were purchased, sold, beaten, killed, and treated as sex objects. One thinks of prominent pastor J. H. Thornwell who, urging the church to be quiet in the face of slavery, argued, "The provinces of church and state are perfectly distinct, and the one has no right to usurp the jurisdiction of the other. The state looks to the visible and outward; the church is concerned for the invisible and inward."[12] For Thornwell, the Christian mission was exclusively and inwardly "spiritual," having nothing to do with social action against grave injustice. Similarly, one thinks of the eight prominent liberal clergymen who rebuked Martin Luther King Jr. for engaging in nonviolent resistance during the Civil Rights Movement, to whom King responded in "Letter from a Birmingham City Jail."[13] As were many German Christians under

[12] Cited in R. Michael Allen, *Reformed Theology* (Edinburgh: T&T Clark, 2010), 170–71.

[13] Martin Luther King Jr., *A Testament of Hope: The Essential Writings and Speeches of Martin Luther King, Jr.*, ed. James M. Washington (New York: HarperCollins, 1986), 289–302; see Bryan Loritts, ed., *Letters to a Birmingham Jail: A Response to the Words and Dreams of Dr. Martin Luther King, Jr.* (Chicago: Moody, 2014).

the Nazis, so were many American Christians complicit in the degradation of an entire class of humanity.

The True Origins of Death and Degradation

Countless other instances could be listed in a genealogy of our culture of death and degradation. But if we trace this genealogy back far enough, we find an origin common to us all. The biblical account of the Edenic fall and its aftermath points all the way back to Adam and Eve, whose rebellion broke God's intended shalom and infected all of humanity. From that moment onward, humans would seek after our own interest rather than that of God and neighbor. Indeed, sin corrupts the world progressively, not limiting itself to a person's inward condition but extending also to the public self and thus to society and culture as a whole. It is like a cancer that dynamically and relentlessly reproduces, leaving the aroma of death in its wake.

Consider the very first narrative after the first couple's sin. Esteeming Abel unworthy of life, Cain laid violent hands on his brother, spilling his blood and catalyzing the culture of death and degradation that have to some extent characterized every human society. Reflecting on this, Dietrich Bonhoeffer wrote,

> It is with Cain that history begins, the history of death. Adam . . . begets Cain, the *murderer*. The new thing about Cain, the son of Adam, is that as *sicut deus* [seeing himself "as God"] he himself lays violent hands on human life. The human being who may not eat from the tree of life grasps all the more greedily at the fruit of death, the destruction of life. Only the Creator can destroy life. Cain usurps for himself this ultimate right of the Creator and becomes the murderer. Why does Cain murder? Out of hatred toward God.[14]

---

[14] Dietrich Bonhoeffer, *Creation and Fall: A Theological Exposition of Genesis 1–3*, ed. John W. de Gruchy, trans. Douglas Stephen Bax (Minneapolis: Fortress, 1997), 145.

This fateful day and its blood-soaked ground, then, betokened not only Cain's fate but also that of all humanity. Instead of repenting, Cain complains that God's punishment is too severe (Gen 4:13–14). Instead of fearing God and lamenting the death of Abel at his own hands, Cain obsesses on himself and his fear of physical and social exposure (4:14). In the wake of Cain's murder, moreover, his progeny of polygamists and murderers is symbolic of godless human culture and its degradation of humanity (4:17–24). Every subsequent era of history, likewise, has experienced the devastating consequences of Cain-like disregard for human dignity.

The Greatest Indignity and the Gate of Hope

Cain's hatred was great, and the consequences of it even greater. Yet the end of Cain's history, and with it all of history, is Christ crucified, the Son of God slaughtered not only *by* us but ultimately *for* us. And with the resurrection, Christ lives.

In the midst of a culture of death and degradation, Christ lives. He restores. And he beckons. He invites the world to experience true life and authentic dignity under his loving reign. Bonhoeffer writes:

> Under the swirling sword, under the cross, the human race dies. But Christ lives. The trunk of the cross now becomes the wood of life . . . and now in the midst of the world, from the wood of the cross, the fountain of life springs up. All who thirst for life are called to drink from this water. . . . What a strange paradise is this hill of Golgotha, this cross, this blood, this broken body. What a strange tree of life, this trunk on which the very God had to suffer and die. Yet it is the very kingdom of life and of the resurrection, which by grace God grants us again. It is the gate of imperishable hope now opened.[15]

---

[15] Bonhoeffer, *Creation and Fall*, 146.

With the gate of hope now thrust open, and with the world invited to experience true life and authentic dignity, the Lord Christ all the more calls his people to represent him to the world, to cultivate a community of life and dignity amidst a culture of death and indignity.

Both an Idea and a Deed

Long is the path that leads from Abel's murder to Christ's return. On that dark day, the voice of Abel's blood cried out from the ground. And so it is, that millennia later the voices of innumerable brothers and sisters join in Abel's cry. They cry out from the lynching ropes, from the concentration camps, from the abortion mills. And if the Lord tarries, countless more innocent voices will be added to Abel's cohort, calling out for justice. The road ahead may darken still. And yet, we must persist.

In considering our calling to fight the culture of death, we do well to remember that the path of death and degradation may be littered with heinous *deeds*, but it is paved by *ideas*—specifically, the idea that we can usurp God's kingship. And a road paved by wicked ideas can be *unpaved* by noble ones. In the *imago Dei*, we have a divine idea capable of putting our culture of death to death. The *imago Dei* carries with it a great dignity and a great humility. The great dignity is that we are all, somehow, like God and thus should be treated with the respect due our humanity. The great humility is that we are *not* God and thus should not give ourselves permission to shed innocent blood or otherwise devalue our neighbors.

Perhaps many of us can remember the first time we came to grips with the culture of death. For me, it was in 2002 when I was a PhD student in Wake Forest, North Carolina. I had acquired the habit of reading *First Things* magazine—especially Richard John Neuhaus's columns—and had been initiated into an ongoing conversation about the culture of death. But in February of that year, I read the column that captured my attention, a reflection by Neuhaus of his recent debate with Peter Singer, in which Neuhaus defended the view that it is always and everywhere wrong to kill an innocent human. Singer, on the other hand, argued that it is permissible and sometimes necessary to kill the innocent.

I learned that Singer—arguably the America's most influential moral philosopher—built his career on a forthright rejection of the *imago Dei*, a dismissal of human immortality, a redefinition of humanity in purely materialistic terms. For him, the Christian notion of human dignity was nothing more than religious nonsense. "By 2040," Singer speculates, "it may be that only a rump of hard-core, know-nothing religious funda- mentalists will defend the view that every human life, from conception to death, is sacrosanct."[16] Rejecting the *imago Dei*, Singer goes on to define humanity as an animal species whose value and dignity resides in its level of consciousness and functionality. Under this view, we should ascribe less value to the unborn, to infants, to the physically or mentally handicapped, and to the elderly or infirm. In fact, a mentally handi- capped baby would be, for Singer, less morally significant than a fully conscious and functioning animal.[17] Having thus defined humans as an animal species without any elevated moral significance, he goes on to argue for an ethic that allows not only for abortion, but also for infanti- cide, euthanasia, and necrophilia.

In Singer's moral philosophy, I saw a great evil at work, an evil similar to the racial and ideological genocides of the twentieth century. Yet surprisingly, Singer's philosophy was allowable, even palatable, to the "enlightened" thought leaders who hired him and who applaud his work. I wondered how a nation known for "liberty and justice for all" could so blithely accept and even promote the use of lethal violence against the weakest and most vulnerable people in our society. I won- dered how we could have learned so little from our history. I wondered if there was worse to come.

But I didn't wonder where I stood. For me, reading Singer was the existential "ground zero" from which I became a lifetime recruit for the pro-life cause.

---

[16] Peter Singer, "The Sanctity of Life," *Foreign Policy* (September–October 2005): 40.

[17] Peter Singer, "Sanctity of Life or Quality of Life," *Pediatrics* 72, no. 1 (July 1, 1983): 128–29.

We Shall Not Weary, We Shall Not Rest

For others, that personal moment of recruitment might have been their first reading of the history of American slavery, the memoirs of a concentration camp survivor, the news of the *Roe v. Wade* decision, or the resurgence of ethnonationalism in recent years. The culture of death is as varied in practice as it is evil in origin. Wherever we find the impulse to consider other human beings unworthy of life and dignity, we find forces of darkness at work. But we also find fresh motivation to continue fighting for the cause of human dignity.

And fight we must. We must fight the culture of death tooth and nail, not only from the pulpit but also from the judiciary bench, the corporate boardroom, and the university halls. We must fight the culture of death no matter how accepted it is and how plausible it is made to sound. We do not know, nor do we need to know, if we will prevail. Our devotion to the pro-life cause is not contingent upon the probability of success but stems from our desire to be champions for our weakest and most vulnerable neighbors; in so doing, we proclaim the hope of the Lord Christ's death and resurrection until he comes.

In this great struggle against the culture of death, we have been recruited by none other than the Lord Christ. And so we remain committed to the cause, through thick and through thin, in victory and in defeat. Addressing the National Right to Life Convention in 2008, Richard John Neuhaus declared,

> The journey has been long, and there are miles and miles to go. But from this convention the word is carried to every neighborhood, every house of worship, every congressional office, every state house, every precinct of this our beloved country [so that] the word is carried that, until every human being created in the image and likeness of God—no matter how small or how weak, no matter how old or how burdensome—until every human being created in the image and likeness of God is protected in law and cared for in life, we shall not weary, we shall not rest.

And, in this the great human rights struggle of our time and all
times, we shall overcome.[18]

We shall not weary; we shall not rest. Some of our neighbors will laugh
in derision as we declare that a baby's right to live outweighs a woman's
right to choose. But we shall not weary; we shall not rest. Others will
mock our concern that the institution of slavery left a culture of death
and degradation in its wake that to this day fosters personal prejudice
and social injustice. But we shall not weary; we shall not rest. Others
will trivialize our opposition to the steadily growing call for legalized
euthanasia and infanticide. But we shall not weary; we shall not rest.

Indeed, some of our neighbors will even indict Christianity as the
scourge of American society. They will wonder aloud if Christians
should not, in fact, be silenced. And in the face of their loathing and violence, we must join with our Savior, who, when reviled, responded with
both hard-hitting truth and warm-hearted grace. We must not weary of
holding out life in the face of death. We must not weary of holding out
hope in a culture that has lost its way. We must never weary of following the path of our Lord, who laid down his very life so that we, though
dead, might live again.

We must not weary. We must not rest.

---

[18] Neuhaus, "We Shall Not Weary," 107.

Chapter 5

Welcoming the Sojourner Leads to Church and Community Renewal

Alan Cross

From one man he has made every nationality to live over the
whole earth and has determined their appointed times and the
boundaries of where they live. He did this so that they might
seek God, and perhaps they might reach out and find him,
though he is not far from each one of us. For in him we live
and move and have our being, as even some of your own poets
have said, "For we are also his offspring."—Acts 17:26–28

The need for a biblical perspective on ministry to and with the
immigrant has never been greater.[1] As a native-born American and

---

[1] In speaking of immigrants or the sojourner, I am referencing all those
who are not native to the United States. I am not attempting to make any
delineations between the kinds of sojourners (legal or illegal) in our country

Caucasian Southern Baptist minister in Alabama, I have noticed a sizable increase in the immigrant population throughout the South over the past twenty years. Scripture instructs Christians to receive the sojourner with sacrificial love and biblical hospitality. Immigrants are full partners in the gospel, and mutual submission to one another must characterize the American Christian's posture as they arrive on American soil. May the church in America have faith to receive one another as ministry partners and pursue God's mission together. We desperately need each other.

The contemporary American social and political climate is often antagonistic toward immigrants and those who minister to and alongside them. Amid shouts of "Build a wall!," the ongoing fear of offering terrorists domicile, and foreigners taking jobs from Americans, the American sentiment toward the sojourner has taken a concerning turn. Patriotic concern easily slips into nativist and xenophobic anger as immigrants are blamed for problems plaguing the average American. Coupled with the racial unrest in America, the rise of anti-immigrant rhetoric has created a toxic environment toward those perceived as the "other." Instead of giving in to this growing sentiment and giving in to fear, evangelicals have an incredible opportunity to "tell a better story" of the gospel in the public square.

Throughout Scripture, the people of Israel are commanded to welcome and love the sojourner ("resident alien" per CSB) as themselves and apply the same protections extended to native-born Israelites. The Hebrew people were told that when foreigners came to their land with a desire to live among them and contribute to their civilization the Hebrews were to welcome and care for them. This is one of the most prominent and recurring commands in the Torah.

---

or to propose any policy solutions to the immigration debates that dominate the news cycle. Although immigration reform and issues pertaining to illegal immigration are complex and it is appropriate for Christians to speak to issues involving vulnerable people (Prov 31:8–9), policy questions are beyond the scope of this chapter. Nevertheless, our posture toward those who are sojourners ought to be straightforward: we demonstrate the sacrificial love and grace of Christ.

Scripture passages that address treatment of the sojourner include the following (emphasis mine):

Exodus 22:21: "You must not exploit a resident alien or oppress him, since you were *resident aliens* in the land of Egypt."

Exodus 23:9: "You must not oppress a *resident alien*; you yourselves know how it feels to be a *resident alien* because you were resident aliens in the land of Egypt."

Leviticus 19:34: "You will regard the *alien who resides with you* as the native-born among you. You are to love him as yourself, for you were aliens in the land of Egypt; I am the LORD your God."

Deuteronomy 10:19: "You are also to love the *resident alien*, since you were *resident aliens* in the land of Egypt."

Isaiah 58:6–7: "Isn't this the fast I choose: To break the chains of wickedness, to untie the ropes of the yoke, to set the oppressed free, and to tear off every yoke? Is it not to share your bread with the hungry, to bring the poor and homeless into your house, to clothe the naked when you see him, and not to ignore your own flesh and blood?"

Zechariah 7:9–10: "The LORD of Armies says this: 'Make fair decisions. Show faithful love and compassion to one another. Do not oppress the widow or the fatherless, the *resident alien* or the poor, and do not plot evil in your hearts against one another.'"

Miguel Ecchevarria says,

While Christians may not be the nation of Israel, loving the immigrant is a principal [*sic*] that applies to all believers. We see this clearly as both Leviticus 19 and Matthew 22 exhort love of neighbor. And, to be perfectly clear, an undocumented person *is* your neighbor. With this in mind, what if Christians treated the immigrant as a neighbor? Would that not lead to a more empathetic view of this vulnerable people group? Would that not lead to more gospel fruit among sojourners, viewing them as persons in need of redemption, or fellow brothers and sisters in Christ, rather than nuisances and threats?[2]

The commands to care for the sojourner, the migrant, and "poor wanderer" are more than just "rules." God's people are called to act upon these commands in response to what God has done on our behalf. This is why such commands often come with the reminder, "For you were sojourners/resident aliens/strangers in the land of Egypt." By reminding Israel of their former slavery and oppression in Egypt, God also reminded them of their deliverance. The apostle Paul echoes this sentiment: "And such were some of you. But you were washed, you were sanctified, you were justified in the name of the Lord Jesus Christ and by the Spirit of our God" (1 Cor 6:9–11).

"For you were sojourners in the land of Egypt" indicates that how you treat the foreigner among you is directly proportional to how believers understand what God has done for them. In Deut 26:5–13, the treatment of the sojourner is tied directly to the tithe and worship. The Hebrews who do not treat the sojourner well fail to understand God's grace and kindness toward them.

Orthodox Rabbi Jonathan Sacks says,

> It is no coincidence that Judaism was born in two journeys away from the two greatest civilizations of the ancient world: Abraham's from Mesopotamia, Moses' and the Israelites' from Pharaonic Egypt. . . . To be a Jew is to be a stranger. It is hard to avoid the conclusion that this is why Abraham is commanded to leave land, home and father's house; why, long before Joseph

---

[2] Miguel Ecchevarria, "Theology: A Biblical Perspective on Immigration," in *Preaching God's Heart for Immigrants & Refugees: Reaching the Nations in North America,* compiled for the Southern Baptist Convention Pastors Conference, Phoenix, AZ, June 2017, 3–4, https://static1.squarespace.com/static/5633 9494e4b0fc0fc2a2633f/t/5978fc48d1758e1a7e9846c6/1501101129014/ Preaching+God%27s+Heart+for+Immigrants+%26+Refugees.pdf.

was born, Abraham was already told that his descendants would be "strangers in a land not their own."[3]

When Christians love, minister to, and advocate for the immigrant, the sojourner, and the refugee, it is not just doing good works or being "political"; God's people bear witness to the reality of God's kingdom, in particular, salvation in Christ, the nature of the church, and the final destination of all nations around God's throne. In a world that seeks to protect, promote, and defend its own "way of life" over and above others, loving the immigrant is a significant way to give prophetic witness to the reality of the gospel and God's character.

The church is an embassy of heaven. When believers minister to and advocate for immigrants, a better story is told—the gospel story. The government has significant questions it needs to answer about immigration, but the church has divinely commissioned responsibilities: "Love your neighbor as yourself" (Mark 12:33), and "preach the gospel to all of creation" (see Matt 28:19). In fact, God's plan may have allowed for the current environment, controversy, and fear to allow evangelicals to love and minister to immigrants and refugees so our light would shine in a world full of fear and anger. Furthermore, the sojourner could be sent by God to foster love and mercy in the church so the world can see the heart of God and the sojourner experience his kindness.

Welcoming the Stranger as a Way of Community Renewal[4]

How believers welcome refugees into our communities, homes, and churches speaks directly to our values and our source of hope.

---

[3] Jonathan Sacks, "Mishpatim (5768)—Loving the Stranger," February 2, 2008, http://rabbisacks.org/covenant-conversation-5768-mishpatim-loving-the -stranger/.

[4] Taken from an essay used with permission from The Restoration Institute. Alan L. Cross, "Welcoming the Stranger as a Way of Community Renewal," The Restoration Institute, September 18, 2018, http://therestorationinstitute.com/

A community that idealizes its past and places hope in reviving the "glory days" is insular and encounters ongoing conflict along racial lines. By contrast, a kingdom community aligns itself with transcendent values that includes newcomers and causes that community to move forward together. Actively welcoming newcomers creates a dynamic experience that helps move a community from what anthropologist Paul Hiebert has called a "bounded set" to a "centered set."

A bounded set is something that is defined by essential or uniform characteristics. This set has clear boundaries and is static, but a centered set "is created by defining a center and the relationship of things to that center."[5] The centered set does not place the primary focus on its boundary, creating a clear division between things moving in and those moving out. Objects within the centered set are not uniform, they are dynamic not static.

The process of "welcoming" newcomers creates a situation where transcendent values are more important than boundaries that keep people in or out. Hiebert's distinction between bounded and centered sets brings synergy and movement toward the center and is more important than where the boundaries are. Indeed, movement helps us understand where boundaries *should* be because believers better understand what the key values really are. As Christians, the "center" is Jesus Christ.

Despite the church being a centered set, this does not preconclude boundaries for the church; they are clearly outlined in Scripture. The person and work of Christ helps the church to understand those boundaries and increases the likelihood of welcoming sojourners, because being embraced is not based on cultural, ethnic, and socioeconomic distinctives. Through centered-set dynamism, the church can model how people from different backgrounds, nationalities, and cultures live together with their unity based in something greater than

---

welcoming-the-stranger-as-a-way-of-community-renewal/?fbclid=IwAR2qA
lQ2pQ4DlaK9NByFxqV_LYZOh1yImZHz6M1R_l3_dMDT3o6FOFPq0WM.

[5] Paul G. Hiebert, "Conversion, Culture and Cognitive Categories," *Gospel in Context* 1, no. 4 (1978): 24–29.

their understood identities because it is rooted in something beyond race, economics, or even shared cultural memory.

Citing Matt 25:35, Hiebert recalls Jesus saying, "For I was hungry and you gave me food, I was thirsty and you gave me drink, I was a stranger and you welcomed me" (RSV). The word translated as *welcome* is the Greek word *synagagete,* from *sunago.* It implies a harvest and means to "gather together, collect, assemble, receive with hospitality."[6] *Sunago* is the root word for synagogue: the assembly of God's people. Christians took this concept, and it became a pattern for the *ekklesia*: the church or "called out ones."

Followers of Jesus are called to welcome those who are far off as Christ welcomed us. This means that Christians should not reject, despise, or keep immigrants beyond our boundaries, but rather receive them with gracious hospitality. The Greek word for hospitality is *philoxenia*, which means "love for or being a friend to the stranger." This is especially true for sojourners who are fellow Christians. For a church or community to welcome the stranger requires adherence to a centered set of transcendent values that move toward unity in Christ. The church is a people moving toward Jesus together that welcomes strangers and sojourners along the way.

As the church "welcomes the stranger," it shows the rest of the world how people from different cultures live together in unity and provides an example to emulate. This unity happens only in Christ; the church's testimony to the community is that Jesus unifies people like nothing else can.

An Opportunity

The high volume of refugee movement into American churches is a fruitful context for discipleship and sanctification. Receiving the sojourner is tangential ministry of the church to join Jesus in his work of proclaiming and demonstrating the gospel to the nations. Conflicts that cause people movements are not to be feared; they are opportunities to positively

---

[6] Greek word, συνάγω (*sunago*), *Strong's Concordance,* usage, accessed January 16, 2019, https://biblehub.com/greek/4863.htm.

impact displaced people and demonstrate the love of Christ to them. Global upheaval offers the people of God an opportunity to show sacrificial love to those in great need. Instead of seeing the influx of foreigners as a threat to our American identity, it is an opportunity to reaffirm a shared kingdom identity. Believers must throw off comfort and a level of cultural security to be ambassadors for Christ to all nations, especially if the nations have moved next door or across the street.

It is important to note that followers of Christ are actually immigrants and sojourners in this world (1 Pet 2:11). Jesus himself was a refugee to Egypt and a homeless wanderer with no place to lay his head (Luke 9:58).

Dr. Ecchevarria says to American Christians,

> The United States of America is not our home. We, along with people from every tribe and tongue, are immigrants, strangers seeking a restored inheritance. That is one of the reasons why we are to love the stranger, for he may be a fellow Christian, sojourning to the same eternal destination. So, we actually have more in common with an undocumented Christian (as a fellow believer) than with our American friend who shares the same political ideology but sleeps in on Sundays. Even if an immigrant is not a Christian, we are still called to love and care for him. Perhaps God might be so kind as to use our witness to win him over to Christ. Is that not more important than preserving our way of life? Is that not more important than spending time and energy on keeping out criminals (who are a small percentage of those trying to enter the country)? If we gave priority to the Bible, and not an elephant or a donkey, would we not spend less time talking about building a wall and more time building bridges to care for the immigrant?[7]

---

[7] Ecchevarria, "Theology," 5.

Contemporary people movements could continue as a global and historic phenomenon that could last for decades. If the church altered its disposition toward the sojourner in ministry, mission, and hospitality, it could position itself to shape the future of the human race and spark a revival.

SPEAK: A Ministry Strategy for Immigrants/ Refugees from Proverbs 31:8-9

Proverbs 31:8–9: "Speak up for those who have no voice, for the justice of all who are dispossessed. Speak up, judge righteously, and defend the cause of the oppressed and needy."

SPEAK is a simple acronym, based on this passage, that serves as a guide to minister to immigrants and refugees who, because they are newcomers, have possibly not yet developed their own voice in society.

S Is for SEE

See the immigrants in our midst. America has approximately forty-five million first-generation immigrants and eighty-five million first- and second-generation immigrants. Statistically, one in four Americans are either first- or second-generation immigrants. It is almost impossible to live in America and not encounter immigrant families. One of the most likely places to engage immigrant families is through the local school system. In many school districts, even in the South, it is not unusual that up to half of the student population is foreign born. Thus a great way for a church to see immigrants in their midst is by connecting with a local school through tutoring and mentoring programs.

Another way to *see* immigrants is to discover where they gather, such as ethnic restaurants or markets. Begin to frequent these places and pursue friendship with the employees and patrons. Learning each employee's story offers insight into their community and their experience in the United States. Most immigrants are candid about their experience, because they want to be seen as participants in American

society. Seeing a person means that the individual is not merely categorized as "other" but is perceived as neighbor and friend.

P Is for PRAY

After we see them, *pray* for them. Christians should proactively pray for
the salvation, well-being, and kind reception of the immigrants in our
midst. Specific prayer requests can be gathered by going to immigrant-
owned restaurants and markets and asking workers and owners how to
pray for them. Identify immigrant-owned businesses and offer prayer
for the owners, their families, managers, and workers. Similarly, connect with exchange programs in local schools and colleges to see what
prayer needs they have. Prayer is a wonderful tool to minimize our wor-
ries about people movements around the world while casting their cares
before the Lord.

E Is for ENGAGE

Seek to *engage* immigrants with good deeds that demonstrate the love of
the Christ that welcomes sinners into the kingdom of God. Engagement
is multifaceted and begins with inviting them to share their stories,
introducing them to your friends, and asking them to dine at your table.
The relational foundation reveals proactive steps to help them acclimate
to the community. A few examples of intentional engagement: Offering
English as a second language and citizenship classes. Identifying social
service organizations that serve immigrants and asking what help is
needed. A women's ministry could offer transportation to and from
OB/GYN appointments. Much of this is less about mechanistic programs and more about sharing life together.

A Is for ADVOCATE

The progression that begins with seeing, praying, and engaging
results in *advocating*. Native-born citizens can use their influence

to bless immigrants by speaking on their behalf in places where they are unable. This assumes a willingness to challenge policies that harm or curtail flourishing among sojourners, and may cause believers to adopt policy positions that challenge long-standing political affiliations. Yet Christians must be the voice of the voiceless on these important issues. In Jesus's parable (Luke 10:25–37), the Good Samaritan risked his own safety and resources to help a beaten man, the "neighbor" whom God put in the Samaritan's path. Believers are called to do the same. This example of expending monetary and relational capital on behalf of another is a fruitful means of building trust with others.

Immigrants have limited social connections and protections. For this reason, God offers them special concern in Scripture. Helping the immigrants connect with resources and relationships is essential to being productive members of society. This is as simple as connecting newcomers to a good immigration lawyer or a public official who will hear their concern.

K Is for KEEP GOING

Engaging in immigrant and refugee ministry requires persistence and perseverance. Mistakes will be made and opportunities will be missed; nevertheless, there is a constant opportunity to love one's neighbor. The best way to persevere in immigrant ministry and advocacy is to reject the impulse to see immigrants as projects rather than people. As Christians interact with immigrants, it becomes evident that they are not to be feared; rather, they are neighbors, friends, and even family—if they are in Christ.

Mixtec People: Case Study in Hospitality Leading to Evangelism and Church Planting

The Mixtec people are an indigenous people from Southern Mexico who came, in large part, to the United States in the 1990s. They are considered an Unreached People Group by the International Mission

Board and have traditionally been closed to the gospel.[8] In the 2000s, Montgomery (Alabama) Baptists discovered that there were thousands of Mixtec who had immigrated to Central Alabama. The church people began to pray for them and try to engage them in ministry and evangelism. The doors were closed until a couple of years ago. After much persistence, prayer, and relationship building, progress was made. Through relationships, Mixtec slowly came to Christ, and a church has now been planted among them. The keys to this process have involved expressing love, sharing meals, joining in deep suffering and great joy, and endeavoring to connect the lives of the native-born and immigrant families.

Several key leaders were involved in the ministry to the Mixtec in Montgomery. Early on, Lisa Chilson Rose, director of Community Ministries for the Montgomery Baptist Association, was the primary initiator of this work. She notes the changes she has seen in her own life through this ministry. "They are 'the stranger' that followers of Christ are told to welcome. They are the ones who are the least of these. They are those who we are commanded to love despite their circumstances. It has brought to life, even more, God's command to love your neighbor as yourself. I am changed because of 'them.' I can see all people through God's eyes even more than I did before. I am grateful that God sent them into my life to refine me and grow me more into the image of God that he desires for me to be."

It should be made clear that immigrant ministry is not merely about what native-born Christians do or the ministry that Americans do for or to immigrants. Immigration ministry is about sharing life together and truly loving strangers who, by God's grace, become neighbors. A Mixtec couple that connected with the Montgomery Baptist ministry says, "It means a lot that this church has helped us to become stronger Christians, to get out of our shells and not be shy any more about our faith. It also feels great to be able to serve others because God has given

---

[8] The International Mission Board describes unreached people groups as those that do not have access to the gospel. See Zane Pratt, "Here's What We Mean by Unreached Peoples and Places," *IMB*, November 22, 2016, https://www.imb.org/2016/11/22/what-do-we-mean-by-unreached-peoples-and-places/.

me the power to tell others about Jesus. We love helping others and especially praying for others who are in need. Because God helped us, we can understand when others are hurting and can help them. It is all because of God's power in us that we are able to do this."[9]

Engaging in immigrant ministry also becomes an incredible way to raise up new leaders for the church from both immigrant and native-born populations. John Halbrooks, a retired school teacher in Montgomery, began working with the Mixtec and eventually was ordained as the initial pastor of the new Mixtec church. He says, "In obeying God to receive Mixtec, God is teaching me that the Gospel is for ALL people! Nothing (immigration status, color, language, culture, etc.) excludes an individual's sin from separating them from God, thus needing the Gospel for salvation. My relationship with the Mixtec has humbled me and caused me to stand on the power of the Holy Spirit to use God's word to change my life and persist as he changes the lives of my Mixtec brothers and sisters. It is a blessing to experience the power of God to save and replace fear with the contentment of joy."

John Wible, who assists in leading worship and discipleship, speaks about how engaging in immigrant ministry led to his own personal change. "Welcoming the Mixtec has been a convicting experience for me. I have been convicted of my own racial and ethnic prejudices and have had to confront them not only with the Mixtec, but with others as well. Second, I have been convicted of my lack of love. I have had to learn to show love by acts of kindness when it was inconvenient. Last, I have been convicted that no true spiritual progress will be made unless I let the Holy Spirit do it through me."

Receiving Faith

Receiving immigrants in a biblical way first requires receiving faith from God to trust him with fears, concerns, and prejudices and to overflow with love for neighbors and even perceived enemies. One must

---

[9] The interviews compiled in this case study were received by me on January 15, 2019.

thoroughly receive God's love and let that love transform and flow through oneself to others. As Acts 17:24–28 says, God determines where people live, and he places them across the earth, establishing their times and boundaries. He does this so the nations of the earth will seek him and find him. God is sending migrants across the earth in what amounts to a great spiritual search. It stands to reason that God has also ordained his people to be on the receiving end of that search, to help them find him.

Over the next several decades, there will be large-scale movements of people groups. As people are on the move in a global and interconnected world, the church should be prepared to receive them in every city and town on the planet. The missional currency of the twenty-first century, in the midst of mass global migration, is love and hospitality. We put this currency into action by helping churches be Jesus-centered instead of ethnic or culture-centered and creating ways to receive sojourners. Instead of fearing the stranger (xenophobia), the gospel calls us to love the stranger (*philoxenia*/hospitality) in ways that are redemptive and transforming—for them *and* us. We will find that as we open our arms, our homes, and our churches to immigrants, we are more blessed than we could possibly anticipate.

When we "welcome the stranger," we will encounter Jesus in our personal lives and churches in new and fresh ways that challenge and ultimately change us and, in time, transform communities and nations. The future of the twenty-first century is being written now, and it will be inhabited by people from every tribe, nation, people, and language bumping up against each other in the megacities and also the rural and suburban areas of our nation and the world. Having the eyes to really see the immigrants in our midst; to pray for them with faith and hope; to engage them with love, good deeds, and the gospel; to advocate for them as Christ does for us; and to keep going in perseverance and joyful hope and love as we journey with them—these are the ways to receive the immigrant and engage the world with the gospel from our hometowns and local churches across the country.

Chapter 6

Apologetics in Twenty-First Century Evangelicalism

D. A. Horton

Introduction

During times of economic disparity, racism, and urbanization in America, church-going African-Americans have turned away from the church to find answers to their life-situational questions.[1] They often become conversant with ethnocentric movements that use the language of nuance to speak to the issues of tension. From the late nineteenth century through the mid-twentieth century, movements such as the Hebrew Israelites, the Moorish Science Temple, and the Nation of Islam successfully wooed wavering hearts away from the Eurocentric Christian faith and welcomed them into one more embracing of their ethnicity.

In the current American social landscape, economic disparity, racism, and urbanization are dominant rhythms. Once again, ethnocentric

---

[1] Paul Harvey and Edward J. Blum, *Guide to Religion in American History* (New York: Columbia University Press, 2012), 228.

movements are actively evangelizing. Professing Christians of color (mainly African-American and Latino) are asking questions and listening to voices outside of the Christian faith. With the use of modern social media platforms such as Facebook, Instagram, and YouTube, the ethnocentric movements mentioned above are seeing a revival of sorts, as they dialogue with inquiring Christians who have a passion to decolonize or reimagine their faith.

The center focus of the questions Christians of color are asking is found at the intersection of their ethnicity, Western church history, and its theological moorings. Inside the spectrum of American evangelicalism, ethnic segregation, especially in houses of worship, is a long-standing issue. Lifeway Research reported 86 percent of the churches polled identified one dominant ethnicity in their regular attendance.[2] This same report asked churchgoers if they would attend a church that placed them in the minority; the response was overwhelming: they would not. Christians of color encounter tension in the "white spaces"[3] of evangelicalism, where they are called to enter into the world of evangelicals without evangelicals, in turn, entering theirs. This truth has even been expressed by Al Mohler,[4] whom *TIME* magazine has called the reigning intellectual of the evangelical movement in the United States.[5]

The questions found at the intersection of ethnicity, Western church history, and theology provide Christians of color with a choice. Do they turn left and become hostile against the church? Do they turn

---

[2] Bob Smietana, "Sunday Morning Segregation: Most Worshipers Feel Their Church Has Enough Diversity," *Christianity Today*, January 15, 2015.

[3] Elijah Anderson, *The White Space*, Sociology of Race and Ethnicity 2015, Vol. 1(1) 10–21 © American Sociological Association, 2014. This examines the history of and tensions attendant to African-Americans progressively being allowed into spaces preoccupied by white-dominant culture. https://sociology .yale.edu/sites/default/files/pages_from_sre-11_rev5_printer_files.pdf

[4] Al Mohler, "The Content of Our Character—King's Dream and Ours," January 16, 2016, https://albertmohler.com/2006/01/16/the-content-of-our -character-kings-dream-and-ours-2/.

[5] Broward Liston, "Interview: Missionary Work in Iraq," *TIME*, April 15, 2003, http://content.time.com/time/world/article/0,8599,443800,00.html.

right and assimilate into becoming color-blind? Do they move forward with biblical guardrails that provide a balance in affirming their ethnicity all the while embracing the tensions of life in the church in a fallen world?

Society has taken notice of African-American millennials leaving the church, having unresolved tensions with Christianity being a tool of oppression.[6] What's also noteworthy is the exodus of Latinos out of Protestantism and Roman Catholicism, as they turn to the "none" or unaffiliated[7] category or Islam. Some one hundred thousand to two hundred thousand Latinos in America have changed their identity from Christian to Islamic[8] for reasons similar to African-Americans who are being challenged to consider the distinctions of the Moors'

---

[6] Leo, "6 Reasons Young Black People Are Leaving the Church," *Atlanta Blackstar*, January 24, 2014, http://atlantablackstar.com/2014/01/24/6-reasons -young-black-people-are-leaving-the-church/4/.

[7] According to Pew Research, during the short span of three years (2010–2013), 15 percent of the Latino population between ages eighteen and twenty-nine who were affiliated with Catholicism left, while the evangelical (those who identified as being "born again") population increased only by 2 percent; the unaffiliated segment leaped by 17 percent. Cary Funk and Jessica Hamar Martinez, "The Shifting Religious Identity of Latinos in the United States: Nearly One-in-Four Latinos Are Former Catholics," Pew Research, May 7, 2014, http://www.pewforum.org/2014/05/07/the-shifting-religious-identity-of -latinos-in-the-united-states/. This same Pew report showed 70 percent of those raised Protestant who are now unaffiliated left because they gradually drifted away from the faith, compared to 66 percent of those raised Catholic who are now unaffiliated. In a separate report from Pew Research, the 31 percent of Latino millennials who are unaffiliated overshadows the 18 percent of Latino adults who say they are unaffiliated; 47 percent of millennials say they pray outside of church services compared to 73 percent of Latinos aged fifty and older. Jessica Martinez and Michael Lipka, "Hispanic Millennials Are Less Religious than Older U.S. Hispanics," Pew Research, May 8, 2014, http://www .pewresearch.org/fact-tank/2014/05/08/hispanic-millennials-are-less-religious -than-older-u-s-hispanics/.

[8] Susmita Baral, *Latin Times*, "Why Are Latinos Leaving Catholicism? New Study Provides Answers on Hispanics Religious Beliefs Changing," November 13, 2014, http://www.latintimes.com/why-are-latinos-leaving-catholicism-new -study-provides-answers-hispanics-religious-275604.

rule in the Iberian Peninsula with the practices of the church during colonization.[9] Dr. Fathi Osman, resident scholar at the Omar
Foundation (an Islamic cultural and educational center), says Latinos
are learning the history of Islam in Spain and how, through eight centuries of rule, conversion to Islam was natural, not forced. Latinos then
are displeasingly juxtaposing the way Muslims treated their Spanish
ancestors with the way Christians treated their ancestors in Latin and
South America.[10]

Taking these facts into consideration, the purpose of this chapter
is to equip the saints in multiethnic settings to minister well with the
ability to (1) identify the ethnocentric movements that are making contemporary appeals to Christians of color, (2) engage their teachings,
and (3) respond with a holistic apologetic that defends the Christian
faith in order to shepherd the hearts of African-American and Latino
Christians. The goal then is to lay an initial foundation for a contextualized approach to apologetics that can be used for dialogue with
Christians of color. Ethnocentric movements such as Hebrew Israelites,
the Moorish Science Temple, and the Nation of Islam will be taken into
consideration alongside Islam.[11]

Identifying the Movements and Their Messages

Hebrew Israelites: The Founders and the Formation of the Movement

The rise of black Jewishness surfaced in America before the Civil War,
as preachers exposed Old Testament narratives that paralleled with

---

[9] Lisa Viscidi, "Latino Muslims a Growing Presence in America,"
Washington Report on Middle East Affairs, June 2003, http://www.wrmea.org
/2003-june/latino-muslims-a-growing-presence-in-america.html.

[10] Viscidi, "Latino Muslims."

[11] Islam has been included not because it is being categorized as ethnocentric, but because of its success in proselytizing Latinos by using their ethnic
heritage as a point of reference.

slaves' reality. This provided them with a "compelling sense of identifi-
cation with the children of Israel and the tendency to dwell incessantly
upon and to relive the stories of the Old Testament that characterized
the religious songs of the slaves".[12] Since there is no one recognized
sect of Hebrew Israelites (as with the Moorish Science Temple and the
Nation of Islam), popular movements claiming similar doctrinal lean-
ings will be mentioned.

In 1800, Gabriel and Martin Prosser worked to free slaves in
Richmond, Virginia, in what was known as Gabriel's Rebellion. As a
means to justify their escape, Martin, a slave preacher, paralleled the
slaves' experiences to those of the biblical Israelites in Egypt.[13] The
Israel United in Christ website references Nat Turner's similar work in
1837 in their timeline of Hebrew Israelite history, before citing William
Saunders Crowdy's establishing of the Church of God and Saints of
Christ (COGASC) in 1896.[14] Crowdy, a Civil War veteran, moved to
Oklahoma to begin a ministry, intending to fulfill Mal 4:5.[15] Crowdy
preached new revelations God gave him; known as the "Seven Keys,"
they frame the doctrine of the COGASC.[16] Crowdy remained the leader
of the congregation until his death on August 4, 1908, after which
Bishop James M. Grove was elected as the new leader.[17]

---

[12] Lawrence Levine, *Black Culture and Black Consciousness* (New York:
Oxford University Press, 1977), 23.

[13] "The Fire of Shem: The Biblical Worldview of Gabriel Posser, Demark
Vesey, and Nat Turner", Hebrew Israelite Nation Times, accessed October 9,
2019, http://hint-magazine.com/shem/

[14] "Brief Israelite History," Israel Unite, accessed January 9, 2016, https://
israelunite.org/brief-israelite-history/

[15] "Prophet William Crowdy," Church of God and Saints of Christ, accessed
January 12, 2016, http://www.cogasoc.net/prophet.html.

[16] "What Are the Seven Keys?," Church of God and Saints of Christ, accessed
February 11, 2016, http://www.cogasoc.net/faq.php. The document authored
by Crowdy can be viewed at the Library of Congress site, http://lcweb2.loc.gov
/cgi-bin/ampage?collId=gdc3&fileName=scd0001_20030506001bipage.db.

[17] "Bishop James Grove," Church of God and Saints of Christ, accessed
January 9, 2016, http://www.cogasoc.net/jamesgrove.html.

In 1886, F. S. Cherry organized the Church of the Living God, Pillar of Truth for All Nations in Chattanooga, Tennessee.[18] His teachings—focused on the blackness of Adam, Eve, and Jesus—argued that whites and white Jews "altered the blackness of biblical figures to fit their purposes, Sabbath worship, and observance of the Ten Commandments. Cherry claimed his call to ministry was given by God to make Blacks aware that their true religion was indeed Judaism."[19] Cherry moved the church from Chattanooga to Philadelphia in the 1940s and remained the leader of the church until his death in 1965, after which, his son Benjamin Cherry took over as the leader.[20]

In 1919, in Harlem, New York, the group known as the Commandment Keepers of the Living God (also known as the Royal Order of Ethiopian Hebrews)[21] began assembling under the leadership of Rabbi Wentworth A. Matthew.[22] The group gained momentum due to its response to events such as the Depression, World War II, and the Italian invasion of Ethiopia.[23] Matthew, born in West Africa but raised in the Caribbean, created a hybrid theology drawing influences from Marcus Garvey and Arnold Josiah Ford to the point he took over Ford's congregation when he left for Ethiopia.[24] Matthew's congregation stayed intact, while other organizations around them were closing

---

[18] Anthony B. Pinn, *African American Religious Culture* (Westport, CT: Greenwood, 2009), 1:167–68.

[19] Pinn, *African American Religious Culture*, 1:167–68.

[20] Pinn, *African American Religious Culture*, 1:167.

[21] Benjamin Sevitch, "When Black Gods Preached on Earth," *Journal of Communication and Religion*, n.d., 28, accessed August 26, 2019, https://umdrive.memphis.edu/ajohnsn6/voices%20of%20the%20black%20church/articles/when%20black%20gods%20preached%20on%20earth.pdf.

[22] Rabbi Sholomo Ben Levy, "The Destruction of Commandment Keepers, Inc. 1919–2007," Black Jews, accessed February 1, 2016, http://www.blackjews.org/Essays/DestructionofCommandmentKeepers.html.

[23] Pinn, *African American Religions Culture*, 1:169.

[24] "Arnold Josiah Ford," Black History Now, accessed October 9, 2019, http://blackhistorynow.com/arnold-josiah-ford/

their doors, most notably Garvey's Universal Negro Improvement Association.

Matthew's views and practices were known to be the closest of all black Jewish movements to Orthodox Judaism, but he taught that original Jews were black, white Jews are products of generational intermarriage with Europeans, and the sufferings of blacks were caused by their violation of God's commandments.[25] Before his death in 1973, Matthew ordained his grandson, Rabbi David Dore, at age seventeen; at the time, he was still a student at Yeshiva High School. A great division ensued between Dore and a contender, Rabbi Chaim White, that lasted more than three decades and eventually led to the group's self-destruction, according to Levy.

Finally, I'll mention the history of the Israelite Church of God in Jesus Christ, Inc., under the leadership of Apostle and Chief High Priest Tazadaqyah. In the 1960s, Eber ben Yomin (also known as Abba Bivens) left the Commandment Keepers and began the Israelite School of Universal Practical Knowledge. Three of Bivens's followers teamed up with four "high priests" to take over the school and were collectively known as the "Seven Heads." These leaders later changed the name of the school to the Israelite Church of Universal Practical Knowledge; to rebrand because of a failed prophecy of Christ's return in 2000, the name was changed to the Israelite Church of God in Jesus Christ, Inc. (ICOGIJC). The current leader, Apostle and Chief High Priest Tazadaqyah, born Jermaine Grant, rose to power after the prophecy of Ahrayah (one of Bivens's disciples) that Christ would return in 2000 to "slay or enslave" all the Edomites (whites) failed to come to pass.[26] Tazadaqyah is known by his followers as the Comforter, a direct reference to the Holy Spirit, and is propagated as such at the website

---

[25] "Rabbi Wentworth Matthew," Tribes of Aboriginal Nations, accessed February 1, 2016, https://www.blackjews.org/biography-of-rabbi-wentworth-arthur-matthew/

[26] "History of Hebrew Israelism," *Intelligence Report*, Southern Poverty Law Center, accessed August 26, 2019, https://www.splcenter.org/fighting-hate/intelligence-report/2015/history-hebrew-israelism.

dedicated to him.[27] The ICOGIJC is the most visual and vocal Hebrew
Israelite group in the urban context of America today.

Islam: The Founder and the Formation of the Movement

The prophet Muhammad was born in AD 570 in the city of Mecca in
present-day Saudi Arabia. Due to his father's death, Muhammad was
raised by his grandfather 'Abdul Muttalib; when Muhammad was age
six, his mother passed away. At the age of twenty-five, he married a
forty-year-old widow, Khadijah, who originally hired him to help sell
goods she produced.

In AD 610, at age forty, Muhammad, while meditating privately in
the cave of Hira, said he had an encounter with the angel Jibril (Gabriel),
who gave him a commission to proclaim the divine message of Allah, to
rid the superstition and ignorance of humankind while leading people
into the light of faith and celestial bliss.[28] Muhammad began his ministry in Mecca and initially received more persecution than converts.
After twelve years of ministry in Mecca, Muhammad and his followers
made a northward *Hijra* (journey) to the city of Medina. Soon their
movement would conquer and unite the Arab people under one political, religious, and spiritual movement.

After the death of Muhammad in 632, four caliphs rose in power to
lead the political and spiritual movement. This led to tensions regarding Muhammad's rightful successor. The result was the creation of two
major sects, the Sunni and Shia (which views Muhammad's cousin and
son-in-law, Ali ibn Abi Talib, as the rightful successor and first imam of
Islam).[29] Both branches have successfully worked to advance the Islamic

[27] The Comforter, http://www.thecomforter.info/.

[28] "The Life of Muhammad the Prophet," Al-Islam, accessed January 19,
2016, http://www.al-islam.org/life-muhammad-prophet-sayyid-saeed-akhtar
-rizvi/early-years#prophet-sawa-born.

[29] "The Origins of the Shiite-Sunni Split," *Morning Edition*, NPR, February 12,
2007, http://www.npr.org/sections/parallels/2007/02/12/7332087/the-origins-of
-the-shiite-sunni-split.

faith from the Arabian Peninsula, into Africa, southeast Europe, Asia, and eventually to North America.

Islam, as a community set to target African-Americans, made its appearance in America through a splinter group known as the Ahmadiyya, which followed the teachings of Mirza Ghulam Ahmad. The Ahmadiyya movement, although deemed heretical by orthodox imams, came from India to America specifically to recruit urban blacks by affirming their ethnic identity as those who are followers of Islam. Their movement started in New York City in 1911, reached Chicago by 1920 and Detroit shortly thereafter.[30] According to Robert Turner, *Awham* and *Tawzih-I Maram*, published between 1890 and 1891, express Ahmad's claim of being the Mahdi of Islam, the promised Messiah of Christianity and Islam, an avatar for Krishna.[31] This claim is what set the foundation for the teachings of Wallace Fard, the founder of the Nation of Islam, to be embraced, as the title of *mahdi* was given to him by his disciple Elijah Muhammad.

Islam's appeal to Latinos has not been as organized or historic as with blacks. The organized development is fairly recent, tracing back forty years. The Alianza Islamica, based in the Bronx in New York City, was founded in 1975. It has seen recent growth because of the appeal of Islam in neighborhoods shared by blacks and Latinos, by Islamic exposure to Latinos in prison, and those looking for a new spiritual path that corresponds with their ethnic heritage.[32]

The latter provides an evangelistic appeal beginning with the AD 711 Moor invasion of the Iberian Peninsula, eventually conquering and ruling through the fifteenth century. Because the Moors intermarried with Spaniards, who eventually colonized most of Latin and

---

[30] Robert Turner, *Islam in the African-American Experience* (Bloomington: Indiana University Press, 1997), 119.

[31] Turner, *Islam in the African-American Experience*, 112

[32] Daniel J. Wakin, "Ranks of Latinos Turning to Islam Are Increasing; Many in City Were Catholics Seeking Old Muslim Roots," *New York Times*, January 2, 2002, http://www.nytimes.com/2002/01/02/nyregion/ranks-latinos -turning-islam-are-increasing-many-city-were-catholics-seeking-old.html ?pagewanted=1.

South America, Muslims are identifying Islam as the natural religion of Latinos, who find their ancestral roots to the Moors from North Africa. This appeal speaks to the hearts of newly immigrated Mexicans but also to established Americans who are second- and third-generation Puerto Ricans. Hisham Aidi, a respected scholar and graduate of Columbia University, whose studies of the Latino Islamic movement in America said the Latino appeal to Islam is grounded in simple truth: Latinos are downtrodden by the American (Judeo-Christian) society and see Islam's progress, from slaves first then to kings, as hope. In particular, in major cities like New York, it is entering into the lower castes of society, that is, the ghettos, streets, and prisons.[33] Although there is not one organized and charismatic leader gathering Latino Muslims, the appeal from Arabs to Latinos' Moorish history is a major element to their evangelistic strategy.

The Moorish Science Temple: Founder and Formation of the Movement

North Carolinian Timothy Drew (1886–1929), later known as Noble Drew Ali, felt his duty was to save nations from the wrath of Allah.[34] Ali taught "Negroes" in America that they were Asiatic, that their lineage traced directly to the Moors of southwest Africa before they were enslaved in North America. Arthur Fauset said that Ali "became obsessed with the idea that salvation for the Negro people lay in the discovery by them of their national origin; i.e. they must know whence they came, and refuse to be called negroes, black folk, colored people, or Ethiopians. They must henceforth call themselves Asiatics, to use the generic term, or more specifically, Moors, or Moorish Americans."[35] Ali

---

[33] Wakin, "Ranks of Latinos Turning."

[34] "Moorish American History," Moorish Science Temple of America, Inc., accessed February 21, 2016, http://www.moorishsciencetempleofamericainc.com/MoorishHistory.html.

[35] Arthur H. Fauset, "Moorish Science Temple of America," in *Religion, Society, and the Individual*, ed. J. Milton Yinger (New York: Macmillan, 1957), 498.

claimed the voice and work of Marcus Garvey[36] paved his way, similar to the role of John the Baptist to Jesus.[37]

In 1913, Ali founded the Canaanite Temple in Newark. The reminded his followers of their Asiatic roots in the land of Canaan. After a congregational split in 1916, Ali changed the name of his movement to the Holy Moabite Temple of the World; in 1925, he moved his congregation to Chicago.[38] In 1926, Ali changed the name of his movement again to Moorish Temple of Science. In 1928, the organization reorganized under the name Moorish Science Temple of America.[39]

During Ali's lifetime, the movement grew to more than thirty thousand followers within New Jersey, Pittsburgh, Michigan, and Illinois.[40] It has been said that up to 70 percent of the African-American

---

[36] Garvey, who started a movement causing an exodus out of the Anglo-dominated church, coupled his teachings of the need for blacks to form an independent society with church dogma, evidenced by his appointment of the former Episcopal rector the Rev. George Alexander McGuire as bishop over the Independent Episcopalian Church that would later be brought under Garvey's Universal Negro Improvement Association. Elmer T. Clark, *The Small Sects in America* (New York: Abingdon, 1949), 172.

[37] Clark, *Small Sects*, 172.

[38] Michael A. Gomez, *Black Crescent: The Experience and Legacy of Muslims in the Americas* (New York: Cambridge University Press, 2005), 215.

[39] Gomez, *Black Crescent*; according to the Moorish Science Temple of America website ("Moorish American History") with the 1928 incorporation came

> a new charter, Divine Constitution and By-Laws consisting of seven acts. There also follows seven additional laws to strengthen the guidelines for better cohesion in the organization. The object of our organization is to help in the great program of uplifting fallen humanity and teach those things necessary to make our members better citizens. The Moorish Movement is still alive today. There are many small temples all over America still following the great teachings of Prophet Nobel Drew Ali. The star and crescent, fezzes, turban, membership card, button, Moorish Flag, and the correction of "El" or "Bey" to the surname signify Moorish identity.

[40] Abdul Noor, *The Supreme Understanding: The Teachings of Islam in North America* (Lincoln, NE: iUniverse, 2002), 4–6.

population in the United States was connected to the movement in some way.[41] In 1929, Ali passed away. Shortly thereafter, at the Second Annual National Convention, controversy over future leadership would split the movement in three ways.

Although these factions exist today, each segment shares the same overall goal as Ali, to see divine salvation brought to their people. In the *Circle 7 Koran*, Ali declares that his pure nation, does not desire to marry the pale skin nations of Europe and serve the gods of the Europeans; they are, therefore, "returning the Church and Christianity back to the European Nations, as it was prepared by their forefathers for their earthly salvation. While we, the Moorish Americans are return-ing to Islam, which was founded by our forefathers for our earthly and divine salvation" (48:6–8).[42]

The Nation of Islam: The Founder and the Formation of the Movement

July 4, 1930, marked the day when Wallace Fard, also known as Master W. Fard Muhammad, or "the Savior," announced that "God is One, and it is now time for Blacks to return to the religion of their ancestors, Islam."[43] His pronouncement led with the affirmation of black ethnicity, which was a core tenet of his doctrine. In 1934, before Fard's disap-pearance or "departure" in a mysterious rapture-like way, his disciple Elijah Muhammad started the *Final Call to Islam*, which serves as the nation's periodical.[44] After a battle with the State of Michigan regard-ing the Muslims self-educating their children rather than placing them under white Christian teachers, Fard and Elijah Muhammad relocated

---

[41] "Who Is Prophet Drew Ali?," accessed February 22, 2016, http://www.themoorishsciencetempleofamerica.org/comments_and_faq.html.

[42] *Circle 7 Koran*, Hogarth Blake, accessed October 8, 2019, http://www.hh-bb.com/circle-7-koran.pdf

[43] "A Historic Look at the Most Honorable Elijah Muhammad," The Nation of Islam, accessed August 26, 2019, https://www.noi.org/hon-elijah-muhammad/.

[44] "Historic Look."

the movement to Chicago. Shortly before Fard, who was facing threats of imprisonment, departed, he gave Muhammad instructions to go to Washington, DC, to study in order to resurrect black men and women and lead the Nation of Islam.

Between 1954 and 1962, membership in the Nation of Islam jumped from four hundred to more than three hundred thousand. The popularity of Malcolm X and the conversion of heavyweight boxing champion Muhammad Ali attributed much to the growth and acceptance of Fard's teachings through Elijah Muhammad.[45] Fard's mission was one that sought to "restore and to resurrect His lost and found people, who were identified as the original members of the Tribe of Shabazz from the Lost Nation of Asia"[46] that were brought to America on slave ships to be dehumanized and forced into slavery.

According to the teaching of Elijah Muhammad, Fard was who the "world had been expecting for the past 2,000 years under the names Messiah, the second coming of Jesus, the Christ, Jehovah, God, and the Son of Man." Muhammad's claim sells Fard as nothing short of being both God the Father and Jesus Christ with this claim; yet, Muhammad was only proclaiming what he was told.

When Muhammad asked Fard to identify himself, Fard claimed he was the Mahdi,[47] the one who "had come in the Early Morning Dawn of the New Millennium to lay the base for a New World Order of Peace and Righteousness on the foundation of Truth and Justice; to put down tyrants and to change the world into a Heaven on Earth."[48] The claim of

---

[45] "Nation of Islam," Southern Poverty Law Center, accessed January 6, 2016, http://www.splcenter.org/get-informed/intelligence-files/groups/nation-of-islam,

[46] Mother Tynetta Muhammad, "Brief History on Origin of the Nation of Islam," The Nation of Islam, March 28, 1996, http://www.noi.org/about.shtml.

[47] The Mahdi in Islam is the "spiritual and temporal leader who will rule before the end of the world and restore religion and justice." *Concise Oxford English Dictionary*, 11th ed. (Oxford: Oxford University Press, 2004), Logos ed.

[48] "Brief history on origin of the Nation of Islam", Nation of Islam, accessed October 8, 2019, https://www.noi.org/noi-history/

Mahdi is not unique to Fard.[49] It is similar to many Jewish revolutionaries claiming to be the Messiah.

An Appropriate Apologetical Approach

When it comes to defending the Christian faith in the complex settings of urban America, a holistic approach is necessary—one that does not focus merely on the theological flaws of other movements but also the brokenness of the FABRIC of the community.[50] We must take into consideration how we as God's people can mobilize to address, with solution-based responses, the brokenness in:

- **Family** structures: How can we best serve the single-parent-led homes, children in the adoption/foster care system, and work toward seeing shalom in the midst of such tension?
- **Authority** structures: How can we build relationships with people as we live in submission to the authority of God's Word, while navigating the tension of repairing relationships between law enforcement and people living in marginalized communities?
- **Business** structures: How can we help mobilize to see fair wages paid to workers (especially women), employment opportunities created for those reentering society from incarceration, and funding for local entrepreneurial enterprise start-ups?
- **Religious** structures: How can we assess the ideologies and philosophies in our proximity that offer ethnocentric teachings that seek to proselytize Christians of color, and develop apologetic resources to help us defend our faith?
- **Institutional** structures: How can we raise the level of local employment or volunteerism in places of elderly or hospice

---

[49] Erwin Fahlbusch and Geoffrey William Bromiley, *The Encyclopedia of Christianity* (Grand Rapids: Eerdmans, 1999–2003), 4:386.

[50] I introduce FABRIC in *Intentional: Kingdom Ethnicity in a Divided World* (Colorado Springs, CO: NavPress, 2019) as part of a suggested plan for the church to respond to the ethnic tensions in America.

care, schools, and jails or prisons to establish a gospel presence in each?

- **Cultural** and artistic structures: How can we reestablish a high view of both creation and the *imago Dei*, all the while creating beautiful and creatively expressed works of art that contribute a biblical worldview to the cultural milieu?

Each of the non-Christian movements listed above has attempted to address spaces of oppression for people living in the urban context. Our efforts of defending the Christian faith in humility will go a long way as we work to establish a community presence that leads to opportunities for proclaiming Christ. Being an involved and caring citizen in your local community, beyond church functions, will likely provide contact with adherents to the movements mentioned earlier. It is wise to be diligent in preparing reasonable responses contextualized to each movement.

Bibliology

When engaging Hebrew Israelites, it's important to keep the focus on the Person and work of Christ, specifically as it relates to his perfect life under the Mosaic covenant (Luke 23:41; 2 Cor 5:21; Gal 4:4–5; 1 Pet 2:22; 1 John 3:5). Communicate that Jesus fulfilled the law; he did not abolish it (Matt 5:17–20), yet when we embrace him as Savior, his perfect right-standing now covers us (Isa 61:10) and has been imputed to our account (Rom 5:12–19). Be prepared to present a case for the sufficiency of Scripture; some Hebrew Israelites use only the King James Version (1611) of Scripture[51]; others hold only to the Old Testament Law and Prophets[52]; still others embrace the KJV, the Apocrypha, the

---

[51] The COGASOC informs its visitors that they use the KJV, http://www.cogasoc.net/faq.php. The ICOGIJC gives a copy of the KJV to those who enter the Baltimore assembly, *Intelligence Report,* August 29, 2008, http://www.splcenter.org/get-informed/intelligence-report/browse-all-issues/2008/fall/ready-for-war.

[52] Commandment Keepers, accessed October 8, 2019, https://www.commandmentkeepersehc.org/

Pseudepigrapha, and the books of Enoch and Jasher as the complete revelation of God that was "removed from the Bible by the so called Roman Catholic Church."[53] The doctrine of each sect is based off its interpretations of the commands found in its accepted body of Scripture.

When engaging members of the Nation of Islam, it's important to understand Elijah Muhammad has declared the Bible is neither holy nor God's Word.[54] He justifies his claim by saying the Bible has been tampered with by the enemy, and the only rightful interpretation belongs to Fard, who passed it on to Muhammad.[55] Yet what's intriguing is that in *The Supreme Wisdom*, Muhammad leverages Scripture to get his point across regarding abstaining from eating pork (Deut 14:8), the 144,000 being the black race that will be saved in whole (Revelation 13–14), and Jesus's rejection of the white race, calling them children of the devil (John 8:42–44).

The Bible declares itself as pure and perfect (Ps 19:7–8; 111:7–8) and inspired (2 Tim 3:16; 2 Pet 1:16–21). When kept in context, each passage shows itself to have been misinterpreted by Muhammad. The Deut 14:8 passage speaks of refraining from eating swine, but through the finished work of Jesus, God no longer holds his people to the same dietary restrictions as under the Mosaic law (Acts 10). The mention of the 144,000 in Revelation highlights the complete salvation of the church,[56] all those redeemed by God's plan of salvation found in Christ, including people from every nation, tribe, and tongue (Rev 7:9). In Jesus's rejection of the Pharisees in John 8, he is addressing their lack of a relationship to God because of their rejection of him being Messiah—nothing relevant to their ethnicity.

---

[53] "The Book of Enoch: Black Adam, Albino Noah, and The Image of God," Black History in the Bible, accessed October 11, 2019, http://www.black historyinthebible.com/hidden-history/the-book-of-enoch-black-adam-albino -noah-and-the-color-of-god/

[54] Elijah Muhammad, *Message to the Blackman in America*," 89.

[55] Muhammad, 94–95.

[56] Got Questions, "Who Are the 144,000?," https://www.gotquestions .org/144000.html.

Theology Proper

When speaking to adherents of the Moorish Science Temple, it is important to take into consideration how they view God's nature. The *Circle Seven Koran* assumes Allah and the God of the Bible are the same being. Allah is said to be the one who sent Jesus (3:20–21), and Jesus taught that Allah is God (7:23–26). This belief rests on the assumption that Allah is mentioned in the Bible. The argument references *alah* (Hebrew) and *elahh (*Aramaic) as both directly speaking of Allah.[57] Yet the Hebrew word *alah* means to "wail"[58] and fails to align with the Arabic term for God. The Aramaic word *elahh* does correspond to the Hebrew *eloah*[59] which means God; however, before one jumps to the conclusion that *Allah* and *eloah* are the same, one should compare the character of the person each name is describing to see if actions and words align. The nature of God, as revealed in the Bible, is triune, meaning he eternally exists as Father, Son, and Holy Spirit. God the Father audibly proclaimed Jesus Christ is his one unique Son (John 3:16–17). Jesus professed he and the Father were one (John 5; 17) and professed the deity of God the Holy Spirit (John 14:16).

Nowhere in Scripture does Jesus connect God the Father to any other deity. Ali claims Jesus taught that Allah is universalistic, saying, "All people worship Allah, the One; but all the people see Him not alike" (10:13). According to Ali, Jesus said everyone sees Allah from a different vantage point; in verses 18–19, he equates Allah with the Brahman Parabrahm, Egyptian Thoth, Greek Zeus, and Hebrew Jehovah. Let it be known, Ali is saying the only true and living God in the Bible is the same as Parabrahm, who is not a tangible deity, but rather an "all inclusive—kosmos," the "highest spiritual sense,"[60] Thoth, the Egyptian

---

[57] "Allah in the Bible—Hebrew Lexicon," accessed January 9, 2016, http://www.allahinthebible.com/.

[58] Robert L. Thomas, *New American Standard Hebrew-Aramaic and Greek Dictionaries,* updated ed. (Anaheim, CA: Foundation Publications, 1998).

[59] Thomas, *New American Standard Hebrew-Aramaic.*

[60] Helena Petrovna Blavatsky, *The Secret Doctrine,* vol. 1 of *The Synthesis of Science, Religion, and Philosophy* (repr., London: Forgotten Books, 2018), 30.

god of wisdom who invented writing and was parallel to Hermes, the messenger of the Greek gods, and Zeus, the chief ruler of the Greeks gods, son of Cronus and Rhea.

Ali's *Circle Seven Koran* paints Allah in a different light, saying he universally dwells in every human; yet, Ali is content in stripping away the full deity of Jesus. The God of the Bible says he is God alone yet has eternally existed as Father, Son, and Holy Spirit. The God of the Bible affirms the full deity and humanity of Jesus, as well as the deity of God the Holy Spirit. Clearly, the God of the Bible and Allah in the *Circle Seven Koran* do not share the same characteristics; therefore, they're not the same being.

As it relates to the Nation of Islam, the primary source of their view on God's nature is Elijah Muhammad. In his book *Message to the Blackman in America*, Muhammad says God is a man, not a spirit.[61] This is in direct conflict with John 4:24, where Jesus says, "God is spirit, and those who worship him must worship in Spirit and in truth." Jesus is speaking of how spiritual regeneration is necessary for acceptable worship to God. According to Muhammad, God is not only a man but a man who is black.[62] This also is contradictory to what the Bible teaches; since God is spirit, he has no ethnicity. In the Bible, God never claims to identify with any specific ethnicity and includes in his plan of salvation a message of hope for the nations (Gen 18:18; Ps 67:5; Isa 49:6; Matt 28:19–20). This view of God as a man who is black is in stark contrast to orthodox Islam, which proclaims Allah to be distant from creation and humans, let alone aligned with a single ethnicity.

In regard to Muhammad's view of the triune nature of God, specifically the coequalness of Jesus and God the Father, he says it's "foolish to say Jesus the Son, is the equal of his Father"[63] and cites Matt 27:46

[61] Elijah Muhammad, *Message to the Blackman in America* (Phoenix: Secretarius Memps, 1997), 27.

[62] Mattias Gardell, *In the Name of Elijah Muhammad, Louis Farrakhan, and the Nation of Islam* (Durham, NC: Duke University Press, 1996), 144.

[63] Gardell, 27.

as his proof text. Muhammad taught there are no Scriptures declaring Jesus to be equal with God; because the Bible says the Father sent the Son, how can God send himself from himself? Muhammad also taught Jesus was a Muslim prophet who is dead and cannot hear the prayers of anyone any more than Moses, who is dead, can.[64] This is a denial of the eternal nature of Christ (John 1:1; 8:58, Col 1:15–20) and his literal and physical resurrection (Matt 28:1–7; Mark 16:1–7; Luke 24:1–7; John 20:1–10).

The doctrine regarding the nature of God according to Muhammad takes an interesting twist when he adds complexity to Allah's being in community with twenty-three others like him. Muhammad claims there is only one God at one time, with a succession of "Supreme Gods" taking place every twenty-five thousand years, which is the time of renewal for the earth, where God rules through the ministry of twenty-four black scientists every cycle.[65] Not only is this teaching not endorsed by the Bible, neither is it substantiated by the Quran, where Allah is known to be one, separated from all, not sitting with or in the circumference of any counsel. This is one of many instances where orthodox Islam and the Nation of Islam disagree vehemently.[66]

Christology

The Islamic view of Jesus conflicts with Scripture. According to Surah 3:44–47; 19:20, Jesus was born of a virgin and is the Messiah. However, this affirmation does not lead Muslims to the conclusion that Jesus is God incarnate. Since Muslims believe Allah is one and completely removed from humanity, there is no room for Jesus to be equal with God, let alone the Son of God. The deity of Jesus is clearly stated by

---

[64] Gardell, 22–32.

[65] Gardell, 145.

[66] For further examination into the differences between Islam and the Nation of Islam, see Dwi Hesti Yuliani-Sato, "A Comparative Study of the Nation of Islam and Islam" (2007), https://etd.ohiolink.edu/.

Jesus himself. Jesus said he was equal to God the Father (John 5:17–18), claimed preexistence prior to the incarnation (John 8:57–59), and declared he and the Father were one (John 10:22–39).

Not only did Jesus claim to be equal with the Father, but he also demonstrated divine attributes during the time of his earthly ministry. He displayed omnipotence (Matt 8:23–27), omniscience (Mark 2:8; John 1:47–51), and omnipresence (Matt 28:16–20). Islam rejects these clear claims and demonstrations recorded in Scripture and opts to project Jesus being a mere prophet, in line with the twenty-five prophets from Adam to Muhammad.[67] The confession of Peter (Matt 16:13–20) and the mount of transfiguration pronouncement by God the Father of Jesus being distinct from Elijah and Moses (Matt 17:1–9) is sufficient biblical evidence countering the Islamic confinement of Jesus to being merely a prophet.

The Moorish Science Temple also violates Scripture's clear description of who Jesus is. The *Circle Seven Koran* contains narratives, known as the Aquarian Gospel of Jesus Christ, about the earthly life of Jesus during the years the Bible is silent.[68] In addition, the *Circle Seven Koram* expands the details of biblical accounts with speculative content. Speaking of Herod (in regard to Matthew 2), Ali says, "He called in council all the wisest men and asked about the infant claimant to his throne. The council said that John and Jesus both were dead; then he was satisfied" (chap. 2:2–3). According to Matt 2:7–12, the wise men were warned in a dream by God not to return to Herod. The Scriptures do not report them saying anything about Jesus or John being dead and neither do they record Herod asking about John.

Chapter 2:20–21 of the *Cirlce Seven Koran* records Ali declaring, "Allah so loved the world that He has clothed His son in flesh that man

---

[67] The Quran gives warrant that every people group will have a prophet sent to them, warning them of Allah's will (Surah 35:24). For the list of the twenty-five accepted prophets of Islam, see "The Twenty Five Prophets Mentioned in the Holy Qur'an," Iqra Islamic Publications, accessed February 21, 2016, http://www.iqra.net/articles/muslims/prophets.php.

[68] The text is available at Levi H. Dowling, *The Aquarian Gospel of Jesus Christ,* http://www.sacred-texts.com/chr/agjc/.

may comprehend. The only Savior of the world is love; and Jesus, son of Mary, comes to manifest that love to men." As stated earlier, since God the Father and Allah are not the same being, and since Allah has no children according to the Quran, to say Jesus is the son of Allah is wrong according to both the Bible and the Quran. John 3:16 expresses the fact that Jesus Christ, the unique and "one of a kind"[69] Son from God the Father, was sent as a demonstration of how God loved the people of the world he created.[70]

Chapter 17:9–14 records an alleged conversation between Jesus and Apollo in which Jesus appears to him and gives him a form of the Great Commission, "Go forth and teach the nations of the earth the Gospel of the resurrection of the dead and of eternal life through Jesus, the love of Allah made manifest to men" (17:12). After expressing this to Apollo, Jesus grabs his hand and says, "My human flesh was changed to higher form by love divine and I can manifest in flesh or in the higher planes of life at will. What I can do all men can do. Go teach the Gospel of the Omnipotence of man" (17:13–14). In essence, Jesus proclaimed his work can be replicated by all of humanity, who is commissioned to preach a "gospel" of declaring the omnipotence of mankind.

This is in direct opposition to the centrality of the gospel message, which hinges on the finished person and work of Christ, who offers salvation as a gift by grace through faith (Eph 2:8–10). John 15:5 records Christ informing his disciples, "I am the vine, you are the branches. The one who remains in me and I in him produces much fruit, because you can do nothing without me." A branch that is not connected to the vine cannot bear fruit; in the same way, anyone who has not been saved

---

[69] William Arndt, Frederick W. Danker, and Walter Bauer, *A Greek-English Lexicon of the New Testament and Other Early Christian Literature*, 3rd ed. (Chicago: University of Chicago Press, 2000), 658.

[70] For further considerations regarding the topic of Christians and Muslims worshipping the same God, see Keith S. Whitfield, "Do Christians and Muslims Worship the Same God?" in *Islam and North America: Loving Our Muslim Neighbors*, ed. Micah Fries and Keith S. Whitfield (Nashville: B&H Academic, 2018).

by Christ cannot bear eternal fruit for the glory of God. Jesus never commissions his disciples to do anything independent of him, let alone depends on their work; rather, the believers' dependency for all things in life, from the provisions (Matt 6:25–34) to every breath taken (Isa 42:5), is on God alone.

Soteriology

According to the Hebrew Israelites, sin is defined by 1 John 3:4, which says, "Everyone who commits sin practices lawlessness; and sin is lawlessness." But on their website, they quote the KJV: "Whosoever committeth sin transgresseth also the law: for sin is the transgression of the law." The explanation given says "laws of Yah can be found in the first five books Scripture which are known as the Torah or Instructions,"[71] which include the Ten Commandments and various dietary laws. *The Law Keepers* say God's people are mandated to

> observe GOD's Holy Seventh Day Sabbath of Complete REST, which starts Friday evening and ends Saturday sundown as HE Commanded in Exodus 16:29 and in 31:12–17 . . . observing all the Holy Days Commanded by YIHOVAH (Leviticus 23rd Chapter): Passover and Feast of Unleavened Bread, Feast of Weeks upon our RETURN to the Land of Israel, Feast of Blowing of Trumpets–Yom Teruah, The Day of Atonement–Yom Kippur, Feast of Tabernacles–Feast of Booths and Ingathering–Shenni Atzeret.[72]

The context of 1 John 3:4 extends from 2:29–3:10, where the apostle John describes those who know God and their continual practice of righteousness. The word translated as "lawlessness" means

---

[71] "The Law, Sin and Love," http://www.angelfire.com/ill/hebrewisrael /Lessons/Lawlovesin.html.

[72] "Fest of the Tabernacles," Israel Unite, accessed October 8, 2019, https:// israelunite.org/feast-of-tabernacles/?doing_wp_cron=1570654142.741833925 2471923828125.

"wickedness" or a "lawless deed"[73] and has the article before it showing that it negates the root word for *law*.[74] John's point refers to a person who ignores the law, not an absence of the law. The question that must be asked is, what law? The answer given is not in harmony with black Hebrew Israelites.

Earlier in 1 John, the apostle says, "This is how we know that we know him: if we keep his commands. The one who says, 'I have come to know him,' and yet doesn't keep his commands, is a liar, and the truth is not in him" (2:3–4). In verse 2, the phrase "we [have come to] know" is written in the perfect tense with a third-class conditional "if" that indicates that keeping the commandments is not something God's people must do to know God; rather, believers know him and will keep his commandments as a demonstration of love toward him.[75] So the answer to the question (what law is John talking about?) is found in 1 John 2:9–10, where John identifies the commandment of Christ (or law of Christ), which is love for one's brother or sister. John reemphasizes by saying, "Everyone who loves has been born of God and knows God" (4:7); "We have come to know and to believe the love that God has for us. God is love, and the one who remains in love remains in God, and God remains in him" (4:16–17); and "We have this commandment from him: The one who loves God must also love his brother and sister" (4:21). John also says that a genuine believer observes God's commands, which are not burdensome (5:1–3).

This thought runs parallel with Gal 5:1–6: if one seeks to keep the whole law, that person has been severed from Christ. Paul says what matters to those who are in Christ is "faith working through love" (5:6); the word *work* is in the present tense, middle voice, saying God supplies

---

[73] Gerhard Kittel, Geoffrey W. Bromiley, and Gerhard Friedrich, eds., *Theological Dictionary of the New Testament,* electronic ed. (Grand Rapids: Eerdmans, 1964), 4:1085.

[74] H. D. M. Spence-Jones, ed., *1 John,* The Pulpit Commentary (New York: Funk & Wagnalls, 1909), 71.

[75] A. T. Robertson, *A Grammar of the Greek New Testament, in Light of Historical Research* (Nashville: Broadman, 1934), 1016.

the believer with the love that energizes our faith.[76] In addition, note the very words of Christ, from the Gospel of John: "If you love me, you will keep my commands" (14:15); "The one who has my commands and keeps them is the one who loves me. And the one who loves me will be loved by my Father. I will also love him and will reveal myself to him" (14:21); "The one who doesn't love me will not keep my words. The word that you hear is not mine but is from the Father who sent me" (14:24); "This is my command: Love one another, as I have loved you" (15:12); and "This is what I command you: Love one another" (15:17). One who truly loves Jesus will keep the words of Christ; this was the revelation he taught, expressing the fact that he was from the Father and demonstrated his deity among humanity (cf. John 3:31–32; 12:47–49; 17:6).[77] The commandments of Christ then are placing trust in his testimony of being fully God and fully man, that he was sent from the Father to be our exclusive way to a right relationship with him, embracing him as our Savior and Lord, and demonstrating our love for him by loving those who have embraced him as their Savior and Lord.

Regarding the Law Keepers' claims of the Sabbath day observation being from Friday evening to Saturday sundown and the mandate of celebrating the holy days named in Leviticus 23, Col 2:16–17 must be taken into consideration. Paul says, "Therefore, don't let anyone judge you in regard to food or drink or in the matter of a festival or a new moon or a Sabbath day. These are a shadow of what was to come; the substance is Christ." Paul here brings a conclusion to his argument against "philosophy and empty deceit" (2:8) by saying the death of Christ has made believers complete in Jesus (2:10); his resurrection allows believers to be spiritually resurrected the moment of salvation (2:12); and through his death he has forgiven all the believers' trespasses, canceled the once-known spiritual debt when he made a public disgrace of rulers

---

[76] F. F. Bruce, *The Epistle to the Galatians: A Commentary on the Greek Text*, New International Greek Testament Commentary (Grand Rapids: Eerdmans, 1982), 232.

[77] D. A. Carson, *The Gospel according to John*, Pillar New Testament Commentary (Grand Rapids: Eerdmans, 1991), 498.

and authorities when he triumphed over them through his completed and perfect work (2:13–15).

All this to mean—worship of God is no longer mandated on one Sabbath day a week; rather, each and every day since Christ is the believers' Sabbath rest (Heb 4:1–16) from trying to earn salvation through perfect obedience to the law.

Since Christ has fulfilled the law in totality, believers are now free to eat and drink no longer in accordance with Lev 7:26–27 and Deut 12:16, 23–24, but rather with Acts 10:9–16; Rom 14:1–12; and 1 Corinthians 8–10. There is now freedom to worship God no longer in accordance with 1 Chron 23:31 (per festival); Ezek 46:1 (per new moon); Exod 20:9–11 and Lev 23:32, 37–39 (per Sabbath) but in accordance with Acts 20:7; 1 Cor 16:2; and Rev 1:10 as associated in commemoration of the "Lord's day" with the first day of the week, the day Christ's resurrection took place (cf. John 20:1, 19, 26).[78]

This gained freedom is rooted in the fact that the dietary laws, festivals, feasts, and Sabbaths were all a "shadow of what was to come; the substance is Christ" (Col 2:17). Paul here is saying that external practices cannot transform the heart of a person. Just as a falling person who reaches and grabs a shadow of something will have only a handful of air, nothingness, so are those who try to place their faith in external practices, never grasping the substance of Christ who is the fulfillment of these practices.

The Moorish doctrine of salvation (*Circle Seven Koran*) is one proclaiming the forgiveness of sins through ceremonial washing and the "purity of life" (4:18). In 4:19–28, the narrative says that as the body is being washed, it is symbolizing the soul's cleansing. Chapter 7:27 records Jesus describing salvation as "a ladder reaching from the heart of man to heart of Allah." In the Scriptures, Jesus himself said that he alone is "the way, the truth, and the life. No one comes to the Father except through me" (John 14:6). Salvation is not a ladder reaching from the desperately wicked heart of a person (Jer 17:9) to God's heart; rather,

---

[78] Warren W. Wiersbe, *The Bible Exposition Commentary* (Wheaton, IL: Victor, 1996), Logos ed.

it is God removing the heart of the stone and replacing it with a heart of flesh (Ezek 11:19; 36:26), thus verifying the supernatural process of regeneration by God the Holy Spirit (John 3:3–8) who makes the sinner a new creature in Jesus (2 Cor 5:17).

Last, the *Circle Seven Koran* teaches heaven and hell are not above or below, because Allah never created a heaven or hell to put mankind in; mankind does this to himself (12:9). Rather than a conscious place in the afterlife, heaven is simply a state of mind; heaven and hell are here and now. The struggles and pain felt on this side of eternity are hell, while heaven is defined as being filled with peace and joy after one has toiled (12:6). To reinforce this teaching, in 12:8 Ali erroneously quotes Jesus as saying, "Heaven is a state of mind."

Again, the recording of Jesus's supposed teaching is not congruent with those recorded in the Bible. John 3:3 records Jesus telling Nicodemus that unless one is born again, one cannot see the kingdom of God; to be in eternal fellowship, one must be born again or regenerated. If heaven were simply a state of mind, why would a spiritual birth be necessary to experience it? In Luke 20:34–38, Jesus articulates a reality of the resurrection—a state of being where death will not be experienced again, showing the resurrected ones were once physically dead. Revelation 20:11–15 records the final judgment of all who rejected the gospel's testimony of Jesus Christ. Their eternal reality will not be merely a state of mind but, sadly, eternal separation from God, consciously suffering in the lake of fire.

Regarding the Nation of Islam, in *The Supreme Wisdom*, Muhammad claims that Jesus was merely a prophet who did his work and died like any other of his time and has no knowledge of all the prayers being said to him.[79] Salvation according to Muhammad is not found in Jesus but in the acceptance of the teachings of Islam, which is the way of freedom, justice, and equality.[80] Muhammad identifies these three elements as being realized when blacks are delivered from the

---

[79] Elijah Muhammad, *The Supreme Wisdom*, 600 of 1667.
[80] Muhammad, 527 of 1667.

oppression of whites and their religion and the white devils meet their inevitable destruction.[81]

The Bible heralds Jesus as God the Son incarnate (Matt 1:22–23; John 1:1–14), who came to give his life as the necessary ransom to redeem sinners (Mark 10:45). Jesus's perfect life (Heb 7:26), substitute death, and literal burial and resurrection provides the only means for salvation from the penalty for sin (Eph 1:7; 1 Cor 15:1–6). Jesus is seated at the right hand of God and has obtained lordship over the universe and all it contains (Eph 1:20–23; 2:6). Jesus's current ministry includes ongoing engagement with the prayers of believers (Heb 7:25), because he is the sole mediator between God and humanity (1 Tim 2:5–6). God the Holy Spirit is also involved in a ministry of intercession (Rom 8:26). Muhammad's claims regarding Jesus are seen to be false.

An obedient Muslim is defined as one who is fully submitted to Allah, evidenced through discipline in fulfilling the duty of every faithful Muslim. This is known as adherence to the five pillars of Islam.

The five pillars are:

1. The Shahada—a verbal confession of faith similar to a prayer in Christianity known as a profession of faith. One becomes a Muslim by verbally saying, "There is no God but Allah and Muhammad is his prophet."[82]
2. The Salat—performing required prayers five times each day while facing the holy city of Mecca. During prayer, one's head must be covered, and the prayers must be recited in Arabic.
3. The Sawm—a mandatory fast during Ramadan, the ninth month of the lunar calendar. From sunup until sundown no food or water is to be ingested, ceremonial meals are to be eaten before the sun rises and after the sun sets.

---

[81] Muhammad, *Message to the Blackman*, 33, 100.

[82] See "How to Convert to Islam and Become a Muslim," The Religion of Islam, December 17, 2018, http://www.islamreligion.com/articles/204/how-to -convert-to-islam-and-become-muslim/.

4. The Zakat—according to Surah 9:60, all Muslims are to pay 2.5 percent of their income as a form of generous giving to those who are poor and oppressed.

5. The Hajj—the spiritual journey from one's geographic location to the holy city of Mecca. While there, mandated rituals must be performed. Every Muslim is required to do this unless stricken by extreme poverty.[83]

The beauty of the gospel expresses a refutation to the five pillars of Islam. Salvation is not based on obedience to traditions, sacraments, or the commands of any deity outside of the triune Godhead. God has determined that salvation, and the process of progressive sanctification, belongs to those who have embraced Jesus Christ the Savior (John 14:6; Eph 2:1–10; Romans 8). The indwelling of God the Holy Spirit is the tangible evidence of God's sanctifying work in the believer (Rom 8:9–13; Eph 1:13–14). Sanctification is not governed specifically by worship service attendance, fasting, ceremonial or ritualistic obedience to Old Testament laws, geographic location, a pilgrimage to Jerusalem, and the financial contributions given to the local church. These practices are beneficial to the believer's walk (Heb 10:24–25), but they do not add to the work of Jesus or take away from it in the context of salvation.

Conclusion

The strongest approach to apologetics in complex urban settings is one that is holistic. It addresses the spiritual and social needs of the people in the community. It will be of great benefit for Christians to study the history, philosophy, and teachings of the ethnocentric movements in their midst by filtering the content through God's Word. Coupling diligent study and prayers that request God's fueling the hearts of believers with compassion for the lost will provide greater potential

---

[83] See Al-Islam.org for comprehensive descriptions of the pillars. Also see Gerald McDermott, "A Thumbnail Sketch of Islam for Christians," C. S. Lewis Institute, *Knowing & Doing* (Winter 2014), http://www.cslewisinstitute.org /A_Thumbnail_Sketch_of_Islam_for_Christians_FullArticle.

for reasonable responses to be given in gentleness and meekness. The harvest is plentiful and the Lord of the harvest is calling his children to be engaged on mission for his glory. May we couple our gospel proclamation with demonstrations of good works. May we build relationships while answering the sincere questions our evangelistic prospects are asking about the faith we have in Christ. May we be found faithful in sowing and watering, and may God bring the increase for the harvest in the urban American mission field.

Part 3

A Practiced Theology

Introduction

Jarvis J. Williams

As the previous essays in this book have shown, Bible-believing Christians must begin the conversation about kingdom diversity with a biblical and theological understanding of sin, redemption, and salvation. Bible-believing Christians must also have a theological understanding of how sin works in individuals and how sin works as a cosmological power to use individuals and systems to create structures of racism and racial injustice. A biblical understanding is necessary because the Bible is God's inerrant (without error), inspired (God-breathed), infallible (trustworthy, reliable, unfailing), and authoritative (the final standard and authority by which we live our lives) word (2 Tim 3:14–17; 2 Pet 1:16–21). Taking the Bible seriously entails intentionally pursuing kingdom diversity in our friendships, churches, Christian organizations, and Christian schools.

Kingdom Diversity and God's Redemptive Plan

The Bible speaks clearly about God's multiethnic vision to redeem individuals from different tongues, tribes, peoples, and nations and to restore the cosmos. Beginning in Gen 3:15, where God promises to crush the seed of the serpent by means of the seed of the woman, to Matt 28:16–20, where Jesus commands his disciples to take the gospel to Jewish and Gentile territories, to John's Apocalypse in Rev 5:9, where John says Jesus purchased some from every tongue, tribe, people, and nation, and to John's remarks in Revelation 21–22 that God through Christ redeems creation and creates a new heavens and a new earth, the Bible teaches God is the God of both Jews and Gentiles because of the redemptive work of Jesus (Rom 3:21–29; Gal 2:16; 3:1–5:1). God's redemptive plan in Christ includes vertical redemption (how sinners become Christians through the death and resurrection of Christ [Rom 5:6–10]), horizontal redemption (how sinners become rightly related to each other through the death and resurrection of Christ [Eph 2:11–22]), and cosmological redemption (how God restores/reconciles the entire universe through the cross and resurrection of Christ).[1]

---

[1] Paul specifically calls this "cosmological" redemptive act of Jesus through his cross and resurrection the disarming of earthly and demonic powers (Eph 1:20–22; Col 2:13–15) and the unification of all things and all people in Christ (Eph 1:9–3:12). Through Jesus's penal substitutionary death on the cross and through his physical and bodily resurrection from the dead, Jesus absorbs the wrath of God for sinners as their penal substitute by becoming what they are and by taking upon himself the penalty for the sins that sinners deserve (Rom 3:25; 4:6–8; 5:8–10; Gal 3:13; 2 Cor 5:21). He reconciles sinners to himself through the blood of his cross and through the resurrection (Eph 2:11–21). He redeems a diversity of people scattered throughout the ages through the blood of his cross and resurrection, and God creates by Jesus's blood and resurrection a diversity of different tongues, tribes, peoples, and nations into one new (but diverse) people who must live in practical pursuit of reconciled community with one another now in this present evil age, an age that is dominated by sin, death, and the devil, as they anticipate the age to come (John 17; Eph 2:11–3:12). God through the incarnation, the death, and resurrection of Jesus

So What?

If kingdom diversity is biblical, then God's vertical, horizontal, and cosmological redemption should move us to action. Ethnically diverse Christians are God's elect people and sanctified by the Spirit according to God's covenantal love for them in Christ (1 Pet 1:1–2). Ethnically diverse Christians are sprinkled with the blood of Jesus Christ (1 Pet 1:2). God caused ethnically diverse Christians to be born again to a living hope in Christ (1 Pet 1:3–12), so that they would practically live in diverse community with one another as the people of God (1 Pet 1:13–5:14). This practical pursuit entails walking in step with the Spirit-empowered fruit of love (Gal 5:14, 16, 22; 6:10).

Practical examples of such love are apparent in the "one another" statements in Gal 5:15-23, including living at peace with others inside the church and outside the church, showing patience, showing kindness, demonstrating goodness, being faithful, showing compassion, exercising self-control in our dealings, not being contentious, divisive, mean-spirited, slanderous, or having outbursts of anger when we disagree. Ethnically diverse Christians should help carry the burdens of

---

Christ begins the renewal of the cosmos now (Romans 8; 2 Cor 5:17–21; Gal 1:4; 3:13–14; 4:4–6; 6:15; cf. Isa 65:17–25). This is not an "overrealized eschatology" but an "inaugurated eschatology" that begins now in this present evil age because of the work of Jesus. Inaugurated eschatology means that God redeemed through Christ a diversity of people to live in harmony with one another and with the cosmos now in this present evil age and in a real transformed and glorified world forever when the kingdom of God will finally be consummated when Jesus returns from heaven to earth, because those from every tongue, tribe, people, and nation whom Christ has redeemed are bound for the promised land of the kingdom of God (i.e., for new creation) (cf. Eph 1:9–5:20; Philippians 1–4; 1 Pet 2:9; 2 Pet 3:7; Revelation 7; 19:11–22:21). Evidence that this inaugurated eschatological reality is experienced now (cf. Joel 2; Acts 2; 1 Cor 10:11; 1 John 2:18) is Jesus's incarnation (John 1:14; Gal 4:4–7), his cross (Gal 1:4; 3:13) and resurrection (Rom 4:25; 1 Cor 15; Gal 1:1), the end-time verdict of justification by faith invading this present evil age here and now (Rom 5:8–10; Gal 2:16; 5:5), and the distribution of the Spirit (Gal 3:14) as the seal of our eschatological inheritance to all who are justified by faith in Christ alone (Eph 1:13–14).

one another with the kind of compassion that the Spirit produces in our lives (Gal 6:1). A diverse body of believers should not "bite" and "devour" one another (Gal 5:15). We should not become conceited toward one another, provoke one another, or envy one another (Gal 5:26). We should not be rude toward one another (1 Cor 13:5). We should not irritate or resent one another (1 Cor 13:5). We should not rejoice when someone does wrong (1 Cor 13:6) but rather should rejoice when the truth is brought to light (1 Cor 13:6). We should worship and do life with one another in our churches (cf. Gal 2:11–14; Eph 2:11–5:21).

Ethnically diverse Christians should also love our neighbors as we love ourselves (Gal 5:14). One-way love is shown by intentionally pursuing the well-being of all people, especially those of the household of faith (cf. Gal 6:10). We should work actively to resist racism and racial injustice with the supernatural weapon of the gospel in ways that are consistent with Jesus's teachings. With God's help, we should intentionally work to care for the marginalized and the most vulnerable in ways that are consistent with Jesus's teachings (cf. Jas 1:27).

Conclusion

For Bible-believing Christians, kingdom diversity is a matter of Christian discipleship because of God's redemptive plan for the world accomplished through Jesus's death and resurrection. The Western tradition tends to make discipleship into a class, a conference, or a special study. Or discipleship has been reduced to individual faith with no regard for the communal, multiethnic, or global nature of the Christian faith. Additionally, we've often failed to understand that discipleship requires us to live as citizens of Jesus's kingdom before the world, to shine our light before others with the intent that they would be drawn to follow Jesus and to glorify our Father in heaven because of our good works (cf. Matthew 5–7). The chapters that follow will consider practical ways to apply the gospel of Jesus Christ to kingdom diversity.

Chapter 7

Shepherding toward Racial Reconciliation

Chris Williamson

Recently a worship pastor of a very prominent church contacted me. He was given the task from his senior pastor of preaching on the subject of racial reconciliation. His church was looking to increase its relevancy, so they decided to cover this topic from the pulpit. They had also hoped this sermon would begin the process of addressing their lack of racial diversity among their ten-thousand-member congregation. As a white man, this staff pastor felt ill equipped to approach the subject of racial reconciliation without speaking to a black pastor first. He knows that my congregation has been racially diverse for nearly twenty-five years, so he reached out to me for wisdom.

As we sat conversing in the local coffee shop, I could see that he was extremely hesitant about the potential backlash he would receive for upsetting the applecart. He was already bracing himself for the unfavorable emails that were sure to come. This young pastor seemed as if he had been told to walk the plank, to preach a message that would get him thrown overboard. I assured him that everything would be all right if his message stayed grounded in Scripture. Even though the senior pastor should have led the way by first preaching on this major topic, I knew this young man would be successful because reconciliation is at the core of the gospel.

It Takes Work for This Thing to Work

When hiring a personal trainer and beginning a comprehensive fitness program, there's a tendency for some people to give up or cheat when things get hard. Others who endure the program sometimes get discouraged when results are not seen quickly enough. In either case, a good trainer tells her weary client, "Don't give up. The program works. It's proven, and it can work for you. You just have to be willing to work the program."

Racial reconciliation works. It is proven, but, for it to work, Christians need to work the program. Things may not change in our lives and ministries overnight, but they will change. We just need to make up our minds not to quit the moment things get difficult. In fact, we should anticipate initial unpleasantries. If racial reconciliation were easy, we would see many more racially diverse churches in our communities. The tragedy is that most of us do not stick around long enough to experience lasting change because we go back to our safe, homogeneous lives, churches, and ministries. We become content (or is it complacent?) to wait until we go to heaven to experience kingdom diversity of a racial kind.

Some of us, however, are not satisfied with waiting until heaven to experience Christ's racially unified kingdom. Some of us want to be a part of this amazing experience now. God's people need to step out of the boat of comfortable Christianity to do what we've never done before and walk with Jesus on the choppy waters of reconciliation, diversity, and justice. I have had numerous adventures and close calls navigating these rapid waters. There were many days when I almost drowned, but, like Peter, I cried out to Jesus for help. Thankfully, he rescued me and lifted me up to walk with him again and again. He stands ready to help you, too. You just have to get out of the boat.

Are You on the Continuum?

I have often said, "If we don't attempt to keep it real, we'll never have a chance to get it right." The church I lead is far from perfect, but one of our strengths is a loving environment that invites open and honest dialogue. God's grace allows us to face the subject of the race head on. Therefore, it is common to hear some of our white members ask or say the following things without condemnation:

- "There's only one race, the human race."
- "Race is not found in the Bible, so why talk about it?"
- "Talking about race only exacerbates the problem."
- "Where's the outrage over black-on-black crime?"
- "Racism doesn't exist in my heart."
- "I'm not a racist."
- "I never owned any slaves."
- "Why do you have to say 'white people' and 'black people'? Can't you just say 'people'?"
- "I resent the term *white privilege*."
- "Why does everything have to be about race for black people?"

You cannot fault people for where they start on the continuum, but you should have concerns if they choose to be stagnant. Over the years, our black congregants have also been freely honest in the conversation about race. Black members ask or say the following things without condemnation:

- "How can we reconcile with a people group that we've hardly been unified with?"
- "I don't trust white people."
- "The black church has been a pillar in the black community for hundreds of years and multiracial churches weaken that legacy."
- "I'm not 'black.' I'm a child of God."
- "Why am I expected to tone down my culture and assimilate to theirs?"
- "Please stop mistaking my passion for anger."

- "Blacks are not a monolithic people. We have diversity of thought."
- "Why do white people feel like they have to always be in charge?"
- "Saying that you're color-blind is not only an insult, it's unrealistic."

Based on these statements and many others, it is easy to see why race remains a challenging conversation in the local church. Even still, the local church is the best place to have these difficult dialogues. Christians have the gospel, which is the only message that brings about reconciliation between divided people. The New Testament word for *reconciliation* means "to change from being enemies to being friends again."[1] The cross of Jesus Christ is what reconciles people back to God, and then it makes believers capable of being friends with one another.

Reconciliation makes Christians one, but it does not make us the same.[2] We can still celebrate our God-given racial diversity and grow in Christian unity. We are always learning within the evolving continuum of racial reconciliation. Some are just starting out on this journey, whereas others have been on this road for decades. There are no experts on the continuum because we are all making personal, spiritual, relational, and historical strides. What matters is that we are on the continuum together, helping each other with questions and providing answers.

Although there are various conflicts between among ethnic groups, the division highlighted in this chapter is the black-white American binary because of America's dreadful, 350-year history of enslavement and segregation. Also, because blacks and whites form the two largest demographics in our southern church, I firmly believe that if blacks and whites can come together, every other ethnic group with less hostile histories will follow.

---

[1] M. Unger and W. White, *Vine's Complete Expository Dictionary of Old and New Testament Words* (Nashville: Thomas Nelson, 1996), 513.

[2] C. Williamson, *One but Not the Same: God's Diverse Kingdom Come through Race, Class, and Gender* (Bloomington, IN: WestBow, 2009), xxiv.

Six Principles to Apply from What Happened in Philippi

The Bible is full of great passages and stories that offer principles for racial reconciliation. One such story is found in Acts 16:16–40. This account takes place during Paul's second missionary journey in the Roman colony of Philippi where he is joined by Silas, Luke, and Timothy.

After casting a spirit of divination out of a slave girl, Paul and Silas were seized, dragged, unfairly tried, lied on, outnumbered, stripped, beaten with rods, wrongfully imprisoned, chained, and placed in a dark, inner cell where their feet were locked in stocks by the jailer. Racism played a significant role in how Paul and Silas were mistreated that day. They were called out for "being Jews" (16:20) by the dominant group who classified themselves as "Romans" (16:21). Racism is much more than harboring prejudice toward another people group; it is when prejudice is enforced with power.

The Lord suddenly made his power known by immediately opening up the prison doors along with the hearts of men. In one night, God turned a negative episode for Paul and Silas into a life-changing experience for a Roman jailer and his family. Men of different ethnicities who were once at odds with each other were now reconciled as brothers in the Lord. I am a witness that the Lord can do the same wonderful things for us if we truly want it. The following principles from Acts 16 are what I shared with the young pastor who needed some direction. There are certain things that racial reconciliation always requires, and I know firsthand that these truths work when applied.

1. Racial Reconciliation Always Requires Mercy

As the text mentions in Acts 16:20–21, race played a part in Paul and Silas's mistreatment and wrongful imprisonment at the hands of the Romans. Any substantive talk about race in America must involve discussing the crippling reality of the prison industrial complex and its effects on black men. According to Michelle Alexander, author of *The New Jim Crow: Mass Incarceration in the Age of Colorblindness*, more black men are under correctional control today than there were under slavery in 1850.[3] Black Americans are incarcerated in state prisons at an average rate of 5.1 times that of white Americans, and in some states that rate is 10 times or more.[4]

Although the Thirteenth Amendment put an official end to slavery, it opened the door to another kind of injustice called mass incarceration. After the Civil War, southern states created Black Codes that made it virtually impossible for free blacks to survive in society. Many blacks were forced to go back to work for their former masters, rebuilding their plantations and working as sharecroppers. The vagrancy laws allowed homeless and unemployed blacks to be arrested and jailed. Once incarcerated, the convict leasing system provided prison labor for plantation owners and businesses. Injustices like these caused attorney and founder of the Equal Justice Initiative, Bryan Stevenson, to say, "Slavery didn't end in 1865, it just evolved."[5]

Like many black men in today's culture, Paul and Silas were victimized by an unjust legal system. When the jailer awakened from sleep and saw that the prison doors were opened, he was about to commit suicide because he knew he would be executed by his superiors. At that moment, Paul's voice echoed from the darkness of the dungeon, saying, "Don't harm yourself, because we're all here!" (Acts 16:28). Don't miss this: Paul told the man who locked him up in the inner prison and fastened his feet in stocks to not kill himself. Paul could have stayed silent in that moment believing that God was taking vengeance on his

[3] Michelle Alexander, "More Black Men Are in Prison Today than Were Enslaved in 1850," October 13, 2011, *Huffington Post*, https://www.huffpost.com/entry/michelle-alexander-more-black-men-in-prison-slaves-1850_n_1007368.

[4] "Black Americans Incarcerated Five Times More than White People—Report," June 15, 2016, *Guardian*, https://www.theguardian.com/us-news/2016/jun/18/mass-incarceration-black-americans-higher-rates-disparities-report.

[5] Emma Seslowsky, "Bryan Stevenson Says 'Slavery Didn't End in 1865, It Just Evolved," December 7, 2018, CNN, https://www.cnn.com/2018/12/07/politics/bryan-stevenson-axe-files/index.html.

enemy. Instead, he and Silas chose to show mercy to their oppressor. In his book *Just Mercy*, Bryan Stevenson writes, "The power of just mercy is that it belongs to the undeserving. It is when mercy is least expected that it's most potent."[6] Demonstrable mercy from Paul and Silas is what opened the door to this man's heart to experience the unlimited riches of God's mercy.

Paul was able to extend the kind of mercy to the jailer that God extended to him when he dragged men, women, and children off to jail because of their faith in Christ (Acts 8:3). The New Testament word for *mercy* can be defined as "the outward manifestation of pity."[7] Mercy withholds the judgment that is deserved and does not give believers what our sinful actions have earned. This is why recipients of mercy should be the greatest dispensers of mercy. One of the greatest contemporary examples of mercy in action was in 2015 when family members forgave the man who murdered their loved ones at Mother Emanuel Church in Charleston, South Carolina, during a Bible study. Nadine Collier, the daughter of seventy-year-old Ethel Lance, one of the slain "Emanuel 9," said to the killer, "I forgive you." And "You took something very precious from me. I will never talk to her again. . . . But I forgive you. And have mercy on your soul."[8] With the nation watching, other family members stepped up to the microphone, lamented, forgave the murderer, and offered God's mercy to him. The power of the gospel was on great display that day.

With this in mind, I have something to say to my black brothers and sisters who may have a problem with white people in general. We must extend the kind of mercy to them that God extends to us every day. We should all ask ourselves, "Who can I show God's mercy to in the way that he shows it to me every day?" If blacks and whites do not start with

---

[6] Bryan Stevenson, *Just Mercy: A Story of Justice and Redemption* (New York: Penguin Random House, 2015), 294.

[7] Unger and White, *Vine's*, 403.

[8] "Mercy for 'Racist' Shooter," June 21, 2015, *City Press*, https://city-press .news24.com/News/Mercy-for-racist-shooter-20150620.

extending mercy to one another, we will never move forward together
in the continuum of racial reconciliation.

2. Racial Reconciliation Always Requires Humility

It was an extreme act of humility for the jailer to fall down in front of
Paul and Silas (Acts 16:29). He could have been ridiculed by his peers
or severely punished by his overseer, but after receiving God's mercy, it
does not matter what other people think. This humble action demonstrated a submissive heart and a teachable spirit. A Gentile jailer chose
to place himself under a Hebrew man's leadership. In a real sense, Paul
became this man's pastor.

Here is a question for my white brothers and sisters: Where in
your life do you voluntarily and regularly place yourself under black
or minority leadership? You have probably never considered that question, but to engage successfully in racial reconciliation, you must. Think
about it, your lawyer is probably white, along with your dentist, banker,
doctor, realtor, professor, grocer, broker, contractor, plumber, babysit-
ter, and elementary school teacher for your children. The police officers
and fire fighters who show up at your house will probably be white.
The neighborhood where you choose to live is probably in the majority,
and the books you read are more than likely written by white authors.
The television shows you watch probably feature whites in leading roles
that are favorable. Your friends on social media are probably primarily
white. To top it off, the church where you choose to attend is probably largely white and has white people in leadership. I would imagine
that when many whites encounter minority leadership, it is usually in
subservient roles to white people. This is not a shaming tactic, but it
is highly probable that you and your children have little experience
submitting to people of color and learning from them.

Making additions to your sphere of influence requires intentionality, bravery, and humility. You will also have to be devoted to developing "followership muscles" you have rarely had to use. The best place to
have healthy interactions with black people is in the local church, and
the local church is the best place to model to your children that you can

willfully submit to black or minority leadership. If you have adopted black children, you may want to strongly consider immersing them in a church with black people and visible black leadership.

Why is it that most efforts for racial reconciliation involve blacks joining white churches? Why is it rare to see whites joining churches led by blacks? Just as blacks have to deal with the mental symptoms of an inferiority complex due to being conditioned in a society built upon a foundation of white supremacy, whites are subconsciously infected with a kind of pride that comes from living in a society that caters to whites. Four centuries of racism that reverberate in this country infect us all, whether we want to admit it or not. The only cure is Jesus, but he only gives grace to the humble and healing to those who can admit to their sicknesses. Latasha Morrison, founder of Be the Bridge, once said, "Part of the racial reconciliation process is supporting efforts led by people of color. I find it interesting when churches with no expertise will try to be the experts. This work requires relinquishing power. The posture of listener is spiritual work."[9] To take the posture of listener, humility must come first.

3. Racial Reconciliation Always Requires Jesus

In Acts 16:30–32, the jailer was so moved by the Spirit of God that he did not wait for Paul and Silas to ask him about salvation that led to his conversion. Instead, he asked them, "Sirs, what must I do to be saved?" (v. 30). He was simply told to believe on the Lord Jesus Christ and he would be saved, along with his household. That is the power of the good news!

In the case of racial reconciliation in the church, Jesus should undoubtedly be at the center of it all. This begs the question, which Jesus are we talking about? Are we talking about a liberal Jesus or a conservative Jesus? Are we looking to a Republican Jesus or a Democrat Jesus? Are we talking about Al Sharpton's Jesus or Robert Jeffress's Jesus? Are we following a Jesus who builds walls or a Jesus who builds bridges? Is

---

[9] Twitter @LatashaMorrison, January 3, 2019.

our Jesus for interracial marriage or does our Jesus strongly discourage "race-mixing"? Does our Jesus support Fox News or CNN?

All of us, if we are honest, have a tendency of making Jesus after our own image, rather than allowing the Holy Spirit to conform us to his image (Rom 8:29). Our overbearing, political bents are hindering our witness to the world. If people do not see and hear the love of Jesus in our public witness, something is wrong. The jailer, however, saw Jesus in how Paul and Silas handled being beaten, arrested, unfairly tried, and unjustly jailed. He witnessed Jesus by how these men suffered when their feet were placed in stocks. He saw Jesus when Paul and Silas extended mercy to keep him from killing himself. No wonder this jailer chose Jesus. Do people see Jesus in you? Do they see Christ in your church? What would you hear if you asked people of other ethnicities to answer these questions?

4. Racial Reconciliation Always Requires Washing Wounds

In Acts 16:33, the jailer washed Paul's and Silas's wounds. What a wonderful act of kindness and tenderness. The jailer may or may not have inflicted the actual wounds on Paul and Silas, but he was a member of the ethnic group and system that did. As a result, he bore some level of culpability and responsibility to see healing occur. His newly regenerated heart compelled him to demonstrate Jesus's love in a way that was tangible and undeniable. This is an example to follow, graciously washing one another's wounds. John Perkins, a pioneer of the Civil Rights Movement, said, "Racial reconciliation occurs when we wash one another's wounds."[10]

Before wounds can be washed, however, believers must first admit the wounds exist. This is a call for us to listen and believe people who share traumatic experiences about race. Making ourselves proximate to them is essential to hear their whispers and wipe their tears. White

---

[10] John Perkins, *One Blood: Parting Words to the Church on Race and Love* (Chicago: Moody, 2018), 82.

believers should be burden bearers who weep with their black friends over the latest unjustified killing of unarmed black people by the police. They should mend the wounds of black friends who tell them of enduring racism on the job or of getting passed over by less-qualified whites. Whites should weep with blacks when their children are called the "N-word" in school.

Conversely, black women must show kindness when white women who are married to black men get wounded by other black women who say, "You stole another black man from us." What about when a white man says that he was robbed at gunpoint by a black man, and since then he's been fearful of black men? He needs compassion from his black brothers in Christ and not a lecture. A church serious about reconciliation will value the need for all of its people to lament from their wounds.

It is not wise, beneficial, or Christlike to argue against someone's feelings. For our white brothers and sisters in particular, compassion is needed instead of defensiveness when the race conversation is being conducted. All of us can better apply the skill of listening to learn instead of listening to win a debate. Christ was anointed to bind up the brokenhearted, and that same Spirit resides in his followers to do the same. The Good Samaritan did not pour salt into his bludgeoned, Jewish neighbor's wounds. He showed love by pouring oil and wine on his lesions (Luke 10:34).

5. Racial Reconciliation Always Requires Fellowship

In Acts 16:33–34, the jailer brought Paul and Silas into his home and placed food before them. A spirit of hospitality spilled out of this man's heart. This was a huge risk, because if it was discovered that he took prisoners out of jail and brought them into his home for a meal, he could have been executed.[11]

---

[11] C. Keener, *The IVP Bible Background Commentary: New Testament,* 2nd ed. (Downers Grove, IL: InterVarsity, 2014), 372.

In first-century culture, sharing a meal together was a sign of acceptance. In preaching about God's diverse kingdom, Jesus said that Gentiles would one day sit down with the Hebrew patriarchs as a sign of mutual acceptance (Matt 8:11). Jesus regularly sat down to eat and drink with sinners as a way to show his love to them (Matt 9:10–11; 11:19). He even sat down with a Samaritan woman and drank out of her cup (John 4:6–7). Sharing a home-cooked meal in any culture has a way of causing people's defenses to drop.

One practical way to see racial reconciliation occur is to regularly open our homes to share meals with people of other ethnicities. We may experience racial integration in some of our churches on Sunday, but real reconciliation is experienced in our homes on Monday. The temptation to debate about race and politics is not as strong with biscuits being passed and when children are present. We must keep in mind that one family cannot do all of the hosting. Fellowship has to reside on a two-way street. Every family must play the role of host because everyone needs to be on both ends of serving and being served. Incarnating into each other's neighborhoods and homes is always beneficial.

6. Racial Reconciliation Always Requires Justice

An injustice occurred in this story when the Romans beat and imprisoned Paul unjustifiably (Acts 16:35–40). Based on a rush to judgment, Paul's rights as a Roman citizen were grossly violated. Had he pushed the matter legally, the magistrates could have been tried, jailed, tortured, and even executed for mistreating a Roman citizen.[12] However, since Paul was being set free and had work to do elsewhere, he chose to show mercy to his persecutors once more. Be that as it may, we must realize that there is a time for the racially oppressed to fight for justice in the courts of law. Changing unjust laws and not simply waiting for unrepentant hearts to change has been the key factor in seeing societal change take place in America on behalf of ethnic minorities.

[12] Keener, 373.

God is a God of justice, and racial reconciliation efforts that do not include a call to justice are weak and unbiblical (Isa 1:17; Amos 5:24; Mic 6:8; Matt 23:23; Luke 18:3). It is ironic how the Bible says so much about justice, yet our pulpits say so little. Citywide reconciliation events that produce great worship, good sermons, and heartfelt hugs are insufficient if those same churches refuse to do justice together. What good is racial reconciliation if certain schools in our community remain substandard? What good is racial reconciliation if police brutality remains an issue for the black community to struggle with alone? What good is a pulpit swap if it doesn't lead to affordable housing initiatives for the homeless, better access to health care for seniors, and job programs for the unemployed? What good is "reconciling" if it doesn't lead to "rebuilding" ruined communities (Isa 61:4)? What good is reconciliation in the church if it doesn't lead to justice outside of the church?

The gospel is found in John 3:16 and Luke 4:18; it has spiritual and social ramifications. The gospel connects people to God and to one another. If a believer's spiritual life is not united with social action, our spiritual activity becomes questionable and social action becomes unprofitable. At the cross of Jesus Christ, the spiritual and the social converge along with justice and righteousness. When Jesus died, justice was meted out to God, and righteousness was imputed to any sinner who believes, regardless of race, class, or gender (Gal 3:28). In the New Testament, the words *right, righteousness, just, justice, justify,* and *justification* all come from the same root word in the Greek language. All of these root words can function as nouns, verbs, adjectives, and adverbs, but all too often Christians want to focus only on the noun of being just and not upon the verb of doing justice.

When churches of different racial makeups come together around a specific justice cause, racial reconciliation occurs faster and always goes deeper. This principle consistently bears fruit in the city in which I live. Amid the ongoing debate across the country about Confederate monuments, a beautiful bouquet of grace blossomed in the middle of this controversy. Black, white, and brown pastors came together for the purpose of telling a "fuller story" about the Civil War in our city.[13] The Fuller Story initiative calls attention to the many contributions African-Americans made during the Civil War. Several churches petitioned our mayor and city leaders with this just cause. After a year of the churches praying and working together, a unanimous vote was passed by the city's administrators that allowed the initiative's leaders to put up historical markers and a statue of a United States Colored Troops soldier adjacent to the Confederate soldier monument. This historic victory would have never happened without the churches coming together around a just cause.

It's Not Easy, but It's Worth It!

At its core, racism is a spiritual problem. It can only be called out and defeated by spiritual forces of light, love, and truth. The six principles of mercy, humility, Jesus, washing wounds, fellowship, and justice found in Acts 16 make racial reconciliation attainable for any individual or church. Shepherding toward racial reconciliation requires pastors to bravely model and teach these and other biblical principles without apology. Intentionality is critical, and it may require putting the words *racial reconciliation* in your church's mission or vision statement.

As you begin or continue on in this journey, keep in mind that some will join you and some will not. Some will walk with you and some will walk away. Whatever you do, do not let unsupportive people discourage you or get you off of God's redemptive mission. God knows how to bring the right people together at just the right time to do the right thing. A racially reconciled church is not easy, but it is definitely worth it!

---

[13] Emily W. West, "National Tragedies Inspired Group to Tell History of Slavery, Civil Rights in Franklin," *Tennessean*, updated January 21, 2019, https:// www.tennessean.com/story/news/local/williamson/2019/01/17/franklin-tn -confederate-statue-group-shares-slavery-civil-rights-history/2536980002/.

Chapter 8

Teaching Scripture with a Kingdom Hermeneutic

Walter R. Strickland II

Introduction

According to the apostle Paul, the "foolishness" of preaching is an essential activity for God's people (1 Cor 1:21).[1] This sacred moment consists of a preacher heralding the gospel's cosmic and contextual (i.e. communal and personal) implications. The gospel's cosmic scope offers hope of a coming kingdom and salvation to anyone who cries out to Jesus as Lord: this message is immediately relevant to all believers. In contrast to proclaiming the gospel's cosmic implications, discerning the gospel's communal implications for a specific church is a contextual matter. This task requires knowing the specific sins that threaten unity in a particular body of believers. Furthermore, on a personal level, the

---

[1] This essay explores the preaching moment as an example of teaching with a kingdom hermeneutic. In complementarian churches, the preaching task is a male-led activity, but the implications of this chapter extend beyond the pulpit into every environment where Scripture is taught by both men and women.

gospel restores a biblically appropriate view of self in the face of satanic lies that threaten each image bearer in unique ways. Thus, preaching, like the gospel, is three-pronged: it is (1) cosmic, and it is contextual in that it is (2) communal and (3) personal.

Upholding preaching's full scope is complicated when the gospel's contextual implications are taken seriously within a diverse body of believers. This task is complex because the preacher's background functions as the primary cultural reference point for the church. This occurs because the preacher's life is the immediate context through which Scripture is understood and most readily applied in sermons. It follows that every preacher communicates most intuitively to people whose lives resemble their own. These dynamics subtly announce the kind of people who feel shepherded most naturally in a church's environment. Even the most experienced expository communicators default to shepherding as if parishioners will endure the same issues, hardships, and concerns the preacher has personally encountered.

Although every believer is encouraged by the cosmic implications of Christ-centered teaching, the enthusiasm is tempered for those on the cultural margins of the church, because the story of redemption is rarely applied to their concerns on a personal level. If illustrations, anecdotes, and application seldom make biblical faith concrete, a parishioner's feelings of functional pastoral abandonment are difficult to navigate. Over time, a lack of spiritual guidance amid life's greatest struggles makes a listener ask, is this the church for me?

Communicating the gospel's full scope is especially intricate among preachers with a high view of the text and fear imposing extrabiblical meaning on Scripture. To avoid culturally captive interpretation, they try to preach the biblical author's meaning to the original audience and limit application to the gospel's cosmic implications. Despite such valiant efforts to attain cultural neutrality, teachers are not able to escape their own cultural contexts. The preacher's burdens, sensitivities, and passions mark each exposition and inform every lesson and sermon.

Books and manuals on exegetical preaching abound, but the preacher's cultural situatedness remains an underexplored variable that complicates hermeneutical accuracy and contextual awareness.

Ironically, preachers who attempt to transcend their personal contexts result in captivity to the contexts from which they desperately desire to be free because the reality of interpretative context is ignored. Among inerrantists in particular, efforts to simplify the interpretative process have functionally eliminated awareness of the preacher's context; this happens when the inerrancy of the biblical text is fused with interpretation. I am a committed inerrantist who affirms the Chicago Statement on Biblical Inerrancy, and my purpose is to critique a negative development that resulted from "the Battle over the Bible"; it is not to do away with this important doctrine. Uncoupling text and interpretation is vital to proclaiming Scripture's cosmic and contextual implications to people of various backgrounds; by extension, it is a nonnegotiable for shepherding a truly multicultural church.

The Arrival of Inerrancy

Throughout the church's history, most Christians believed in some form of biblical authority. At minimum, Scripture was inspired by God and speaks with divine power. However, the concept of inerrancy as commonly defined today did not emerge until the nineteenth century.[2] Inerrancy's formulation was prompted by a growing number of educated elites who concluded that traditional religion grounded in Scripture restrained the human race from reaching its potential for peace, prosperity, and happiness.[3] Against this backdrop, cultural shifts were coupled with discoveries of historic texts and ancient biblical history that comprised the foundation of biblical "higher criticism."[4]

Ongoing threats to Scripture's integrity resulted in Western Christians verbalizing what previously had been an intuitive confidence

---

[2] Mark Noll, "A Brief History of Inerrancy, Mostly in America," in *The Proceedings of the Conference on Biblical Inerrancy 1987* (Nashville: Broadman, 1987), 10.

[3] Noll, "Brief History," 10.

[4] Noll, "Brief History," 10. "Higher criticism" is defined as a branch of literary analysis that investigates the origins of texts in order to understand the world behind the text itself.

in Scripture.[5] The most tumultuous period establishing American's contemporary account of inerrancy spanned three decades (1955–85) that J. I. Packer dubbed the "thirty years' war."[6] During this period, the Evangelical Theological Society (ETS) emerged as a fertile proving ground for inerrancy's contemporary expression.[7] The ETS annual meeting, regional convenings, and academic journal provided the infrastructure for initial deliberations and ongoing refinement of the doctrine. As inerrancy grew in significance, the battle over the Bible came to a head in 1978 with the establishment of the International Council on Biblical Inerrancy and the adoption of their seminal statement, the Chicago Statement on Biblical Inerrancy.

Since ratifying the Chicago Statement, numerous evangelical organizations affirm a form of inerrancy. Moreover, multiple evangelical institutions, including Southeastern Baptist Theological Seminary where I serve, require faculty to sign the statement "without hesitation or reservation."[8] Although a commitment to inerrancy provides a firm foundation for preaching and teaching God's Word, it does not require interpretive uniformity.

---

[5] As an aside, the doctrine of inerrancy was most prevalent among Anglo-American Christians because the threat to Scripture was predominant in educational environments where white clergy were trained.

[6] J. I. Packer, "The Thirty Years' War: The Doctrine of Holy Scripture," in *Practical Theology and the Ministry of the Church, 1952–1984: Essays in Honor of Edmund P. Clowney,* ed. Harvie M. Conn (Phillipsburg, NJ: P&R, 1990), 25–46.

[7] Since its 1948 establishment, an affirmation of inerrancy was required for membership. The society's succinct doctrinal basis reads, "The Bible alone, and the Bible in its entirety, is the Word of God written and is therefore inerrant in the autographs. God is Trinity, Father, Son, and Holy Spirit, each an uncreated person, one essence in power and glory." The statement's commitment to Scripture is elsewhere distilled, asserting, "The ETS is devoted to the inerrancy and inspiration of the Scriptures and the gospel of Jesus Christ." "About the ETS," Evangelical Theology Society, https://www.etsjets.org/about.

[8] In addition to Southeastern Seminary, The Southern Baptist Theological Seminary, Moody Bible Institute, and the Council on Biblical Manhood and Womanhood are among those required to affirm the Chicago Statement.

The Expansion of Inerrancy

Affirming the Chicago Statement did not deter the conflation of the biblical text and human interpretation. In fact, it seems that proponents of inerrancy are more susceptible to this misstep in a subconscious effort to safeguard the text from interpretative practices that locate authority in the reader or their community. In *Five Views on Biblical Inerrancy*, Michael Bird questions the fusion of text and interpretation in the classical articulation of inerrancy. Bird suggests that while some proponents defend biblical inerrancy, they practice the inerrancy of their interpretation.[9] Moreover, Bird argues that when inerrancy of the text and interpretation are merged, to disagree with an interpretation is, functionally, to deny the inerrancy of the text.[10]

At the 1987 Conference on Biblical Inerrancy sponsored by the six Southern Baptist seminaries, Richard Land insisted that

> the fundamentalist coalition's agreement on the Scripture's inerrancy clearly illustrates that inerrancy was concerned with the origin and the nature of Scripture, not interpretation. B. B. Warfield [a covenantalist] and C. I. Scofield [a dispensationalist], exemplifying divergent segments of the fundamentalist's coalition, disagreed acrimoniously and vehemently concerning what they understood the Bible to say about many things, but they agreed that it was God's inerrant and infallible Word.[11]

---

[9] Michael F. Bird, "Response to R. Albert Mohler Jr.," in *Five Views on Biblical Inerrancy*, ed. J. Merrick and Stephen M. Garrett (Grand Rapids: Zondervan, 2013), 69.

[10] Bird, "Response," n. 53. Bird offers the example of Mohler accusing Michael Licona of denying inerrancy by claiming in his book *The Resurrection of Jesus: A New Historiographical Approach* that Matt 27:51–54 is a poetic metaphor and not a literal narration of saints of old coming back to life. Bird, "Response," 69.

[11] Richard Land, "Response," in *The Proceedings of the Conference on Biblical Inerrancy 1987* (Nashville: Broadman, 1987), 34.

At the same gathering, James Carter affirmed that disagreements on nonessential interpretative matters are not an occasion to break fellowship: "The Baptist strength has always been the ability to accept one another as brothers and persons of integrity while differing on some matters of interpretation." And he offered the admonition, "This must never be surrendered!"[12]

The warning from Bird, coupled with the admonitions of Land and Carter, demonstrate that a high view of the text does not necessitate a single interpretative paradigm. A reasonable hermeneutical scope allows the preacher to take the cares of the congregation into the exegetical moment. This is necessary because it affords ministers the opportunity to take the concerns of their congregants before the word of God and encourage their congregations with the cosmic hope of the kingdom and shepherd them by bringing the text to bear on their lives. Nonetheless, the fear of misinterpretation, together with the near papal influence of evangelical interpretative gatekeepers, obligates ministers to mimic the exegetical patterns of their role models—even if it requires abandoning their unique ministerial concerns.

Flattening Context

To arrive at uniform exegetical conclusions, inerrantists often minimize or eliminate as many interpretative variables as possible, including the exegetes themselves. They assume that diminishing the interpreter's contextual situatedness (i.e., in this case, their cultural and ministerial concerns) resists the possibility of cultural captivity that inflates the role of culture over Scripture itself. Robert L. Plummer's interpretative approach, described in his widely circulated *40 Questions about Interpreting the Bible*, conveys a common hermeneutical model among inerrantists. He states, "Reader-created meanings are at times self-consciously driven by various philosophical or social concerns (e.g., the Marxist reading, the feminist reading, the homosexual reading, the environmentalist reading,

---

[12] James Carter, "Response," in *The Proceedings of the Conference on Biblical Inerrancy 1987* (Nashville: Broadman, 1987), 27.

the liberationist reading)."[13] Plummer associates readers who consider
context, to any degree, with the chiefest of interpretative sinners. These
self-consciously contextually aware interpretations are intended to stand
in contrast with Plummer's self-conscious pursuit of reading Scripture
untarnished by the stain of cultural context. Plummer's readers are left
to conclude that any interpretative approach that considers the reader's
context is socially motivated and therefore inappropriate.

When Plummer cites oppression, for example, he belittles it as a
biblical concern and deems it a matter of culturally captive interpreters.[14] He argues:

> Another issue often underlying a reader-response approach to
> literature is the assumption that language is an instrument of
> oppression. That is, texts are primarily used to assert power
> rather than to convey and receive information. While it is
> true that texts, including the Bible, do bring about action and
> change, one must be quite cynical to reduce the reading and
> writing of texts to underhanded power plays.[15]

Plummer's concern of reducing texts to powerplays is warranted, but
being sensitive toward the abuse of biblical texts demonstrates not cynicism but an awareness of Scripture's reception history. In *The Civil
War as a Theological Crisis*, Mark Noll details how Scripture was used
to manipulate and subjugate an entire American race for generations.[16]

---

[13] Robert L. Plummer, *40 Questions about Interpreting the Bible* (Grand
Rapids: Kregel, 2010), 127.

[14] To be clear, oppression references the mistreatment of one image bearer
by another, not unorthodox positions on gender, sexuality, etc.

[15] Plummer, *40 Questions*, 128.

[16] Cultural biases leading up to the Civil War caused slave masters to assume
their reading of Scripture, which affirmed slavery was a "plain" or "normative"
reading. Generally these believers had an implicit trust that the Bible was a plain
book whose authoritative declaration could be apprehended by anyone who simply opened Scripture without the effect of any cultural influences. This "common
sense" reading of Scripture, which dominated evangelical Protestantism in the
nineteenth century, gained a prominent place in public life. The Baconian model
successfully intermingled an affirmation of the status quo with the Christian faith

Biblical interpreters capable of reducing a historically founded concern to cynicism are likely blessed with testimonies that do not include significant experiences with oppression.

Plummer's logic leads to wary skepticism—that pastors or scholars, even those with inerrantist convictions, who read Scripture with a ministerial concern or an awareness of American history are practicing an agenda-driven exegetical approach. In this schema, the only viable pathway that respects inerrancy and the biblical author's intended meaning is to flatten all contextual concerns, to avoid the slippery slope toward theological liberalism. In an effort to achieve interpretative accuracy, a rigid method is employed to flatten extrabiblical concerns that allegedly impede healthy biblical interpretation.

Context Cloaked by Method

The desire to pursue a foolproof interpretative model, coupled with the assumption that contextual consideration is anathema, can lead inerrantists to seek a more scientific approach to interpretation. Missionary theologian Paul G. Hiebert argues,

> [Science] was equated with "positive" knowledge about the natural world based on empirical observation. Physics and chemistry, which became known as "hard sciences," served as the models for all other sciences with regard to their rational presuppositions, empirical foundations, and logical rigor reflected in their use of mathematics.[17]

---

under the guides of a "simple reading" of Scripture. The human proclivity toward cultural biases remains today. Being aware of that fact is essential to pursuing an accurate reading of Scripture. Mark A. Noll, *The Civil War as a Theological Crisis* (Chapel Hill: University of North Carolina Press, 2006), 20. These interpretative patterns are virtually unquestioned in explorations of the antebellum period. For further reference, see George M. Marsden, *Fundamentalism and American Culture*, new ed. (New York: Oxford University Press, 2006), 55, 215.

[17] Paul G. Hiebert, *The Missiological Implications of Epistemological Shifts: Affirming Truth in a Modern/Postmodern World* (Harrisburg, PA: Trinity Press, 1999), 17.

These developments are in concert with the modern academy, which encouraged students to transcend their cultural context to pursue universal and certain knowledge. Philosopher Nicholas Wolterstorff recalls,

> The modern university aspires to universal knowledge. It was a fundamental presupposition that the kind of learning that took place in the modern university was a generically human enterprise: Before entering the university halls of learning we are to strip off all our particularities of gender, race, nationality, religion, social class, age—and enter purely as normal adult human beings.[18]

Such positivist thinking infiltrated theological discourse in the era of Charles Hodge, who viewed theology as an inductive science. In his view, Scripture is a storehouse of facts, and doctrine is the result of explaining the biblical data.[19] Surefire scientific methods created an unhealthy trust in a fallible exegete's handiwork rather than in the final form of the biblical text.

The Transcultural Interpretative Fallacy

Insistence upon universalizing Western biblical and theological constructs produced an outcry from the global Christian community.[20] African theologian Kwame Bediako laments, "Western theology was for

---

[18] Cited in Kevin J. Vanhoozer, "One Rule to Rule Them All? Theological Method in an Era of World Christianity," in *Globalizing Theology: Belief and Practice in an Era of World Christianity*, ed. Craig Ott and Harold A. Netland (Grand Rapids: Baker Academic, 2006), 86.

[19] Vanhoozer, "One Rule to Rule Them All?," 93.

[20] Among Westerners, this discovery is not new. To begin, racial minorities in the West have continually asserted that dominant culture interpretative practices are not universal. Furthermore, the contextual nature of Western theology was also apparent to missionaries tasked with carrying the message of Scripture to the ends of the earth. See Harold A. Netland, "Introduction: Globalizing Theology Today," in *Globalizing Theology: Belief and Practice in an Era of World Christianity*, ed. Craig Ott and Harold A. Netland (Grand Rapids: Baker Academic, 2006).

so long presented, in all its particulars, as the theology of the Church, when, in fact, it was geographically localized and culturally limited, not universal."[21] Likewise, Kevin Vanhoozer argues that

> interpreters are never disembodied minds but embodied persons, persons who are male or female, persons who inhabit a particular place in space and time and so are susceptible to historical and cultural conditioning. Is exegesis without cultural presuppositions possible? It is not. Biblical interpreters have identities that cannot simply be checked at the door upon entering the academy. A human being, we might say, is always [embodied], never generic.[22]

Despite attempts to mask contextual considerations, the preacher's contextual concerns are never eliminated, only cloaked by method. Because cultural dynamics always influence interpretative practice, it raises the question, whose contextual concern became inherent to "inerrantist interpretation"?

Cultural Normalization

The battle over the Bible resulted in the contextual concerns of dominant-culture evangelicals becoming normative in the interpretative process. Cultural normalization occurs when the most influential culture serves as the rubric by which all other cultures are judged. As a result, it is considered culturally neutral. Thus, it is advantageous for preachers to align their interpretive priorities with dominant-culture evangelical power brokers; it is viewed as being equivalent to reading Scripture from a neutral position and achieving the misguided goal of cultural transcendence. It follows that cultural assimilation is the real objective, not cultural neutrality. It follows that "having culture" is the property of nondominant persons and is therefore a less-than-ideal context to pursue exegetical

---

[21] Kwame Bediako, *Jesus and the Gospel in Africa: History and Experience* (Maryknoll, NY: Orbis, 2004), 115.

[22] Vanhoozer, "One Rule to Rule Them All?," 94.

fidelity. Functionally, affirming inerrancy evolved into (1) upholding the "normal" evangelical interpretative context and (2) making specific claims about the plenary verbal inspiration of the text. These interpretative assumptions impede genuinely engaging the needs of parishioners from different cultural contexts because the conflation of text and interpretation delegitimizes their concerns worthy of biblical consideration.

The Consequences of Inerrant Interpretation

Leaders are charged with proclaiming the cosmic story of the "good news" to their parishioners in the areas where they experience brokenness. The disturbing nature of sin is that it manifests commonly among all people and uniquely in different communities. Unfortunately, in multicultural ministries, the brokenness of nondominant communities is often addressed from the Scripture only if the brokenness coheres with the concerns of the dominant culture.

Biblical vs. Social Issues

Interpretations raised by inerrantists marshaled a hermeneutical justification for downgrading "biblical issues" to "social issues." In recent history, it is no secret that traditional marriage and abortion are of deep importance for evangelicals. Yet other ills that are equally "social," including matters of education equality, racial justice, and immigration reform, are often relegated to a social-issues status. Every case above has significant implications for human flourishing, but the latter set of hardships more consistently characterizes life on the margins of the American story. Because these concerns have not marked the lives of the most influential evangelicals, they have been sidelined as social issues and have been inconsequential in prevailing interpretative concerns among inerrantists. If the ethical issues that are most pressing to church members are not addressed from Scripture, parishioners are vulnerable to employing secular or unbiblical approaches to social problems, because their spiritual leaders neglected to address them.

Positivist Leadership

Concerning issues that arrest the evangelical conscience, well-known figures who claim inerrancy garner the unquestioned support of Christians with a high view of Scripture. Lay people tend to mimic the social or political posture of their leaders, because the infallibility of text extends not only to interpretation but implicitly to the social sphere in which the leaders make judgments with nearly divine authority. Said differently, the conflation of text and interpretation is constructed in such a way that to disagree with a leader's social or political ideals amounts to an attack on Scripture itself. Preaching ought to exhort listeners to unity in Christ, rather than uniformity on nonessentials. For example, embodying biblical wisdom supersedes political partisanship or converting parishioners to the preacher's position on the right to bear arms.

Fickle Unity

Christians are called to live as one (John 17:21) and embody the new humanity made possible by the resurrection (Eph 2:15). Sin thwarts unity within the body of Christ and is apparent in distinct ways to different people. To some, division in the church is a matter of relational brokenness characterized by false assumptions, stereotyping, and attitudes toward others. As a result, if individual relationships are mended, unity within the body is restored. Others are convinced that the way the faith is expressed and prescribed privileges some and disadvantages others. Because Scripture reading normalizes the dominant cultural context, it is often assumed that the majority culture has a more appropriate understanding of the dynamics that thwart unity. This dynamic invalidates the grievances of church members on the margins and breeds unhealthy assimilation. The minister's responsibility, however, is to see beyond himself, with the help of others, and identify all the ways division manifests within the flock and bring about healing.

Cultural Hierarchy

Conflating text and interpretation also promotes the normative culture as the "appropriate" context in which to pursue Christlikeness. By extension, it implies that nondominant cultural environments are less advantageous spaces for pursuing righteousness. As a result, "follow me as I follow Christ" means appropriating the dominant culture's language, demeanor in corporate worship, and standards of dress to become more like Christ. Because God-honoring cultural forms can emerge from any community, it is imperative that Christian leaders foster an environment where sanctification does not mean developing an uncanny resemblance to the dominant culture. This dynamic breeds a form of cultural superiority that assumes that those of the normative culture have everything to teach and nothing to learn from minority brothers and sisters. Leading a multicultural church requires the assumptions that (1) every culture has something to offer the corporate body and (2) ministers must strategically plan for each culture to enrich the community with its presence.

Where Do We Go from Here?

At this point, the question might be raised, what about just preaching the gospel? This question commonly implies that the gospel is "Christ crucified for sinners so we can have eternal life" (i.e., penal substitutionary atonement). Human finiteness situates each minister and limits one's ability to discern all the ways resurrection power is at work. The fullness of the gospel must be accounted for in the preaching moment.

The question may also be raised, what happened to just preaching the text? Exegesis rooted in a high view of Scripture is essential to sermon preparation, but preaching is a far cry from simply reading an exegesis paper in the pulpit. The goal of an exegetical paper is to discern the biblical author's intended meaning, but the shepherd's work does not end there. Building upon a sound exegetical framework, ministers are charged to bring biblical truth to bear on the cosmic and contextual dynamics of a body of believers.

A Task of Multiple Contexts

Several contexts are at play when Scripture is taught appropriately: (1) that of the original text, (2) that of the preacher, and (3) that of the listeners. Since all preaching is, in part, contextual, expositors are called to "fuse the horizons" of the biblical text, the preacher, and the listener.[23] First, on the horizon of the biblical text itself, there is a great deal to be said about interpreting the text before focusing on the reader, but it has been done at length elsewhere so I will not attempt to do so here, but suffice it to say that Scripture is the authoritative horizon where the others find their meaning and significance.[24] Second, in an effort to fuse the horizons of the text and preacher, Anthony Thiselton explains, "The nature of the hermeneutical problem is shaped by the fact that both the text and the interpreter are conditioned by their given place in history. For understanding to take place, two sets of variables must be brought into relation with each other."[25] He continues:

> Even if, for the moment, we leave out of account the modern reader's historical conditionedness, we are still faced with the

---

[23] Hans-Georg Gadamer's imagery of fusing horizons offers a helpful description of the preacher's primary task. The term *horizon* was first used in Gadamer's magnum opus, *Truth and Method* (New York: Crossroad, 1991).

[24] For a helpful introduction, see Craig G. Bartholomew, *Introducing Biblical Hermeneutics: A Comprehensive Framework for Hearing God in Scripture* (Grand Rapids: Baker Academic, 2015).

[25] Anthony Thiselton, *The Two Horizons: New Testament Hermeneutics and Philosophical Description* (Grand Rapids: Eerdmans, 1980), 15. While Gadamer is tremendously insightful, Thiselton explores the concept with a more robust foundationalist epistemology that aligns more closely with the presuppositions employed in the development of this essay. The intersection of the horizons brings forth ideas conveyed in contextual language, idioms, and word pictures, but the authoritative horizon is the biblical text, not the contemporary horizon.

undeniable fact that if a text is to be understood there must occur an engagement between two sets of horizons, namely, those of the ancient text and those of the modern reader or hearer. The hearer must be able to relate his own horizon to those of the text.[26]

Unfortunately, few books on biblical interpretation offer interpreters tools to identify and address their cultural blinders.[27] Exegesis itself transpires within a culture's presuppositions; therefore, reading Scripture well includes more than looking for the author's intended meaning. In essence, biblical interpreters must know how to read themselves in order to read Scripture with more precision. Reading the text with greater accuracy requires discerning the assumptions projected onto the Bible that obscure the author's meaning.[28] This is what prompted Protestant Reformer John Calvin to insist that "nearly all wisdom we possess, that is to say, true and sound wisdom, consists of two parts: the knowledge of God and of ourselves."[29]

Calvin's assessment acknowledges that interpreters introduce contextual variables that are not neutralized by employing a scientific interpretative method. Acknowledging human situatedness does not preclude humanity's ability to discern truth. Rather, it allows us to better understand how our cultural conditionedness can cause us to misread it. In essence, this is a call for greater humility as biblical interpreters and is, by no means, an effort to diminish the text's truth value. Finite persons are prone to read Scripture motivated, to some degree, by self-interest. Although we can be made aware of these tendencies, it will not be overcome fully until glorification; reading Scripture with believers conditioned by different cultural situations offers the possibility of seeing beyond our individual limitations. Scripture is far richer and more

---

[26] Thiselton, *Two Horizons*, 15.

[27] E. Randolph Richardson and Brandon J. O'Brien, *Misreading Scripture with Western Eyes: Removing Cultural Blinders to Better Understand the Bible* (Downers Grove, IL: InterVarsity Press, 2012), 15.

[28] Richardson and O'Brien, *Misreading Scripture*, 16.

[29] John Calvin, *Institutes of the Christian Religion*, 1.1.1.

wonderfully complex than any individual or homogeneous community can discern. Although Scripture's authority is never found in a group of interpreters, this does, however, emphasize the importance of our collective effort to understand Scripture as the people of God.[30] In this sense, reading Scripture in community, not as rugged individuals, is an imperative for interpretative fidelity.

The third horizon of the learner is an addition to Gadamer's imagery of fusing horizons. Teachers read Scripture not only for themselves but also to communicate it to others. This third horizon is complicated because not every listener shares the horizon with the teacher nor with other listeners. This overwhelming realization ought to impart humility to preachers and incite a keen dependence on the Holy Spirit in the teaching moment. With this challenge in mind, Robert Smith Jr.'s imagery of the preacher as an exegetical escort serves as a helpful framework for applying the biblical text to the lives of listeners:

> The priest asks, "Is there no balm in Gilead? Is there no physician there?" The priest gives spiritual medicine and spiritual messages. Jesus the priest invites, "Come unto me, all you that labor and are heavy laden, and I will give you rest" (Matt. 11:28). Instead of the priest offering a balm, the prophet indicts the people and delivers a bomb to those who are at ease in Zion. Preachers need to know when and how to use the bomb and the balm, depending on whether people who are afflicted need

---

[30] When the goodness of situated persons is denied, reading Scripture in community is, as Plummer insists, to access the insights of gifted teachers (Plummer, *40 Questions*, 105). Without denying the significance of the spiritual gift of teaching and the value of theological training, if the only benefit of reading Scripture in community is to access the gifts of clergy-types, an interpretative hierarchy ensues that fortifies the hermeneutical practices of those who are culturally "neutral." Rather, reading Scripture in community should draw upon the expertise of gifted teachers, but also use the insights of the people of God from different stages of life, socioeconomic status, and cultures.

to be comforted or whether people who are comfortable need to be afflicted.[31]

This admonition assumes that the shepherd "knows the sheep" and is aware of when to administer the balm and when to drop the bomb in the sermonic moment.

This does not mean that every sermon must engage each demographic, but it implies that, over time, parishioners know if the preacher in the midst of sermon preparation and delivery was burdened by their sorrows and sharing in their joys. To be a shepherd from the pulpit, and not a stale academician, sermon preparation does not begin in the study but in the midst of ongoing pastoral responsibility including sitting next to hospital beds, in the counseling room, and visiting with parishioners around their dinner tables. New Testament scholar Robert Stein's interpretative notion is correct: "Where you start determines where you finish."[32] Although the "field work" commences prior to formally studying the text, Scripture remains authoritative, and the teacher's job is to let the people know how God's universal redemptive narrative upends the brokenness they experience each day.

Although a more extended treatment of this topic is warranted, it is appropriate to conclude that preaching is a cosmic and contextual activity. Shepherding multicultural, not merely multiethnic, churches requires preachers to acknowledge their situatedness to reach interpretative understanding and see beyond themselves to minister to the flock. Uncoupling text and interpretation in the preaching moment is a subtle yet essential step toward ministering to God's multicultural people. May God give us grace as we proclaim the cosmic and contextual implications of the gospel to those the Lord places under our care.

---

[31] Robert Smith Jr., *Doctrine That Dances: Bringing Doctrinal Preaching and Teaching to Life* (Nashville: B&H Academic, 2008), 77.

[32] Robert H. Stein, *Jesus the Messiah: A Survey of the Life of Christ* (Downers Grove, IL: IVP Academic, 1996), 18–24.

Chapter 9

Men and Women in the Body of Christ

Amber Bowen

It all started when I walked into the provost's office at my institution, existential crisis in tow. I had recently enrolled in a master's program that would prepare me for a PhD. I had long felt the call to be involved in theological education at the university level and finally had the opportunity to begin the process of becoming a professor; that is, until a tidal wave of fear and apprehension knocked me off my feet. The provost had been a college professor of mine whom I trusted and looked up to. I knew he would help. As soon as I sat down at the table across from him, I let it out.

"If I get a PhD, will it harm the church?" I asked.

He tilted his head with curiosity. "Explain to me what you mean."

I took a breath. "My heart's desire is to build up the church and to use my gifts for God's glory. But I am afraid that if I get a PhD, especially in something like philosophy, I will not be an *encouragement* to my brothers; I'll be a *discouragement* to them. Rather than feeling

163

empowered to lead and grow, I fear they will feel intimidated and shrink back. I would rather quit now than risk that happening."

Leaning his elbows on the table, he carefully chose his words. "I know you may feel that would be the case based on your experience, but that is not the way the church is designed to work," he responded. "God has gifted you for this, and there are so many ways your training can be used to build up the church, which includes your brothers in Christ. I want to encourage you to do this."

"Really?" I replied with shock. I came thinking he would give me solid parameters for how to hold myself back to avoid invading my brothers' territory.

"Go produce show-stopping work," he said. "Speak with grace and love like all Christians should, but do not sit in the back of the classroom afraid to let your voice be heard. Do not feel like you don't belong in the theological academy as a woman, because you do. Do not think your investment is a risk to the church's sound doctrine rather than a contribution to it. And don't you stop with just the master's. Get into the best PhD program you can. Write an excellent dissertation that offers a real contribution to both the academy and the church. I can only imagine where God will take you and how he will use you!"

What I received that day was encouragement. We often think that *encouragement* means making someone feel better or paying them a compliment. However, the original meaning of the word offers much more. It means *to give courage* to someone. The Bible repeats the command for those in the church to "give courage" to one another to grow in maturity in Christ and to follow him in obedience (1 Thess 2:12; 4:18; 5:11; Heb 3:13, 10:24–25; Col 4:8). As lovely as the idea of giving courage to one another sounds, applying it gets tricky when we think about the current conversation on gender roles in the church. In recent times, many men and women have called for a reconsideration of what it means to faithfully live out a complementarian framework in the church. There has been much fruitful discussion on ways to include women in all areas of church life and ministry outside of the office of pastor/elder.[1] However, at times this conversation can become charged and frustrating. It can quickly devolve into a territory battle.

Territory battles can make us think that for one side to expand, the other side must diminish. Territory battles can also pit two sides in opposition to each other. One side can easily be classified as the invader and the other as the oppressor. Both sides develop dispositions of fear and suspicion toward the other. Under these conditions, the command to *encourage* one another is nearly impossible. Each feels the need to protect itself rather than *give courage* to the other.

To advance the conversation on how faithfully to live out the complementarian vision for the church, we need to see the discussion, and one another, with fresh eyes.[2] To help us do this, I would like to invite

---

[1] As reflected by the positions offered in James Beck and Stanley Gundry, eds., *Two Views on Women in Ministry* (Grand Rapids: Zondervan, 2005), a person qualifies as a complementarian if he or she believes that the role of pastor/elder and head of the household are reserved for men who are called to those roles. For additional key resources in the dialogue, see Kathy Keller, *Jesus, Justice, and Gender Roles: A Case for Gender Roles in Ministry* (Grand Rapids: Zondervan, 2012); John Dickson, *Hearing Her Voice: A Case for Women Giving Sermons* (Grand Rapids: Zondervan, 2014); Owen Strachan, Jonathan Parnell, and Denny Burk, eds., *Designed for Joy: How the Gospel Impacts Men and Women, Identity, and Practice* (Wheaton, IL: Crossway, 2015); Alice Matthews, *Gender Roles and the People of God: Rethinking What We Were Taught about Men and Women in the Church* (Grand Rapids: Zondervan, 2017); Aimee Byrd, *No Little Women: Equipping All Women in the Household of God* (Phillipsburg, NJ: P&R Publishing, 2016); Wendy Alsup, *Is the Bible Good for Women?: Seeking Clarity and Confidence through a Jesus-Centered Understanding of Scripture* (New York: Multnomah, 2017); Jen Wilkin, "The Complementarian Woman: Permitted or Pursued?" The Gospel Coalition, April 25, 2013, https://www.thegospelcoalition.org/article/the-complementarian-woman-permitted-or-pursued/.

[2] There is a pressing question that needs to be addressed. Does this perspective shift, away from territory lines and to the distinctiveness of the person, make it then illogical to affirm male headship? Upon what basis would one claim that the role of pastor and head of the home biblically rests on men? In his forthcoming work *Heirs Together: A Theology of the Sexes* (Crossway), Alastair Roberts notes the conversation on men and women has often fallen

an unexpected voice to the table: nineteenth-century Christian philosopher, Søren Kierkegaard. Kierkegaard's texts may not directly address
gender dynamics in the contemporary church, but they do help us learn
how to resee God's image bearers. The first thing Kierkegaard says we
need to do is go for a walk—in a meadow.

---

to a discussion on roles and regulations. The Bible is often approached as a
rule-book dictating brute norms that God has decided and that must be
obeyed. Often complementarians insist on holding fast to male headship simply because God says so. They are viewed as uncompromising and courageous
followers of God's Word even when such a position is unpopular and even
offensive to our culture. Women often feel a pressure not just to affirm the
rule of exclusive male headship, but to be glad hearted about it—to be happy
about not being allowed to occupy such positions. For many women especially,
the question becomes, why? They struggle to believe that they are indeed of
equal value, when key positions in the church are out of bounds for them. The
problem is a hermeneutical and an ecclesiological one. The Bible is a dramatic
story of creation, fall, redemption, and restoration. As such, it must be read
more like a dramatic story than a stagnant rule book. Roberts shows how the
narrative—from Genesis to Revelation—is full of symbolism, typology, echoes,
and foreshadowing. The way the church is structured is not an arbitrary organizational technique that God has mandated. Rather, it is an embodiment of
God's redemptive story. One example of the symbolic and typological nature
of the church's institutional practice is in the role of the pastor. The pastor
stands before God on behalf of the people and is also charged with proclaiming God's Word to them. His role is a priestly one. He symbolically points to
Christ, who is the ultimate High Priest and lovingly cares for his bride, the
church. Therefore, his maleness is not simply an arbitrary requirement God
decided to throw in, but part of the deeply symbolic nature of the role. In our
modern context, however, where pastors are reduced to CEOs, spiritual advisers, or motivational speakers, it becomes very difficult to understand why a
woman could not occupy such a position. After all, women make excellent
CEOs, spiritual advisers, and motivational speakers. However, there is something deeper going on in the way the church lives out not just Christian principles but the gospel story. Approached this way, the concept of gender "roles"
is recast. There are different "roles" in this story, but they are less like a specific
division of labor and more like a character to play.

How to See a Meadow

In *Works of Love,* Kierkegaard includes a discourse, "Love Does Not Seek Its Own," that addresses our sinful tendency to seek our own rather than the "other's own." He begins with an observation:

> Love does not seek its own, for there are no mine and yours in love. But "mine" and "yours" are only relational specifications of "one's own." . . . Justice is identified by its giving each his own, just as it also in turn claims its own. This means that justice pleads the cause of its own, divides and assigns, determines what each can lawfully call his own, judges and punishes if anyone refuses to make any distinction between *mine* and *yours*.[3]

It is not difficult to appropriate this observation to our own discussion on gender. Territory negotiations center on dividing, assigning, and determining what is biblically permissible to call "women's" territory, "men's" territory, or "shared territory." Biblical guidelines for the church are incredibly important to establish. However, if we reduce ourselves to border patrols, we keep our eyes locked on what is rightfully ours instead of seeing what the other could become. For example, if a woman gets an opportunity in the church, perhaps some men think, "It's difficult being a man in this day and age. You can't expect to get anything unless you are a woman." When a man gets an opportunity, perhaps some women think, "That position would have been appropriate for a woman to have. But, yet again, it goes to a man." Do men and women live in different realities? No, we are just fixing our eyes on the wrong thing. We are *looking* at our own territory line or gender block instead of *seeing* the other.[4]

---

[3] Søren Kierkegaard, *Works of Love,* trans. Howard V. and Edna H. Hong (Princeton, NJ: Princeton University Press, 1998), 265.

[4] Esther Meek gives insight to the problem of looking versus seeing as endemic of what she calls a defective epistemic default in (post)modern society. She writes, "We have caricatured seeing itself so that it involves us in a looking at the exterior of something, as opposed to any sensitive indwelling of it. Seeing has led us, not to empathy, but to criticism. Seeing empathetically has been virtually non-existent as a feature of our prevailing epistemology. At least,

Kierkegaard suggests we readjust our gaze: "The truly loving one does not love his own distinctiveness but, in contrast, loves every human being according to his distinctiveness; but his 'distinctiveness' is what for him is his own."[5] Explaining this concept, De Vries writes, "[The] refusal to seek one's own, the refusal to look out for one's own interest, implies also that we seek, positively, the 'distinctiveness' of the other. In referring to the distinctiveness of the other, Kierkegaard refers to God's creation of each person, *ex nihilo*, in his or her particularity."[6] To train our eyes to see distinctiveness, Kierkegaard suggests we take a walk in a meadow:

> Just recollect what you yourself have so often delighted in look-ing at, recollect the beauty of the meadows! There is no differ-ence in the love, no, none—yet what a difference in the flowers! Even the least, the most insignificant, the most unimpressive, the poor little flower disregarded by even the most unimpressive, the poor little flower disregarded by even its immediate surround-ings, the flower you can hardly find without looking carefully— it is as if this, too, had said to love: Let me become something in myself, something distinctive. And then love has helped it to become its own distinctiveness, but far more beautiful than the poor little flower had ever dared to hope for. What love! First, it makes no distinction, none at all; next, which is just like the first, it infinitely distinguishes itself in loving the diverse. . . . Just suppose nature were like us human beings—rigid, domineering, cold, partisan, small-minded, capricious—and imagine, yes, just imagine what would happen to the beauty of the meadow![7]

---

it has been nonexistent *as seeing*. We might have called it pity, or intuition—but not seeing, or knowing. Seeing has turned into, not *insight*, but objectifica-tion." Esther Lightcap Meek, *Loving to Know: Covenant Epistemology* (Eugene, OR: Cascade, 2001), 24.

[5] Kierkegaard, *Works of Love*, 279, quoted in Roland J. De Vries, *Becoming Two in Love: Covenant Epistemology* (Eugene, OR: Pickwick, 2013), 189.

[6] De Vries, *Becoming Two in Love*, 89.

[7] Kierkegaard, *Works of Love*, 270.

There are two ways to walk through a meadow. The first is to look at it with broad strokes, enjoying the scenery while you occupy yourself with other things. The second way is to stop, to stoop down, and to find a single flower that is part of that meadow. When you attend to it, or focus your attention on it, you notice how it is unlike every other flower. You see the existence of something God created as a particular act of his creativity and wisdom. When you turn your face toward the flower and marvel at it, there is a sense in which you usher it into existence. Instead of being lost in the background of the category *flowers*, you now see something specific, something *more* than you saw before. G. K. Chesterton echoes this very idea: "It may not be automatic necessity that makes all daisies alike; it may be that God makes every daisy separately, but has never got tired of making them. . . . The repetition in Nature may not be a mere reoccurrence; it may be a theatrical encore."[8] By noticing each individual act of creation in its distinctiveness, you honor it, and you honor the One who made it.

This single flower gives you a window of depth into the meadow. Instead of the meadow being one dimensional, you realize it is made up of millions of examples of God's particular acts of creation interwoven in such a way that neither flattens their distinctiveness nor makes their distinctiveness a threat. The unique plants, flowers, shrubs, rocks, and wildlife dwell in concert with one another, together forming a harmonious ecosystem that is bursting at the seams with life!

Imagine if brothers and sisters learned to "see" one another like this. Instead of classifying one another in broad-stroked categories, they would pay particular attention to the person in front of them. Their focus would be on actively identifying ways he or she is distinctly created by God, marveling at God's creativity and wisdom. Brothers and sisters would imagine how God could use the other to build up the church and perhaps even facilitate ways the other's gifts could be cultivated. When brothers and sisters regard each other in this way, they affirm the goodness of each other's existence. They build each other up.

---

[8] G. K. Chesterton, *Orthodoxy* (New York: John Lane, 1909), 106.

In short, they *give courage* to one another. They outdo one another in showing honor (Rom 12:10).

When a brother looks out for the growth of his sister, and a sister looks out for the growth of her brother, both expand. The need to hold one back so the other can have space becomes irrelevant if the mutual focus is the expansion of the other. They discover that it is not the absence of the other, but their *presence* that encourages the one to grow. The result is not a flattening of the genders or even the pursuit of bare equality, but generosity, harmony, and mutual growth.[9] There is no law of diminishing returns. There is no land grabbing. The church operates on a fundamentally different logic. When brothers and sisters *give courage* to one another, the church, like the meadow, bursts at the seams with life.

The walk in the meadow is not an alternative to the overdue discussion on what it means to live out a complementarian vision in the church; rather, it is a perspective shift within it that takes us *deeper* than merely changing the landscape. The complementarianism discussion rightly calls attention to ways we have allowed our (sub)culture, more than the Bible, to influence our ideas about men and women. It exposes extra fencing we have placed around the office of pastor/elder, and it encourages the church to imagine ways both men and women can be built up for the glory of God and the benefit of the church. However, the walk in the meadow reminds us that the body of Christ is more like an ecosystem than a machine. There is no need to hold your own when you are mutually looking out for the "other's own," championing it as far as you can within the precinct of our complementarian conviction. When brothers give their sisters courage to explore all the ways their

---

[9] It is important to note that the Bible talks about gender not as variegated but as binary: male and female (Gen 1:27; 5:2). The metaphor of the meadow can be used to point out how sexual difference can be expressed through a variety of giftings rather than by collapsing giftings and sexual difference into one category. The meadow metaphor does not teach us to be gender blind, nor does it lead us to become gender fluid. Rather, it teaches us to develop an eye for distinctiveness in gifting as creatively expressed by both men and women so that it may be encouraged and honored in the church.

gifts could be used outside of the pastorate, sisters no longer need to advocate for themselves. Likewise, not all brothers are called to be pastors, so sisters must also give nonpastor brothers courage to explore all the ways their gifts could be used outside of that office. Rather than being exclusively fixated on parameters to protect against dysfunction, the walk in the meadow helps us pursue conditions that bring health. It escorts the conversation beyond the mechanics of either segregation or equal representation to a verdant space of mutual love, flourishing, and growth. Our discourse no longer takes the tone of negotiation but of invitation.

Masculine Despair and Its Consequences

The meadow teaches us what it is like to delight in the distinctiveness in creation and in one another. Yet Kierkegaard suggests two ways of being that render us incapable of delighting in the "other's own," much less seeking it above our own: (1) by being domineering and (2) by being small minded. These dispositions bear strong resemblance to what one of Kierkegaard's pseudonymous authors, Anti-Climacus, describes as "masculine" and "feminine" despair.[10] Before moving forward, it is nec-

---

[10] Kierkegaard uses the literary technique of indirect communication across his authorship. Rather than deceiving or teasing the reader, this technique is intended to invite the reader into a conversation. When truth is communicated directly, it can become merely a transmission of information that remains in the head without shaping the heart. When truth is communicated indirectly, as Nathan does for David in 2 Samuel 12 or Jesus does through his parables, there is a greater chance readers or hearers will see themselves in relation to that truth and will allow themselves to be changed by it. Kierkegaard's authorship is composed of works signed by him and those signed by pseudonyms. These pseudonyms are fictional characters that Kierkegaard created. They have different personalities and different perspectives on faith. Some, like Johannes Climacus and Johannes De Silentio, admit they are not (yet) Christians. They observe what faith looks like from where they stand. Anti-Climacus, however, is a Christian. Together, these voices form a dialogue in which they give different perspectives and opinions. For this reason, reading Kierkegaard's texts for the first time can be confusing. The aim of the corpus as a whole is not

essary to make one thing clear. Although Anti-Climacus labels these two types of despair as *masculine* and *feminine*, they are not gender specific. Men can experience small-minded "feminine" despair, and women can experience domineering "masculine" despair.[11] Additionally, Kierkegaard is not directly associating men with being domineering or women with being small minded. His point is far deeper than that. He is saying that we must reject both types of human despair to be able to *give courage* to the other to grow up in Christ. These insights on the sin of despair help us understand why giving courage to the other can be extremely difficult.

Anti-Climacus suggests that God created the human self to be formable rather than fixed.[12] Our job in the world is to be occupied with the task of growing, filling, and *becoming* alongside other image bearers in creation under the loving gaze of our Creator. Just like the rest of creation, we are bursting with possibility of how we could expand in the world and what we could "become."[13] The life of the cre-

---

to perplex the reader, but to *edify* her; to encourage her faith and assist her in her flourishing as a self before God. By pointing out similarities between Kierkegaard's description of the domineering person and the small-minded person and Anti-Climacus's description of masculine and feminine despair, I am showing how the two interlocutors reinforce each other and each contribute to the discussion. For introductory resources on Kierkegaard's authorship, see Mark Tietjen, *Kierkegaard: A Christian Missionary to Christians* (Downers Grove, IL: InterVarsity Press, 2006); C. Stephen Evans, *Kierkegaard: An Introduction* (Cambridge: Cambridge University Press, 2009); Christopher Ben Simpson, *The Truth Is the Way: Kierkegaard's Theologia Viatorum* (Eugene, OR: Cascade, 2011); and Steven M. Emmanuel, *Kierkegaard and the Concept of Revelation* (Albany: State University of New York), 1996.

[11] Silvia Walsh, *Kierkegaard: Thinking Christianly in an Existential Mode* (Oxford: Oxford University Press, 2009), 101–2.

[12] Søren Kierkegaard, *Sickness unto Death*, trans. Howard V. and Edna H. Hong (Princeton, NJ: Princeton University Press, 1983), 13.

[13] Human selves, Anti-Climacus says, are both *finite* and *eternal* and have both *necessity* and *possibility*. There is something transcendent and eternal in each of us, yet we are also embodied creatures rooted in God's world and designed to flourish as such. Moreover, we each have certain things about us that are determined—like when and where we were born and if we were

ated self is one of active discovery, exploration, and cultivation of possibilities under the providential hand of God. We acquire new skills, take risks, create new things, give birth to new ideas, and grow in ways we never imagined. We can be formed and shaped in many different ways, but we become our truest selves when we are shaped by God's story through his Word and alongside his people.[14] However, because sin is also involved in that story, we often respond to this call with despair rather than faith.

Masculine despair, says Anti-Climacus, occurs when the self defiantly insists on the kind of self it wants to be:

> The self in [masculine] despair wants to be the master of itself or to create itself, to make his self into the self he wants to be, to determine what he will have or not have in his concrete self. . . . In other words, he wants to begin a little earlier than do other men, not at and with the beginning, but "in the beginning"; he does not want to put on his own self, does not want to see his given self as his task—he himself wants to compose his self.[15]

This self wants to create itself, ex nihilo, according to the expectations it has crafted or adopted. According to Anti-Climacus, this self is "an acting self, it constantly [relates] itself to itself only by way of imaginary constructions." In other words, by trying to recreate itself rather than stewarding the distinct self God created, it becomes a fake self rather

---

created male or female. This is what Anti-Climacus means by "necessity." However, we are also bursting with possibility of how we could expand in the world and what we could "become." God's providential hand is the sustainer, what Anti-Climacus calls the "synthesis" of finitude and infinitude, necessity and possibility. See Kierkegaard, *Sickness unto Death*, 13.

[14] Stanley Hauerwas's description of the Christian narrative identity of the self in *The Peaceable Kingdom* (Notre Dame, IN: Notre Dame University Press, 1983) expresses a similar view of human personhood as formed rather than fixed and put on display in a narrative that involves community.

[15] Kierkegaard, *Sickness unto Death*, 68.

than an authentic self. It defies rather than delights in God's creation, which Anti-Climacus identifies as demonic.[16]

When this kind of despair is turned outward, not only does this person demand "its own" for the kind of self it becomes, but it also demands "its own" for the kind of self the other becomes. In other words, it tries to create the other into the form it wants. Kierkegaard writes,

> The rigid, the domineering person lacks flexibility, lacks the pliability to comprehend others; he demands his own from everyone, wants everyone to be transformed in his image, to be trimmed according to his pattern for human beings. . . . If the rigid and domineering person cannot ever create, he wants at least to transform—that is, he seeks his own so that wherever he points he can say: See, it is my image, it is my idea, it is my will. Whether the rigid and domineering person is assigned a large sphere of activity or a small one, whether he is a tyrant in an empire or a domestic tyrant in a little attic room essentially makes no difference; the nature is the same: domineeringly refusing to go out of oneself, domineeringly wanting to crush the other person's distinctiveness or torment it to death.[17]

The outward expression of masculine despair can be what Caroline Simon calls fiction-making. She writes, "We often fool ourselves into thinking that we love when in fact we are indulging in fiction-making:

---

[16] Kierkegaard, *Sickness unto Death*, 72. Kierkegaard stands in sharp contrast to existentialists such as Jean Paul Sartre who insist that humans have the ability to self-make through the projects they pursue. Sartrean self-creation is in the air that our culture breathes and particularly notable in how the secular world views gender. See Jean Paul Sartre, *Existentialism Is a Humanism*, trans. Carol Macomber (New Haven, CT: Yale University Press, 2007). Kierkegaard's self is a *theological* self. It does not make itself ex nihilo nor does it self-govern, rather it is a created being that is given the call to become the fullest expression of itself *coram Deo* or under the face of God. The voices of community should point us back to the truth that we are created beings that exist before God and encourage us in our stewardship of that gift.

[17] Kierkegaard, *Works of Love*, 270–71.

seeing people as who we wish they were rather than who they are."[18] Fiction-making, she says, is a counterfeit love. She continues,

> [There is a] contrast between seeing what may not yet wholly exist, but should (imagination), and seeming to see either what should not and will not exist or what does or will exist, but should not (fiction-making). Fiction-making can confer its own kind of coherence, for rationalizations also connect the beginnings of stories with their middles and endings, but in fiction-making the story we tell does not cohere with God's story.[19]

Love requires imagination, the ability to see the person's God-given possibilities located in God's story. Imagination elicits the other person's best self. When we see the other in terms of expectations or overly descriptive roles that are actually more our idea than God's, we do not truth-tell. We fiction-make.

Although difference between the sexes is part of the diversity of creation, it goes awry when we become *overly* descriptive on what the differences are and overly prescriptive on how they should be lived out in areas beyond the pastorate. These prescriptions can be constricting for men as well as women, though in different ways. Moreover, while complementarianism affirms that the office of pastor/elder is reserved for men, many fall into inconsistency when they create a distinction between what nonpastor men and women can do in the church. It is not up to extrabiblical norms to maintain the distinctiveness between the genders. Rather, as the brothers and sisters kingdom-build alongside one another, their genders, which include their embodied realities that shape their experiences and situate their vantage points, add an irreducible dimension to how they serve. Men and women can share the same kinds of gifts, but their genders bring a unique aspect to them that shapes and enriches the way they embody those gifts. Flattening gender difference would be just as unfortunate as becoming "color blind." It falsely

---

[18] Caroline J. Simon, *The Disciplined Heart: Love, Destiny, and Imagination* (Grand Rapids: Eerdmans, 1997), 1.

[19] Simon, *Disciplined Heart*, 14.

avouches the idea that diversity is not an essential part of God's good creation and his mission. Women exercising their gifts in the church is not about proving that girls can do everything that boys can. It's much deeper than that. Womanhood adds an irreplaceable value to how that gift is exercised and uniquely used to build up the body.

Our gender-based conversations can also be unproductive if we don't critically examine how we think about difference. Throughout the history of Western philosophy, we've been challenged by the issue of difference, or how differing entities relate. The broad assumption is that difference is either alienating or annihilating. The first assumes that difference is so absolute that there can be no relationship whatsoever, like oil and water. Claims that men are from one planet and women are from another exemplify how this assumption has been imported into the complementarian gender conversation. It assumes that the absoluteness of gender difference will result in a degree of perplexity and dissonance in the relationship between the sexes. The second philosophical assumption about difference is that it is annihilating. Two differing entities cannot exist in a mutually shared space without one being a threat to the other. One will always consume the other or insist that the other become just like it. Those who overemphasize "sameness" between the sexes risk falling into homogeneity. Yet Scripture opens up our interpretive closure of difference as being either alienating or annihilating. Genesis 1–2 portrays the world neither as a mechanistic system of cause and effect nor as indeterminate flux, but as a *creation*. As we see in the meadow, the distinctiveness relates in harmony. Difference neither repels nor consumes but mutually enhances. God's image bearers are created male and female, and their differences are designed to interrelate harmoniously rather than be segregated.

Although one side of the negotiation table despairs by overfencing the office of pastor/elder, the other side can despair by becoming so focused on equal representation in all nonpastoral areas of church life that it begins to see the gender before it sees the gendered person. Although their heart is to break down the extrabiblical wall of division between men and women in the church, the risk is aiming to fill a gender disparity rather than first noticing a woman's God-given gifting and then encouraging her to expand those gifts in the church. Becoming more gender centered than person centered will create trophies or cookie cutters. Neither trophies nor cookie cutters are true, full, distinct selves. They are made in our image, a result of fiction-making rather than courage-giving.

Feminine Despair and Its Consequences

If masculine despair is seeking to become the *wrong* self or the self God did not create, Anti-Climacus says feminine despair is refusing to be a self. People who experience this kind of despair do not try to become their fullest self or cultivate their own distinctiveness. Rather, this kind of self is caught up in "the immediate":[20] the laundry, dishes, activities, bills, and schedules of everyday life. Some prefer to lose themselves in such things and not think too deeply about life. Others feel they are under the tyranny of the immediate and do not have the privilege of pursuing their gifts in this season. Some single women who desire marriage and children may even fear that pursuing gifts, passions, and opportunities that are considered "weighty" could be viewed as a liability by a prospective spouse. To make themselves more desirable to men with a strong sense of self, they become "lighter" selves. Men and women can prefer to float on the surface of life without taking weightier questions about life and growth too seriously or making meaningful investments in it. Anti-Climacus rightly points out that there is defiance in this kind of despair. Even though it takes on a form different from masculine despair, it is still a refusal to be the self God created, and it can be a pitfall for both men and women.[21]

The outward expression of feminine despair corresponds to what Kierkegaard calls small-mindedness. He writes:

[A small-minded person] has no distinctiveness, that is, it has not believed in its own and therefore it cannot believe in anyone

---

[20] Kierkegaard, *Sickness unto Death*, 50–51.
[21] Kierkegaard, *Sickness unto Death*, 49.

else's either. The small-minded person has clung to a very specific shape and form that he calls his own; he sees only that, can love only that. If the small-minded person finds this, then he loves. Then small-mindedness holds together with small-mindedness; they grow together, which, in a spiritual sense, is just as pernicious as an ingrown toenail.[22]

If a small-minded person cannot see his or her own distinctiveness, he or she may not have a skilled eye for truly identifying the distinctiveness of others. Kierkegaard says such individuals grow uncomfortable when they are stretched or pulled out of the "shape and form they call their own." Thus, they tend to gravitate toward other small-minded people who allow them to stay in their comfort zones.

Being small-minded does not mean being unintelligent; it means being shallow. The church should be a place where we pull one another out of our own small-mindedness. Not all people are made to be academics—thank goodness!—but none of us are called to be shallow in our understanding about God or about living in his world. For those who find themselves buried under the "tyranny of the immediate," encouragement likely comes in the form of actively creating space and opportunity for those struggling with this kind of despair to grow as distinct selves. Kierkegaard points out that "the creature in relation to God does not become nothing even though it is taken from nothing and is nothing but becomes a distinctive individuality."[23] In other words, becoming conformed into the image of Christ does not mean the self becomes a transparent, nonself; rather, it becomes a cross-shaped self that is gloriously distinct as a member of Christ's body.

Many Members, One Body

The discussion on how the church can faithfully live out complementarianism must continue down a fruitful and life-giving path instead

---

[22] Kierkegaard, *Works of Love*, 272.
[23] Kierkegaard, *Works of Love*, 271–72.

of becoming a frustrating stalemate. Walks in the meadow help. All metaphors, including the metaphor of the meadow, are limited. The Bible speaks of the church in a variety of ways, and we need them all acting in concert to gain robust conceptual purchase on the reality of what Christ has secured for his people. The metaphor of the meadow is not designed to describe church polity or governing structure, but simply to give us a phenomenological perspective shift on how we view one another within the body. The meadow helps us recover a vision for the life of the church as expansive, beautifully variegated, and fruitful. It reminds us that we are each distinctively created by God with specific gifts and strengths. These strengths do not need the absence of the other to flourish; they need the other's courage-giving presence. To be sure, men must also give courage to other men, and women must do likewise for other women. However, being intentional about cross-gender encouragement is especially important today.

Is the idea of creating harmony through encouragement overly idealistic? According to the world's logic, it is. However, according to Christian Scripture, it is simply a description of the reality secured for us by Christ. First Corinthians 12 speaks of a variety of gifts: "One and the same Spirit is active in all these, distributing to each person as he wills" (v. 11). The body consists of not one member, nor one kind of member, but of many. The foot should not compare himself to the hand and determine his own distinctiveness is a hindrance to truly belonging in the body (v. 15), and the eye cannot say that it is unfortunate she was not made like the ear (vv. 16–17). If distinctiveness was eliminated and the whole of the body was made like one part, there would be so much the body could not do. It is the withholding of gifts that takes away from the body not the cultivation and appropriate use of them. Paul continues:

> The eye cannot say to the hand, "I don't need you!" Or again, the head can't say to the feet, "I don't need you!" On the contrary, those parts of the body that are weaker are indispensable. And those parts of the body that we consider less honorable, we clothe these with greater honor, and our unrespectable parts

are treated with greater respect, which our respectable parts do
not need.

Instead, God has put the body together, giving greater
honor to the less honorable, so that there would be no division in the body, but that the members would have the same
concern for each other. So if one member suffers, all the members suffer with it; if one member is honored, all the members
rejoice with it. (vv. 21–26)

The body of Christ is designed to function through mutual care of
its various members. There is no atomized division of labor or silos.
Instead, each part protects, empowers, and honors the other parts.
Rather than seeking "their own," members of the body are occupied with
seeking each other's own. Rather than pushing the other away through
criticism, suspicion, demands, or extrabiblical divisions, brothers and
sisters are called to give courage to one another. When this happens, the
church bursts at the seams with life, just like a meadow.

Chapter 10

Men and Women as Partners in the Gospel

Tony Merida

Missional women have always played a vital role in the advancement of the gospel. The church—as the bride for whom Christ bled, died, and was raised to life—ought to be a place where women are encouraged, loved, taught, respected, heard, and deployed for service. They should thrive as Christ's ambassadors to the world, as they are built up in him.

Faithful, humble, gospel-centered leadership in the church will foster the kind of environment in which women are seen and valued as true partners in the gospel. Godly women will be viewed as active participants in the mission, not relegated to sidelines. Before we consider some biblical foundations and practical suggestions for achieving this dream, allow me to share two personal stories of missional togetherness.

Marriage and Student Ministry

I became a follower of Jesus in college, and it was not uncommon to have women doing all sorts of things in our campus ministries. I don't ever remember hearing a woman say she wanted to be a pastor, but it was very clear that women were playing a vital role in making the gospel known on our campus. The same was true for my youth-camp experiences; men and women together were engaging students with the gospel.

I began working at summer-long youth camps in 1998. I eventually met my wife, Kimberly, at a youth camp called Centrifuge in 2002. She was a fellow staff member. In fact, she was one of the camp directors. The following summer she would be the main camp director (though I worked at a different camp that year). We were married at the end of 2003 after she finished a master's degree at Southeastern Baptist Theological Seminary. In 2004, we worked together on the same camp staff, where I was the camp pastor, and she was again one of the camp directors. I tell people, "I'm still the pastor, and she's still the director!"

We were all college and seminary students, and we ministered to thousands of middle and high school students for about ten weeks. Those years on camp staff have forever impacted my life. It was there that I learned to work hard, to communicate the Bible in a way that people can understand it, and to give great attention to those who are not Christians. Further, it taught me to work together with teammates, both men and women.

The women didn't preach during nightly worship gatherings, but they assisted in other ways. During the day, they were leading Bible studies, leading various tracks during the day (from sports to classes), and active in all the general decisions of the staff. I absolutely loved working with these women, and they became like sisters to us guys.

Unfortunately, not all complementarians[1] have such an experience of working on a mixed-gender ministry team. Because this kind of camp ministry was my first ministry experience, it has forever marked me. I not only believe that women should be allowed to perform certain

---

[1] Defined as those who reserve the office of pastor for qualified *men* only (1 Tim 3:1–7; Titus 1:5–9). See the appendix for a more thorough definition.

ministry functions; I believe the mission suffers if they don't! Moreover, these years of camp made me more aware of female concerns, and it gave me much-needed perspective on the various heart issues particularly relevant to women.

Having Kimberly working alongside me in camp ministry impacted our marriage and our future ministry together in the local church. We have not known each other outside of ministry. Sometimes people ask, "How do you balance your time between marriage and ministry?" I don't even know how to answer that question. So I often say, "I do life and ministry *with* my wife." When I write sermons, I talk to her about it. When I'm struggling with matters of ministry, we talk about it. When she is doing work in the world of justice ministry, I listen and learn as I encourage her. When she is playing piano and preparing for Sunday morning musical worship, I sit and worship with her.

We regularly have people live with us. We adopted five kids, which we often say is like running a youth camp! Kimberly is on the front row when I preach. She is the biggest encourager I have. And besides all the work she does teaching women's conferences, leading musical worship, and advocating on behalf of the oppressed, she's a wonderful mother to our children. She's not just a "pastor's wife." She's a gospel-centered, missional woman in her own right! I often tell people, "Kimberly doesn't need me to have a ministry; she would have a ministry without me."

But she's never wanted to be a pastor. She's always had a "sign of submission" about her; that is, a vibe that she is happily submissive to her husband and our church's leadership. And I have never wanted her to be a pastor. I believe as long as I pursue a Christlike, lay-down-your-life attitude of service toward her and the church, then, far from feeling put down, she (and others) will be lifted up. It's possible to be a complementarian and encourage women (as Amber said in chap. 9), causing them to feel as if they can flourish in their giftings.

Scripture, not my experience, has the final say on matters, but my experience has shown me how this vision of men and women as partners in the gospel can look. I wish other complementarians could have a similar experience.

Planting Imago Dei Church and Romans 16

On September 11, 2011, Imago Dei Church held its first public worship service. But long before then, we (a group of men and women) had been planning and working to plant a new church.

I had wanted to plant a church for about ten years. After pastoring churches in New Orleans and Hattiesburg, Mississippi, we eventually set out to do it. I was able to recruit seven people from Mississippi, three couples and a fifty-seven-year-old widow. We then added a few more couples once we arrived in North Carolina, and we spent the first three months together. We learned together; we laughed together; we took trips together; we prayed together; we did outreach events together. After getting on the same page theologically and philosophically, we soon invited others to join us in our house for a weekly worship service. We soon outgrew our house. We split into three small groups, and then on September 11, 2011, we rented an auditorium and held our first public service.

During our last core team meeting, I read Romans 16, a chapter filled with names. The apostle Paul honored several men and women who were true partners in the gospel. I have always been struck by this passage because of its diversity in age, ethnicity, gender, and class. As our team studied Romans 16, I simply encouraged them and expressed my thankfulness for sacrificing much for the mission. While we had a robust ecclesiology, our women were viewed as vital participants in the mission. We could not have planted Imago Dei Church (IDC) without them.

Now we have grown to about twelve hundred people and have planted multiple churches. We have worked hard to promote that same spirit of men and women in biblical community, together on mission. Admittedly, the growth of the church and other factors has made this goal challenging. We still have room to grow at IDC. And every week our staff elders seem to be discussing how we make steps to encourage, disciple, and empower our women for ministry—for the good of this broken world, for the good of the church, and to the glory of God.

Most recently, we have appointed twelve directors and coordinators of various ministries, about half men and women. These folks will serve under and with pastors in important ministries—discipleship classes, childcare, worship development, local outreach, student ministry, missionary care, small group care, membership assimilation, and event planning. The inclusion of these gospel partners has already changed the entire spirit of the church office and has brought a new level of health to the various ministries. The women in particular bring a very important perspective and set of gifts that we desperately need in order to shepherd the flock skillful and faithfully.

To achieve this vision of missional complementarianism, I find myself regularly articulating, defending, and championing four biblical foundations: (1) men and women as image bearers of God, (2) men and women as disciples and disciple makers, (3) men and women as brothers and sisters in the family of God, and (4) men and women as partners in the gospel.

Men and Women as Image Bearers of God

Long before we planted the church in Carolina, Kimberly and I discussed possible names. We landed on the name Imago Dei long before we planted the church. In fact, I have some old sermon notes where I was teaching on the *imago Dei* (image of God); I said, "If I ever plant a church, I want to call it Imago Dei." We chose that name not because it was cool, but because of what it communicates theologically about humanity. We wanted to be a church that truly believed everyone matters to God and therefore should matter to us. Every person is worthy of dignity, value, and basic human rights. Every person should hear the gospel. The *imago Dei* changes the way we see people, from the womb to the tomb (and beyond the tomb!).

God—who eternally exists in a triune relationship—created the universe out of nothing. He created the heavens and the earth, and his special creation: human beings. We read that on the sixth day—

God said, "Let us make man in our image, according to our
likeness. They will rule the fish of the sea, the birds of the sky,
the livestock, the whole earth, and the creatures that crawl on
the earth."

So God created man in his own image;
he created him in the image of God;
he created them male and female. (Gen 1:26–27)

Being made in the image of God means that people have the capacity to think, feel, reason, love, rejoice, reproduce, choose, and most of all
know God personally and eternally through Jesus Christ. God made us
intimately, uniquely, and as male and female distinctly. He also made us
purposefully: "to glorify him and enjoy him forever," as the Westminster
Confession puts it.

Throughout the Bible, as Martin Luther King Jr. stated, we find
that there are no gradations in the image of God. The rich, the poor,
the black, the white, the educated, the not educated, are all made
in God's image, and worthy of dignity. Further, we find in Scripture
that if you dishonor anyone made in God's image, you dishonor God
himself (Prov 14:31). When describing the destructive nature of the
tongue, James says, "With the tongue we bless our Lord and Father,
and with it we curse people who are made in God's likeness" (Jas 3:9).
Sinning with your words is an assault on the *imago Dei*. We must
treat both men and women with great dignity and care in both word
and deed.

When we dishonor people, we dishonor God himself. This is an
important starting point for any discussion on gender. Men and women
share in equal value. Martin Luther King Jr. gave the following picture,
regarding race relations, but it can also be applied to complementarian
ministry relationships:

There are no gradations in the image of God. Every man from
a treble white to a bass black is significant on God's keyboard,
precisely because every man is made in the image of God. One
day we will learn that. We will know one day that God made us

to live together as brothers and to respect the dignity and worth of every man. This is why we must fight segregation with all of our non-violent might.[2]

Gospel men and women on mission together are like the black and white keys on a piano. Together, we make beautiful music unto the Lord.

We are not only made uniquely by God, but also distinctly as male and female. God, in his infinite wisdom, designed two complementary genders. As the biblical writers communicate in the unfolding of the story of the Bible, God describes how men and women have two complementary roles within the home and the church. We should recognize these responsibilities as acts of grace and wisdom, not as statements of importance or superiority (Gen 2:18–25; 1 Cor 11:2–16; 14:33–35; Eph 5:22–33; Col 3:18–19; 1 Tim 2:8–15; 1 Pet 3:1–7). God has designed men and women to work together, as male and female, for the purpose of human flourishing to his glory.

Men and Women as Disciples and Disciple Makers

Recently I was in California talking with friends who serve together at a church plant. The wife of a church planter shared a story that highlights a problem among some complementarians. She approached her pastor on one occasion advocating for women to be given the opportunity to learn theology. She, like many women, had grown tired of the lack of depth in many women's ministries. In response to this sensible, mature request, the pastor responded, "Okay. But just as long as you don't think women should be theologians!"

Whatever you make of the ways in which women can and should teach in the local church, surely, we can agree that women should be learners of theology! A disciple is—among other things—a learner.

---

[2] Martin Luther King Jr., Sermon, 1965, Ebenezer Baptist Church, cited in Timothy Keller, *Generous Justice* (New York: Dutton, 2010), 86–87.

Unless you have some version of discipleship that doesn't involve learning, a pastor must be for the growth and maturing of all disciples, male and female. Therefore, we desire for women to become good theologians because all Christians ought to pursue good theology

To every female reader: learn theology. Study the Bible. Learn hermeneutics. Study the storyline of Scriptures. Learn the biblical languages, if possible. Don't settle for "cotton candy" teaching; but dig into the meat of theology. You are a disciple, and that means you are a theologian, and you should make it your practice to engage in theological dialogue, just like your brothers in Christ.

Women are also *disciple makers*. The often-quoted Great Commission in Matt 28:18–20 is not reserved for men only. All women are called to make disciples of all nations. New Testament scholar James Edwards says this about women in the Gospel of Mark:

> Women play especially important roles in the Gospel of Mark (1:1–16:8). Not only are they mentioned frequently, but *the highest acclaim of Jesus in the Second Gospel goes to women.* . . . To be sure, some women appear in negative roles. . . . Fifteen of the twenty-two mentions of women, however, appear in unusually positive contexts. The value and dignity of women—and girls—are signified by the fact that Jesus heals them (1:30–31; 5:25–34; 5:23, 41–42; 7:25). In their following and serving of Jesus and the Christian fellowship *women are models of discipleship* (1:30–31; 15:40, 47; 16:1). In special instances they play prominent roles, even preeminent roles, *receiving the highest praise that Jesus gives in the Gospel.* On two occasions women appear in the heart of the sandwich technique as the ideal of faith (5:21–43) and devotion (14:1–11). The woman with a hemorrhage is a model of faith for Jairus, the synagogue president (5:25–34); and the Syrophoenician woman is a model of faith for all "outsiders" (7:25ff.). The widow in the temple is praised for giving more than everyone else, "her whole life" (12:42–44). And above all, the anointing at Bethany is so

exemplary that the proclamation of the gospel in the world is a commemoration of her act (14:9).[3]

The Bible portrays women as models of discipleship.

It's interesting that in my denomination, the Southern Baptist Convention, many are hesitant to give women certain disciple-making opportunities, even though we take up annual missions offerings named after Lottie Moon and Annie Armstrong! Those were missional women who made a tremendous impact on the world. Like Mary Magdalene and the Samaritan woman at the well, they were faithful witnesses to Jesus Christ, and the world was blessed because of their obedience.

Some may push back and say, "Well, they weren't pastors of churches." Granted, but there are many nonpastoral roles in evangelicalism (like the academy, various training positions, and various ministry roles in the church) that still seem off limits to most women. If you view them as disciple makers, then some of these opportunities should open up.

Men and Women as Brothers and Sisters in the Family of God

I'm convinced that one reason complementarians hold extreme positions (such as patriarchy) and neglect to encourage and empower women for ministry is because they don't know how to relate very well to the opposite sex. A secure male leader, who is content in his singleness or his marriage, should be able to have regular conversations with women without awkwardness or fear of the conversation leading toward sinful behavior.

How can we develop this kind of healthy interaction? It seems that a first step involves recovering the biblical idea of the church as a family of adopted brothers and sisters. The church is not a building we visit, or an event we attend, but a family to which we belong. Neither is it a

---

[3] James R. Edwards, *The Gospel according to Mark* (Grand Rapids: Eerdmans, 2002), 417, emphasis mine.

factory either with rigid silos but a family with real relationships. The more men and women can interact in purity, the better we will fulfill God's idea of the church.

Paul speaks of this, saying, "Do not rebuke an older man, but exhort him as a father, younger men as brothers, older women as mothers, and the younger women as sisters with all purity" (1 Tim 5:1–2). Treat people in the church as family—because that's what we are. There are mothers, fathers, brothers, and sisters in the church. The way you interact in purity is not by avoiding one another, but by pursuing God and godliness personally, while interacting with one another wisely, appropriately, and lovingly.

Like a family, men and women should practice the "one anothers" together: serving one another (Gal 5:13); having the same concern for one another (1 Cor 12:25); praying for one another (Jas 5:16); bearing one another's burdens (Gal 6:2); loving one another as brothers and sisters (Rom 12:10a); showing honor to one another (Rom 12:10b); building up one another (Rom 14:19); instructing one another (Rom 15:14); teaching and admonishing one another in all wisdom; being kind to one another and forgiving one another (Eph 4:32); encouraging one another (1 Thess 4:18); seeking to do good to one another (1 Thess 5:15); stirring up one another to love and good deeds (Heb 10:24); not grumbling against one another (Jas 4:11); showing hospitality to one another (1 Pet 4:9); clothing ourselves with humility toward one another (1 Pet 5:5); loving one another (1 John 4:7). What a glorious vision of biblical community! It's a vision of brothers and sisters who are one in Christ (Gal 3:28), sharing life together and living on mission together.

In this beautiful but fallen world, where do we go to find strength in the midst of stress and discouragement? We go to the gospel, and we go to Christian brothers and sisters. Peter said in his Pentecost sermon twice that God has poured out his Spirit on both men and women alike (Acts 2:17–21). Both men and women have spiritual gifts to be used for the common good.

In the book of Acts, it's striking to observe how often Paul spent time with his Spirit-filled friends, which included both his brothers and sisters in Christ. It's striking to see how intentional he was in spending time with them, also. It took sacrifice to be with them. Paul, the mighty apostle, did not do ministry alone! We read about Barnabas, Titus, Silas, Luke, Priscilla and Aquila, Lydia, Onesiphorus, Epaphroditus, Ephesian elders, and many unnamed brothers and sisters in the churches.

Paul prioritized friendships. He spent time with ethnically diverse brothers and sisters; Jews and Gentiles; weak and strong; men and women. He stayed with them. He visited them. He worked alongside them. He got beaten alongside them; was imprisoned with them. He sang in prisons with them. He encouraged them. He—at times—disagreed with them. He also—at times—reconciled with them. Paul's constant contact with brothers and sisters wasn't due to a deficiency in his life! It wasn't the result of an extroverted personality. He needed Christian friends for the same reasons we do: he was an image bearer of God and thus made for community, and he was a justified sinner in need of support and encouragement.

Regarding Paul's need for support and encouragement, he says to the Romans, "For I want very much to see you, so that I may impart to you some spiritual gift to strengthen you, that is, to be *mutually encouraged* by each other's faith, both yours and mine" (Rom 1:11–12, my emphasis). Jesus's sufficiency is often expressed through other brothers and sisters. To the Corinthians, Paul says, "But God, who comforts the downcast, comforted us by the arrival of Titus, and not only by his arrival but also by the comfort he received from you" (2 Cor 7:6–7a). Notice Paul says that when he was downcast, God sent Titus to lift him—and his lifting of Paul was the result of the church's lifting of Titus! We need one another. The writer of Hebrews says, "Watch out, brothers and sisters, so that there won't be in any of you an evil, unbelieving heart that turns away from the living God. But encourage each other daily, while it is still called today, so that none of you is hardened by sin's deception" (Heb 3:12–13). Our hearts are prone to wander. Sin never sleeps. Satan rages because he knows his days are short. In light of this war, we need to come alongside of our brothers and sisters with gospel-centered encouragement.

Men and Women as Partners in the Gospel

Just a quick glance at Paul's ministry shows that he sought to equip and encourage women in the gospel. In Philippians 4, Paul says that Euodia and Syntyche had "contended for the gospel at my side" (Phil 4:3). That doesn't sound like they served only in the kitchen and in childcare! Paul also mentions women like Lydia (Acts 16:15, 40) and Nympha (Col 4:15) in relationship to various house churches; elsewhere we read of female prophets in the early church (Acts 21:9; 1 Cor 11:5).

The most extensive list of female gospel partners is found in Romans 16. We read of Phoebe (Rom 16:1), who heads the list. She may have had an official role, like that of deacon. Whatever the case, she was important to the church. He names Prisca/Priscilla, who is mentioned several times in the New Testament (Acts 18:2, 26; Rom 16:3; 1 Cor 16:19; 2 Tim 4:19). Paul goes on to mention Mary, Tryphaena, Tryphosa, and Persis; each person "worked hard in the Lord" (Rom 16:6, 12). He also mentions Junia, who had apparently been in prison with Paul (and Andronicus), and both Andronicus and Junia were "noteworthy in the eyes of the apostles" (v. 7). He speaks a sweet word about Rufus's mother, who had been like a mother to Paul (v. 13). In verse 15, he mentions Julia and the sister of Nereus. In total, out of about twenty-eight people that Paul wants to greet in Rome (vv. 1–16), ten of them were women. That's a significant number in its own right, but when you consider it occurs in a male-dominated culture, it is very striking. When we consider not just Paul's ministry, but also the whole sweep of the New Testament, along with significant women in the Old Testament, it is clear that the mission of God is not reserved to men.

What I find particularly instructive and inspiring about Romans 16 is how this gospel partnership is *emphasized*, *established*, and *experienced*. Regarding the *emphasis*, it's clear that people mattered to the apostle. He mentions men, women, couples, households, slaves, persons of honor, fellow Jews, and non-Jews. It is a vivid expression of Christian togetherness.

Regarding the *establishment* of this gospel partnership, this too is clear. What brings diverse people together? It's the gospel! They called Jesus, "Lord." Notice this theme (emphasis added):

v. 2: "Welcome her *in the Lord.*"

v. 3: "My coworkers *in Christ Jesus.*"

v. 5: "The first convert *to Christ.*"

v. 7: "They were also *in Christ* before me."

v. 8: "My dear friend *in the Lord.*"

v. 9: "Our coworker *in Christ.*"

v. 10: "Apelles, who is approved *in Christ.*"

v. 11: "Greet those . . . who are *in the Lord.*"

v. 12: "Greet [those] who have worked hard *in the Lord.*"

v. 12: "Persis, who has worked very hard *in the Lord.*"

v. 13: "Rufus, chosen *in the Lord.*"

These were former unbelievers, from various backgrounds, and Jesus changed them. Each person's new identity in Christ resulted in new friendships and partnerships. Because Spirit-filled Christians share a common passion in Christ, people who may not have otherwise spent time together can become great friends and serve a common mission.

Finally, consider from Romans 16 how these friendships are *experienced.* The short answer is "love." In addition to specific expressions of love (e.g., "my dear friend," like a mother to me), love is specifically conveyed through the giving of *honor*, through the mention of various forms of *hospitality*, and even through physical *affection* ("a holy kiss" v. 16).

Concluding Reflections

When you think about your local church, how might gospel partnership among men and women look?

Regardless of how you come down on specific "roles" within your church's government, we all should share a common idea about the "spirit" or "culture" of the church regarding men and women. We must seek (1) a culture of *honor* (based on the *imago Dei*), (2) a culture of *learning* (based on the priority of discipleship and theology), (3) a culture of *family* (based on the familial nature of the church) and (4) a culture of *encouragement* and *support in mission* (based on the gospel partnerships exemplified in the New Testament).

In terms of specifics, in our corporate gatherings at Imago Dei Church, our women do not preach on Sunday mornings, but they do participate in a number of other meaningful ways, such as prayer, Scripture reading, testimonies, and musical worship, just to name a few. Regarding weekly ministries, they may also serve in small group facilitation, small group hosting, counseling, visiting, various diaconate ministries, administration, childcare, and in various forms of teaching.

Concerning the church scattered, we use an acronym to describe our global mission: PEACE. This stands for Plant churches, Evangelize the world, Aid the poor and the sick, Care for the orphan and the oppressed, and Equip leaders. In some way or another, women may engage in each of these ministries, along with other men.

For me, Scripture is clear about God's design for male eldership in his church. But when Paul taught that women shouldn't teach Scripture or exercise authority over men (1 Tim 2:12), he never intended for women to become sidelined in the church's mission. This point is clear when one considers the whole sweep of the New Testament. The space for women to make disciples and serve outside of the role of elder is a large space. Sadly, in many churches, it's also an empty space. Our sisters are valuable partners in kingdom work. It's time we release our fears of inviting women into appropriate church ministry and be the kind of men that God intends by lifting up our sisters for the good of the church. God desires to see men and women working alongside one another in his strength and for his glory.

Chapter 11

Tales from the Trenches

Daniel Im, Amy Whitfield, R. Marshall Blalock, and Dwight McKissic

Introduction
Dayton Hartman

Application is often the most difficult step in the pursuit of change. Theories regarding the *why* of change and conjectures regarding the *how* of change are easily produced. Nevertheless, change only occurs with action. This section features multiple testimonies of men and women who have moved beyond theory to practice and are pursuing kingdom diversity in deed—and not just word. These *tales from the trenches* are real-world applications of the concepts and convictions being argued for in this book. These stories are meant to provide courage and an example for readers who desire to move from theory to application. It can be done. These stories prove that it has been done.

Daniel Im

A couple of weeks after moving to the States, I remember the moment when my little girls shared what they had learned in preschool. It was simultaneously adorable and shocking. After singing a few songs, they recited words I've never said and never thought I'd hear from my own flesh and blood, "I pledge allegiance to the flag of the United States of America, and to the Publix . . ." Yes, the grocery store chain!

Don't get me wrong, I'm by no means antipatriotic. I'm just not an American. As a Korean Canadian, I never grew up pledging anything to anyone. For me, the closest thing to patriotism was Hockey Night in Canada on Saturday night television. So the fact that my own flesh and blood were reciting a pledge—to a country and a flag that was not their own—made me cringe. This was especially jarring because it was within weeks of moving to a foreign nation! Sure, it was adorable that they mixed up the words with the name of a grocery store chain, but after hearing them, my wife, Christina, and I were speechless. We were shocked, and something felt "off," but we didn't quite know why.

After living in three countries and six different cities, I'm usually asked where "home" is. Although I was born and raised in Vancouver, Canada, the fact is, I moved away when I was nineteen. So every year that passes, it feels less and less like my home. Korea is not home either—even though Christina and I lived and worked there for a couple of years. Sure, ethnically I'm Korean, but it just didn't feel like home. Ottawa, Montreal, Edmonton, and Nashville don't quite feel like home either, even though we've developed deep friendships and community everywhere we've lived.

And now, for my children, not only are they Canadians living in America, but they're also half Korean and Chinese. So regularly around the dinner table, although I need to remind them that they're Chorean-Canadians living in America, that still doesn't quite fit the definition of "home."

The concept of home is interesting, isn't it? The idea of "home" is tied to our identity, which is linked with our ethnicity, nationality, what we do, and who we know. While each of these aspects contributes to our identity, none of them is sufficient. They all fall short.

I wonder if the reason I was so disturbed with my children reciting the Pledge of Allegiance was because they were embracing an identity or "home" that wasn't actually true of them. In fact, I wonder how often Christians do this, when we place our identity in everything other than our kingdom citizenship?

As a Christian, you are not what your passport says you are, nor are you what your genetic tests say. You are, instead, an exile, alien, and stranger here on earth because this is not your home (1 Pet 2:11). Your citizenship is not here on earth, but it is in heaven (Phil 3:19–20).

Does that mean we're all the same and that our earthly citizenship and ethnicity don't matter? Of course not! That's why we read that one day, "every nation, tribe, people, and language" will stand before the throne of God (Rev 7:9). However, we often live more focused on the latter than the former. And what would change if we shifted the order around? What would that mean for the Church? For evangelism and outreach?

The moment we start living, not as earthly citizens with allegiances to everything that is temporal, but rather as heavenly citizens with eternity in mind, the world will begin noticing the church as a city on a hill that can't be hidden (Matt 5:14).

Amy Whitfield

I have been a Southern Baptist for nearly twenty years and not just on Sundays.

Since 2000, I have been a member of six Southern Baptist Convention (SBC) churches in four different states. I have served as a Bible teacher, nursery volunteer, member of the building committee, women's ministry director, church pianist, wedding coordinator, AWANA commander, children's ministry greeter, and more.

My professional career has been spent entirely as a denominational employee. I've worked for three different SBC entities in a variety of roles, from part-time contractor to full-time director of marketing and communications.

At the cooperative level, I serve on a committee for my state convention, and I volunteer at the SBC annual meeting to do my part in helping the process run smoothly as an assistant parliamentarian. In my spare time, I use different avenues of communication to tell the Southern Baptist story and help others know how they can get involved.

I guess one could say, I'm all in. I never set out for it to be that way. I was called to minister alongside my husband, and I was looking for a job while he completed his degree. My entrance into denominational service came through a job posting, and I just never took an exit ramp.

As you can imagine, one of the questions I am asked most often is, what is it like to be a woman in the Southern Baptist Convention? My typical answer is, it honestly depends on the day.

Some days I feel encouraged. Some days I feel hopeful. Some days I want to give up. But at the end of all of it, I keep working.

Being an active member of a church in the SBC means sometimes you see people who are full of joy and excitement, and sometimes you see people who are struggling and hurting. Being a denominational employee in the SBC means sometimes you see the beauty of cooperation, and sometimes you see the pain of conflict and strife. Being a woman in the SBC means sometimes you stand out, and sometimes you are invisible—and every now and then you experience the paradox of both things happening at the same time.

Walking into rooms where you are the only female can feel like being a square peg in a round hole and makes for days all over the emotional spectrum. Some people will say things that are a little awkward, and I may just laugh it off inside. Those are strange days. Some people will say things that are truly offensive, and I may never tell a soul. Those are bad days. And some people will say things that communicate that they see me and they value me. Those are good days.

But being part of the SBC is not about how I spend my days. It's about how *we* spend *our* days, working together for a common mission.

We are part of a bigger story that's being written, and one in which we already know the end. Because of that, the most important moments for me as a Southern Baptist are the ones when I get to really see the point. Counting ballots raised in the air so we can do more together than we can do apart, working with men and women on projects that make a difference, seeing students arrive on a seminary campus for the first time as they answer their calling, sitting with church members in Bible study and watching them learn something new, watching missionaries being commissioned to take the gospel to the ends of the earth, getting on a plane with other Southern Baptists to go to the other side of the world, celebrating someone coming to know Christ—those are the things that make up the best days.

On any given day, I may feel encouraged, hopeful, or ready to give up. But at the end of every day, I choose to keep working in this family because this is where God called me to use my gifts. And I keep praying that others will join our cooperative efforts because we are better together, and we all bring unique gifts and experiences to the table.

I am a Southern Baptist because I believe this great story we tell, I stand by our Statement of Faith, and I think that cooperation is better than going it alone. And the cooperation I love to see the most is when brothers and sisters are working together on mission for the glory of God.

R. Marshall Blaylock

I serve as pastor of the First Baptist Church of Charleston, South Carolina, the oldest congregation among all Southern Baptist Churches, founded in 1682. Southern Baptist history has deep roots here, the first Association, the first women's missionary society, the first international missions offering, the roots of The Southern Baptist Theological Seminary can be traced here, along with a list of luminary leaders who are a virtual who's who of Baptist history that include Richard Furman, J. P. Boyce, Basil Manly, and revered evangelist Vance Havner. This great history has one deep, nearly indelible stain: African slavery and the racism that affirmed it.

In the more than 150 years before the emancipation of the slaves, First Baptist Church welcomed enslaved people to hear the gospel, to be baptized, to share communion, and to worship—but not alongside the white, free members who had pews on the main floor reserved for their families. Slaves were relegated to enter by a side door, to ascend stairs to the gallery (the balcony), where they would stand for worship. The church had conflicting values, wanting the enslaved people to have the gospel, but denying their dignity and freedom. Regarding slavery, the church had adopted the culture of the day rather than the eternal truth of God. Sadly, it was not a revival or a deeper understanding of Scripture that ended slavery at First Baptist Church; only a costly and inhumane war would do it.

Once the Civil War ended, the freed slaves were invited to stay in the church, but they understandably chose to begin churches in close proximity to their homes, churches where they would find refuge, where their dignity and worth was celebrated and honored. One of those churches was Morris Street Baptist Church.

June 17, 2015, reshaped my life, and it has never been the same. It was a Wednesday night when churches throughout downtown Charleston were gathering for Bible studies on a beautiful summer evening. The historic Emanuel AME Church was one of those churches. Myra Thompson was teaching the parable of the soils. As the study closed in prayer, nine black Christians were brutally murdered by a young white man, who, by his own testimony, wanted to start a race war. The city and the nation were equally stunned by the horror of the killings and by the racial hatred that motivated the killer. What happened to me that night was transformational.

As I grieved for these heartbroken families, God spoke to my heart. Identifying racism as evil was nothing new to me. As long as I can remember, I have believed everyone is made in God's image and is of worth and value. I had some good relationships across the racial divide in the city. And yet I had never felt the pain of racism in such a personal way until that heart-wrenching night, the blood of nine black brothers and sisters in the Lord crying out to me as I prayed for their families.

My journey began with listening more deeply to people of color and learning the realities of the experiences I had never lived myself. I began to see there was much I could not comprehend until I had deeper and more genuine relationships. I realized that much of my compassion over the years had been paternalistic. The experience was humbling for a number of reasons; the most difficult was wondering how I could have been so blind when I thought I knew better.

Since that night, my life has changed. By the patience and grace shown to me by many, my heart is being reshaped to have authentic friendships, which become the bridges for racial understanding and reconciliation. By God's grace, I have had the privilege to lead meaningful change in our community, to help bring the conversation to the Southern Baptist Convention in St. Louis in 2016, and to lead the South Carolina Baptist Convention to make Building Bridges the theme of the annual meeting in 2018. The highlight of that gathering was a worship service in the sanctuary of Emanuel AME Church. Everyone in the sanctuary sensed the depth of God's grace and heard the powerful testimony of Anthony Thompson, whose wife, Myra, was brutally murdered, yet he forgave the killer and shared the gospel with him face to face. That worship service was unforgettable and transformative for all who were present.

These events, as moving as they were, are not the goal. Only relationships can lead to the goal of racial reconciliation. Morris Street Baptist Church was formed shortly after the Civil War. Now, 150 years later, their pastor is Leonard Griffin, a great-hearted pastor who loves Christ and his church. I thought it would be good for the two of us to be friends since our churches shared a history, and I was trying hard to get to know my black colleague. After several attempts to develop a meaningful friendship, I was perplexed by the distance I could still feel. One day, I was meeting with Leonard, and I asked him for some advice on a personal subject. His whole countenance changed in that moment. For the first time, he felt that I was treating him as an equal by asking him for his insight and wisdom. I had a blind spot to my own paternalism, and that was a humbling moment for me.

Years later, Pastor Griffin, our wives, and I share life together as true friends. On November 11, 2018, he and I stood together at the front of the sanctuary of First Baptist Church to unveil a plaque in memory of the enslaved members of the church who had for centuries been unnoticed. As the great cloud of witnesses who had worshipped in the balconies surrounded us, we embraced through tears to honor the lives of those who had been unjustly enslaved and ignored. We have more ground to cover to see racial reconciliation in the church and community, but by the infinite power of God's grace, we are seeing glimpses of Rev 7:9.

Dwight McKissic

I'm the pastor at Cornerstone Baptist Church in Arlington, Texas. We joined the SBC thirty-five years ago, and it has been a mutually beneficial partnership. The SBC needs pastors and multicultural congregations like the one I pastor to accomplish our shared mission to evangelize the entire world for Christ.

Believe me, there are plenty of things in the SBC that make me uncomfortable, and I don't always agree with the decisions made by its most prominent leaders. On one occasion in 2006, I spoke out against certain now-reversed policies of the SBC's International Mission Board regarding missionaries. Everyone did not appreciate my criticism, and I considered leaving the SBC, but I stayed.

Some have called me "the racial conscience of the SBC" as I have spoken on the need for racial inclusion and empowerment. Many SBC leaders are uncomfortable with discussing racial inequity within the ranks. It is equally uncomfortable for me and some of my colleagues to feel like we are in someone else's house—invited for dinner but told to sit at the kids' table.

For consideration at the 2017 SBC Annual Meeting, I submitted a resolution dealing with the alt-right movement and the white supremacist ideology that animates it. Even though it ultimately passed in an edited form, the Resolutions Committee initially rejected it. Whether the committee's members consider it a factor in their decision, the panel is largely made up of people who are white, people with historical power and privilege. You have what you are born with, but people with power and privilege need the voice of racial minorities to understand our different experiences. Because the committee contained only one

African-American member of ten members, the panel failed to prioritize the need to subvert white supremacy in all its expressions. Minority underrepresentation does not reflect the demographics of our convention, and it eliminates the opportunity to sharpen each other across the denomination.

Unfortunately, some people view my church's dual alignment with the National Baptist Convention (NBC)—the country's largest majority-black denomination—as "two-timing." How quickly some forget the SBC has not always cooperated with pastors who share my skin color. There's nothing wrong with having two friendships, one long and reliable, the other new and growing.

Despite these challenges, I am remaining a Southern Baptist for three reasons.

First, my roots with and respect for the SBC run deep. My childhood home was always filled with Southern Baptist books, hymnals, and literature. We often shared positive and powerful interactions with Southern Baptists in various venues and contexts. One reason for that is the fraternal and fiscal support the SBC gave the National Baptists and black Southern Baptists.

At the 2016 SBC Annual Meeting in St. Louis, Ronnie Floyd, former president of the SBC (2014–16), shared the stage with Jerry Young, the current president of the NBC, a visible sign of hope. The reality is the relationship between the SBC and NBC has been strained but could be on the precipice of returning to the fellowship once enjoyed between the two conventions.

Second, my indebtedness to the SBC is immense. I want to give back to the SBC for having poured into NBC fellowships, camps, and gatherings in my early youth, college, and church-planting years.

The SBC provided a sponsoring church for my church plant in Arlington, Texas, and substantial funding for its first three years. I was told that our church plant received more funding than most white SBC church plants because SBC national leaders really wanted us to succeed.

The SBC provided health, life, and disability insurance at a reasonable cost. The SBC delivered a chapel building, free of charge, in which our church could incubate after we outgrew my home garage. The SBC delivered a sponsoring church, Tate Springs Baptist, which taught our children and youth with theirs in Sunday school while I taught our adults. The SBC delivered a loan of $330,000 within ten months of our church starting in 1984, a loan that was cosigned by two local SBC congregations. In 1996, the SBC provided a $3 million loan for us to purchase forty acres and build a twenty-nine-thousand-square-foot facility.

In return, over the past thirty-five years, Cornerstone Baptist Church has given close to $2 million to the SBC's primary funding channel, the Cooperative Program, and other SBC causes, including gifts to SBC church plants.

Third, my vision for the future of the SBC requires interracial composition. Although it has been officially integrated since 1951, the SBC is marginally interracial; most of its churches remain segregated. I choose to work from the inside to improve the racial makeup of the SBC, to see the fulfillment of Jesus's prayer in John 17:21 that his church would be one. If all ethnic minorities abandon the work of racial reconciliation, we will abandon Jesus's prayer for oneness.

When the SBC is persuaded to address the needs of African-American communities—such as building up the black family, assisting ex-convicts with employment, removing payday loan offices from our neighborhoods, addressing disparities and inequities in the criminal justice system, and addressing police brutality—it will have a huge positive impact on black SBC churches, we will then see real change and leave a better SBC for our grandchildren.

A common perception among African-American pastors and churches is that in order to be welcomed, we have to fully accept a white-dominated culture and park our brains, history, politics, worship practices, critical-thinking skills, and autonomy at the door. The SBC needs to make it clearer that this is not the case, so we can draw more churches to cooperate with the SBC.

Not everything in the SBC is what it should be, but I am called to work within it to help it become what it can be.

That's why I remain.

Conclusion

In Pursuit of the Vision of the Lamb

Daniel L. Akin

The school I have the honor of leading, Southeastern Baptist Theological Seminary, has become well known for its commitment to kingdom diversity, a school that welcomes and embraces men and women from every ethnic, racial, and social background. This commitment grows naturally from a biblical and theological vision that runs throughout Scripture but finds a special emphasis in the last book of the Bible, the book of Revelation. There, the Lion who is a Lamb, the Lord Jesus Christ, has "purchased people for God from every tribe and language and people and nation" (5:9). There is a heavenly family standing before the Lamb and the throne of God, "a vast multitude from every nation, tribe, people, and language, which no one could number" (7:9). The body of Christ is all together in relationship with the same Father, worshipping the same Savior and indwelt by the same Spirit. This vision of the Lamb motivates and drives us to build churches and schools on earth that look like the church in heaven.

God has been kind to our college and seminary in this regard. We are more diverse in our ethnic makeup on all levels than at any time in our history. We have made great strides, but we have not arrived. We still have much work to do. But, by God's grace, we will stay in pursuit of the vision of the Lamb until his glorious return.

As we have pursued this biblical agenda of kingdom diversity, we have learned a lot through our successes and failures. And, we are still growing and learning. We face new challenges constantly. Reflecting on the past several years, there are a number of lessons we have learned that I hope would encourage and help those walking the same path. Let me simply note four.

First, we must be intentional in pursuing kingdom diversity. This was true in the first century, and it is true in the twenty-first century. Jews and Gentiles did not just naturally come together even after they were converted. The book of Acts and Paul's letter to the Galatians make this clear. The pursuit of unity required work and intentionality. It was hard work. Cultural, ethnic, and social differences are real and are not easily transcended. The transforming power of the gospel is necessary to get beyond these divides. Further, it requires an intentionality on the part of the body of Christ to be obedient to all of Scripture and to live out the clear implications of the gospel. Intentionality requires a definite strategy. It necessitates a commitment, especially from the leadership—in our case, our administration, faculty, and staff. Fortunately, we have had tremendous buy-in among our team. We have, of course, experienced bumps in the road. That is to be expected. But we have continued to make progress and move forward. This mind-set is becoming a part of our institutional DNA, which I pray will sustain this vision for the future.

Second, actions speak louder than words. We all know this to be true, but it is certainly the case here. It is one thing to shout, "y'all come!" It is entirely different to actively go out and recruit ethnic minorities and women and then provide a campus atmosphere that feels like home to everyone. This effort, of course, has been the area that has stretched us the most. We had to make changes in budgets, personnel, and institutional structure. At times, it has been trying and difficult. But I have no doubt whatsoever it has been worth it.

Third, listen more than you talk. This sounds simple, but it is hard. It is not something many of us excel at doing. To truly be a family means we invest the time needed to get to know one another, to hear one another's stories and experiences. Different communities have different perspectives. They have distinct questions and concerns. I confess that I was quite blind and tone deaf on this issue. Surrounding myself with brothers and sisters from backgrounds different from my own and actually listening to their life's experiences has greatly broadened my perspective on life. Sometimes it has been very painful. Why didn't I see that before? How could my point of view have been so myopic and narrow? James 1:19 reminds us to "be quick to listen, slow to speak." That is always good counsel, but it is invaluable in building a community of faith on earth that looks like the one in heaven.

Finally, be prepared to be misunderstood and misrepresented. The school I lead is proudly confessional in the Baptist, evangelical tradition. We hold, without mental reservation or hesitation, to biblical inerrancy, the exclusivity of the gospel, penal substitution, and complementarianism. We are steadfast in our stand against abortion and homosexual behavior. To both issues, we seek to "speak the truth in love" (Eph 4:15), but speak the truth we must. Nevertheless, because we are in passionate pursuit of a kingdom vision of ethnic inclusivity, loving our sisters in Christ, and biblical justice, we have been criticized, mostly but not exclusively from afar. We have been accused of compromising or even abandoning the gospel. We are accused of promoting cultural Marxism. We are accused of seeking the approval of the secular world. We are accused of being social-justice driven rather than Great-Commission driven. Now, I could dismiss out of hand these inaccurate caricatures and just move on. However, I once heard Billy Graham say that some of his best counsel comes from his critics. So I will always be willing to listen and learn, challenged and critiqued. I will be ever aware of the dangers of drifting into theological liberalism and a social gospel that ultimately is a dead end. At the same time, I will not waiver from a rock-solid commitment to both orthodoxy and orthopraxy. I will never lose sight of the fact that the gospel is and always will be the main thing while also recognizing that the good news of King Jesus has implications for life. As Article XV of the *Baptist Faith and Message 2000* correctly says,

> All Christians are under obligation to seek to make the will of Christ supreme in our own lives and in human society. Means and methods used for the improvement of society and the establishment of righteousness among men can be truly and permanently helpful only when they are rooted in the regeneration of the individual by the saving grace of God in Jesus Christ. In the spirit of Christ, Christians should oppose racism, every form of greed, selfishness, and vice, and all forms of sexual immorality, including adultery, and pornography. We should work to provide for the orphaned, the needy, the abused, the aged, the helpless, and the sick. We should speak on behalf of the unborn and contend for the sanctity of all human life from conception to natural death. Every Christian should seek to bring industry, government, and society as a whole under the sway of the principles of righteousness, truth, and brotherly love. In order to promote these ends Christians should be ready to work with all people of good will in any good cause, always being careful to act in the spirit of love without compromising their loyalty to Christ and His truth.

The heavenly vision of the Lamb for his eschatological people is a glorious vision indeed that will one day be a reality. Until that day arrives, let it be the vision that captivates his churches on earth.

Appendix

A Statement on Complementarianism

Matthew Y. Emerson

What Is Complementarianism?

Much of this book assumes rather than explains in detail a "soft" version of a theological position called complementarianism.[1] The core belief of complementarians is that God made men and women equal in dignity and worth as his image bearers (Gen 1:26–28) but distinct in their roles within the home and the local church. Complementarianism stands in contrast to egalitarianism, which states that men and women are equal not only in their status as God's image bearers (an equality that complementarians readily affirm) but also in their roles in the home and the church. Complementarians maintain such a distinction between the

---

[1] Although we have opted for the language of *soft* and *hard* complementarianism, we find commonality with the formulation of *narrow* and *broad* complementarianism as described by Jonathan Leeman, "A Word of Empathy, Warning, and Counsel for 'Narrow' Complementarians," 9Marks, February 2, 2018, https://www.9marks.org/article/a-word-of-empathy-warning-and-counsel-for-narrow-complementarians/.

sexes in these two arenas of home and church, because they believe that this distinction is rooted in the created order (Gen 2:18–25) and is not merely a result of the fall. Regarding sin's effects on the relationship between men and women, complementarians do acknowledge that the entrance of sin into the world certainly affects the relationship between husband and wife (Gen 3:16). But they argue that sin affects marriage not through introducing complementarity but by subverting it; the wife in Gen 3:16 tries to grasp leadership in the home when God's natural order has already bestowed it upon the husband, thus creating tension in the home. Further, ungodly misogyny, sexism, sexual, physical, and verbal abuse, and other sinful activity related to how men treat women are attested by Scripture and especially in the narrative sections.

The rest of Scripture maintains these basic commitments, including both sexes' status as divine image bearers, the created order's distinction between the sexes with respect to roles within the home and the church, and the effect of sin on God's design. While a comprehensive examination of pertinent texts is not possible here, what follows is a brief survey of the most relevant passages. Regarding the full equality of men and women, we could note the way that both the Old and New Testaments speak of humanity in general (i.e., in a way that is inclusive of men and women) as the triune God's image bearers who glorify him. In fact, the Bible does not distinguish between men and women when talking about bearing God's image or giving him glory, apart from one difficult passage that will be discussed below (1 Cor 11:1–6). Whatever else we say about how the two sexes complement each other, we should start and end with this: that men and women both fully and equally possess the image of the triune God, and men and women are both fully and equally able to give glory to the triune God.

The Bible does, however, distinguish between men and women in terms of their roles in the church and home. The most explicit texts in this regard are found in the New Testament, although the rest of Scripture bears witness to the same reality, ultimately rooted in God's created order. Some of the most important are Eph 5:22–31; 1 Tim 2:12; and 1 Pet 3:1–7. In the Ephesians and 1 Peter passages, wives are called to submit to their husbands, a submission that is rooted in the created order and also in the mystery of the gospel. A wife's submission to her husband is compared by Paul to the relationship of Christ and the church, but this analogy cuts both ways as husbands are called to love their wives sacrificially and selflessly. In the third passage, 1 Tim 2:12, Paul restricts the functions of the office of overseer (synonymous in the New Testament with the terms *pastor* and *elder*) in the church to men. These functions—spiritual authority and teaching—are not restricted to men because only men have the capacity to do them, but because, once again, this design reflects God's created order. Additionally, it works against the effects of the fall and points people to the gospel (1 Tim 2:12–15). Thus, complementarianism is, at its core, an affirmation that the Bible clearly speaks to the full equality in dignity and worth of men and women while distinguishing between their complementary roles in the home and in the church.

"Hard" Complementarianism

The basic beliefs of complementarians, fairly simple and clear as they may be, are often applied in divergent ways in both the home and the local church. Scripture does not offer much more in terms of instructions about how this vision is to be worked out practically. Because of this, there are at least two different streams of complementarianism today. One stream, what I and others have called "hard" complementarianism, believes the Bible gives strict guidelines for how these broad parameters of equal dignity and complementary roles are to be worked out in the home. They point to passages such as Titus 2:3–5: "older women are to be reverent in behavior, not slanderers, not slaves to excessive drinking. They are to teach what is good, so that they may encourage the young women to love their husbands and to love their children, to be self-controlled, pure, workers at home, kind, and in submission to their husbands, so that God's word will not be slandered."

In the home, according to "hard" complementarians, submission often includes refraining from working outside the home ("working from home"). Additionally, "hard" complementarians often make strong delineations in the home between the wife's responsibilities as the homemaker and the man's responsibility as the breadwinner. In this kind of complementarianism, anything related to homemaking—namely, cooking and cleaning and tending to children—is primarily the responsibility of the wife and should not be added to the husband's responsibility due to his primary role as breadwinner and leader.

In the church, "hard" complementarians often affirm 1 Tim 2:12 in such a way that it restricts all teaching of adult men to male teachers. In other words, there is never a scenario in which a woman should teach a crowd that includes adult men; she can teach only women and children (as mentioned by the Titus passage above). Additionally, this brand of complementarianism often restricts most ministry positions from women, including the office of deacon. First Timothy 3:8 and following, which gives instructions for the qualifications of the office of deacon, is seen by "hard" complementarians as restricted to men; thus, the two offices of the church, elder/pastor and deacon, as discussed in 1 Tim 3:1–13, are restricted to women. If women lead or teach in the church, it must be in areas that (1) do not include men and (2) are not functioning in the offices of elder or deacon.

Two additional facets of "hard" complementarianism should be mentioned before we move to the alternative. First, these complementarians often extend their understanding of gender roles beyond the home and the church to society at large. Certain offices or vocations are seen as contrary to God's design for men and women, and so women should refrain from participation in them (e.g., police officers, the military, and, in some cases, positions of the highest authority in an organization or government). Likewise, certain recreational activities or hobbies should be restricted to one sex or the other (e.g., boys should not play with dolls; girls should not play contact sports with boys, etc.).

Second, "hard" complementarians often posit a straight line between gender roles, specifically the requirement that wives submit to their husbands, and the nature of our triune God. First Corinthians 11:3 is one of the passages most often employed: "But I want you to know that Christ is the head of every man, and the husband is the head of the woman,[2] and God is the head of Christ." For "hard" complementarians, it is not just biblical commands or the effects of the fall or even the created order, as important as all those are, that demands complementarianism. Ultimately complementarianism (in this version) reflects the very nature of God; wives submit to their husbands as the Son submits to the Father in eternity and in the incarnation. Instead of "hard" complementarianism, we could refer to this version as "maximal" complementarianism. Roles of men and women are maximally delineated in the home and church as well as society, and there is a maximal relation between the Creator's nature and his created order regarding the relation between the sexes.

"Soft" Complementarianism

A second version of complementarianism agrees with its "hard" counterpart about the foundations of complementarity—men and women are fully equal in dignity and worth, while also distinct but complementary with respect to roles in the home and church—while refraining from the maximal explication of those differences in the previous version. In this regard, we could refer to this second version as minimal, in contrast to maximal, complementarianism. This version of complementarianism fully affirms the distinction of men and women in the two arenas delineated in Scripture, the home and the church; it affirms Scripture's call for wives to submit to their husbands and for husbands to love their wives as Christ loves the church; and it maintains that the office and function of elder is restricted to men. "Soft" complementarianism does not, however, go much further than that in terms of offering specific rules of how that is worked out in the home or church. It also does not extend those distinctions into society at large. The reticence to make strict delineations beyond those mentioned in Scripture in all three arenas (home, church, society) rests on the conviction that

---

[2] Wording per CSB footnote.

Scripture does not speak further on the subject. For this reason, "soft" complementarians do not wish to add restrictions or rules to believers' lives that are not found in God's Word.

Regarding the home, "soft" complementarianism does not see Scripture restricting women only to the vocation of homemaker and therefore barred from working outside the home. Instead, it views Titus 2:5 in light of other scriptural passages, such as Prov 31:10–31 and Acts 16, which portrays women as working outside of the home. They do not view these passages in conflict, but rather see Titus 2 as giving a general picture of wives rather than a specific command related to never working outside the home. Additionally, "soft" complementarians do not attempt to restrict men from helping with housework, nor do they believe wives are lacking submission when they expect their husbands to help with housework.

With respect to the church, "soft" complementarians maintain that Scripture restricts the office and function of elder to men, but they do not believe that this restriction includes all forms of teaching or leadership by women when men are involved. Rather, the restriction includes only leading and teaching as elders and pastors. Additionally, many "soft" complementarians do not restrict the office of deacon to men (although some do), but instead believe that 1 Tim 3:8 leaves open the idea of female deacons, or deaconesses. This is because "soft" complementarians believe that Scripture does not portray deacons as the primary shepherds of the church, but rather as those who lead in service and under the authority of the pastor(s)/elder(s).

With respect to society and the Trinity, "soft" complementarians often take a much more minimal approach than do "hard" complementarians. Regarding complementarianism's necessity in wider culture, "soft" complementarians believe the distinction in roles for men and women includes only the home and the church, not society at large. A "soft" complementarian might point in this respect to Deborah (Judg 4–5), who served as a political and military leader of Israel. Finally, regarding the Trinity, "soft" complementarians often maintain that there is no straight line between God's nature and gender roles. It is, beginning with the incarnation and not in eternity past, in Christ's humanity that he submits to the Father. God's life is one in which the three persons—Father, Son, and Holy Spirit—are fully equal in divinity and authority, no one person submitting or being less in authority than the other. Passages such as 1 Cor 11:3 are thus about Christ submitting to the Father in Christ's humanity, not eternally in his divinity.

Which Version?

Ultimately every church must wrestle with Holy Scripture by the illuminating power of God the Holy Spirit in order to articulate what they believe about complementarianism and how to work it out in their context. Neither "hard" nor "soft" complementarians—nor theologically conservative evangelical egalitarians, for that matter—are any more or less committed to the inerrancy and authority of God's Word. If either version of complementarianism were less committed, they probably would not hold even the most basic tenets of the position given how radical it is in the twenty-first-century West. Nevertheless, the reader should note that, of the different contributors to this book who hold to complementarianism, most hold to the "soft" version. If readers are interested in wrestling with which version to adopt or adapt in their church, the resources listed in the Bibliography are recommended. This list includes both versions, and the author does not intend to promote one view over the other here.

BIBLIOGRAPHY

Akin, Danny, Kevin DeYoung, and Darryl Williamson. "What's (Not) Essential to Complementarianism?" The Gospel Coalition. January 15, 2019. https://www.thegospelcoalition.org/podcasts/tgc-podcast/whats-not-essential-complementarianism/.

Bird, Michael F. *Bourgeois Babes, Bossy Housewives, and Bobby Haircuts: A Case for Gender Equality in Ministry.* Fresh Perspectives on Women in Ministry. Grand Rapids: Zondervan, 2012.

DeYoung, Kevin. "9 Marks of Healthy Biblical Complementarianism." The Gospel Coalition. April 22, 2016. https://www.thegospelcoalition.org/blogs/kevin-deyoung/9-marks-of-healthy-biblical-complementarianism/.

Duncan, J. Ligon, and Susan Hunt. *Women's Ministry in the Local Church.* Wheaton, IL: Crossway, 2006.

Keller, Kathy. *Jesus, Justice, and Gender Roles: A Case for Gender Roles in Ministry.* Fresh Perspectives on Women in Ministry. Grand Rapids: Zondervan, 2012.

Leeman, Jonathan. "A Word of Empathy, Warning, and Counsel for 'Narrow' Complementarians." 9Marks. February 2, 2018. https://www.9marks.org/article/a-word-of-empathy-warning-and-counsel-for-narrow-complementarians/.

Wilson, Andrew. "Why Women Can Give Sermons." Think Theology. February 13, 2013. https://thinktheology.co.uk/blog/article/why_women_can_give_sermons.

———— "Women Preachers: A Response to John Piper." Think Theology. May 6, 2015. https://thinktheology.co.uk/blog/article/women_preachers_a_response_to_john_piper.

EDITORS AND CONTRIBUTORS

Editors

Dayton Hartman, lead pastor of Redeemer Church in Rocky Mount, NC, and adjunct faculty for Southeastern Baptist Theological Seminary and Judson College.

Walter R. Strickland II, assistant professor of systematic and contextual theology and associate vice president for diversity at Southeastern Baptist Theological Seminary.

Contributors

Daniel L. Akin, president, Southeastern Baptist Theological Seminary.

Bruce Riley Ashford, provost and dean of faculty and professor of theology and culture, Southeastern Baptist Theological Seminary.

R. Marshall Blalock, pastor, First Baptist Church, Charleston, SC.

Amber Bowen, PhD candidate at the University of Aberdeen.

Alan Cross, senior pastor, Petaluma Valley Baptist Church, Petaluma, CA.

Stephen Brett Eccher, assistant professor of church history and reformation studies, Southeastern Baptist Theological Seminary.

Matthew Y. Emerson, associate professor of religion and holds the Dickinson Chair of Religion at Oklahoma Baptist University.

J. D. Greear, president of the Southern Baptist Convention and pastor of The Summit Church in Raleigh-Durham, NC.

Keith Harper, senior professor of Baptist studies at Southeastern Baptist Theological Seminary.

Steve M. Harris, Policy Director, the Ethics and Religious Liberty Commission of the Southern Baptist Convention.

D. A. Horton, pastor of Reach Fellowship in Long Beach, CA and assistant professor of intercultural studies at California Baptist University.

Daniel Im, senior associate pastor of Beulah Alliance Church, Edmonton, Alberta.

Dwight McKissic, founder and senior pastor of Cornerstone Baptist Church in Arlington, TX.

Tony Merida, founding pastor of Imago Dei Church in Raleigh, NC.

Josh Wester, director of strategic initiatives in the office of the president at the Ethics and Religious Liberty Commission of the Southern Baptist Convention.

Amy Whitfield, associate vice president for convention communications of the Southern Baptist Convention Executive Committee.

Jarvis J. Williams, associate professor of New Testament interpretation, The Southern Baptist Theological Seminary.

Chris Williamson, senior pastor, Strong Tower Bible Church, Nashville, TN.

NAME AND SUBJECT INDEX

SCRIPTURE INDEX